TAIPEI

JOSEPH R. ALLEN

TAIPEI

CITY OF
DISPLACEMENTS

A McLellan Book

University of Washington Press
Seattle & London

Taipei: City of Displacements is published with the assistance of grants from the McLellan Endowed Series Fund, established through the generosity of Martha McCleary McLellan and Mary McLellan Williams, and from the Chiang Ching-kuo Foundation for International Scholarly Exchange. The University of Minnesota was generous in providing additional support.

University of Washington Press
PO Box 50096, Seattle, WA 98145, USA
www.washington.edu/uwpress

LIBRARY OF CONGRESS CATALOGING-IN-PUBLICATION DATA
Allen, Joseph Roe.
Taipei : city of displacements / Joseph R. Allen.
p. cm.
"A McLellan book."
Includes bibliographical references and index.
ISBN 978-0-295-99125-2 (cloth : alk. paper)
ISBN 978-0-295-99126-9 (pbk. : alk. paper)
1. Taipei (Taiwan)—Description and travel. 2. Taipei (Taiwan)—Social life and customs. 3. City and town life—Taiwan—Taipei—History. 4. Public spaces—Taiwan—Taipei—History. 5. Architecture and society—Taiwan—Taipei—History. 6. National characteristics, Taiwan. 7. Taipei (Taiwan)—Politics and government. 8. Political culture—Taiwan—Taipei—History. 9. Regime change—Social aspects—Taiwan—Taipei—History. 10. Social change—Taiwan—Taipei—History. I. Title.
DS799.9.T36A44 2011
951.24'9—dc23   2011017750

Printed and bound in the United States of America
Designed by Ashley Saleeba
Composed in Warnock Pro and Folio

FOR MY MOTHER,

Marguerite M. Allen

Contents

Preface

This study of Taipei City began in a most pedestrian way. During my first year in Taiwan, 1977–78, Lauren and I lived in the little town of Danshui (Tamsui) on the coast. Now a well-known tourist attraction at the end of the Red Line, Danshui was then a sleepy town of temples, fish markets, and questionable tea houses, all with an interesting colonial overlay. The reasons for our living there were entirely capricious. I had been sent to Taiwan by the University of Washington to study Chinese at the Inter-University Program (IUP) in Taipei, and, thanks to a friend, Lauren and I had been offered teaching jobs at Tamkang College (now University) out in Danshui. We had to commute one way or the other; the choice was easy and fortunate. The artist Yang Weizhong, younger brother of my mentor and soon to become a dear friend, lived and worked in Danshui. He found us an apartment on "first hill" amidst the residences of the former British legation and with a commanding view of Guanyin Mountain.

Every morning that year I rode the rickety no. 5 bus or the local train (built in 1901 by the Japanese) into Taipei to take classes, and back again in the afternoon to teach English. My exposure to Taipei City consisted primarily of the dingy train station, the crowded North Gate area, where we could catch "pheasant" taxis (*yejiche*) to Danshui, and the campus of National Taiwan University, formerly Taihoku Imperial University. The rest of the city was basically terra incognito. Some mornings I would sleep through my bus stop and wake up somewhere down the line. I might be miles away or just a block or two from my stop, but it all looked the same to me. Perplexed, all I could do was walk across the street and catch the no. 5 back to campus.

In graduate school I had studied classical Chinese literature, primarily early poetry, with some old-fashioned philology thrown in for ballast. I was also drawn to contemporary poetry, but C. H. Wang, who was my advisor and a famous poet, urged me to stick with classical poetry, preferably before 755 CE. So I did. When I graduated, I got a very nice job teaching Chinese language and literature at Washington University in St. Louis. A few years later I returned to Taiwan to attend classes and read classical poetry with Professor Qiu Xieyou of National Taiwan Normal University. This time I lived in the Taipei International House, a particularly unattractive residence on the edge of the Xinyi Road shantytown. That year—1985—I began to walk the city and think about things Chinese in post-755 CE terms.

Deciding that I would try to expand my research to contemporary poetry, I landed a Fulbright Fellowship and returned to Taiwan in 1987–1988 to study post-war poetry and society. Again I enrolled in language tutorials at IUP, reading with Yang Jiu and Zhou Changzhen. Through my friendship with Stephen Durrant, I also discovered mountain biking. I was living in the university area, and as we biked across town, headed for the nearby mountains, I began to develop a sketchy mind-map of the city, giving the space some logic and scale. Meanwhile, walking and biking around the university district filled that small locale with assorted, often fascinating, details, such as the old abandoned Japanese houses that I raided for furniture. This was when the city really became "visible" to me.

In the 1990s, the appeal of poetry studies began to wane and my interest in semiotics grew. I applied for another Fulbright Fellowship to begin a study of Taipei City "as a text," an idea I rationalized as an extension of poetics but which was probably simply a desire to live in Taiwan again. The rules allow for two Fulbright Fellowships for an individual; I got my second and never looked back.

The next year, 1999, I lived in the oldest section of Taipei (Wanhua) in a ramshackle apartment building owned by zany Mr. Guo. I carried out my reading and research across town at the new, modernistic National Library, which faces the grandly neoclassical, some would say ostentatious, Chiang Kai-shek Memorial. Every morning, I walked across the old intramural city from West Gate to East Gate, and back again in the evening, often stopping in Taipei Park along the way. During later visits to Taipei, I would explore many other parts of the city, but when I began to write this book, the spaces and places of that daily walk from west to east and back again, especially through the park, were most on my mind.

In the summer of 1999, I accepted a position as chair of the newly established Department of Asian Languages and Literatures at the University of Minnesota, Twin Cities. Finishing my Fulbright that fall, in January 2000 I drove through a heavy Wisconsin snowstorm to begin work. It was a sudden, unexpected change for me, but it turned out to be a very good one. Over the next eight years our small department recruited a new group of young scholars, and I benefited very much from learning about their research, which was primarily grounded in cultural and media studies. Our many conversations and my readings of their work gave me new perspectives on my Taipei project. Although my research slowed to a crawl while I was chair, I still managed to visit Taipei every year. Over ten years, amazing changes were seen in research facilities, archival materials, and studies related to Taipei City: the old run-down Taiwan Branch Library became National Taiwan Library in elegant new quarters; old and new archives welcomed researchers and digitization made more materials available on line; and publishers such as SMC Publishing released scores of new studies and reissued many older works.

Every visit produced a second piece of luggage full of materials for the return trip. Even as I complete this manuscript, I keep discovering important publications that I need to read. Yet, as Paul Valery said, "a poem is never finished, only abandoned," so now I must abandon this book to the printer.

Acknowledgments

My list of acknowledgments will be long, even with the inevitable inadvertent omissions, so I will begin with the institutions. First are the Fulbright Fellowship Program of the Council for International Exchange of Scholars in Washington, D.C., and the Foundation for Scholarly Exchange in Taiwan—their generous fellowship launched this project so many years ago. Special gratitude goes to Wu Jing-jyi (Wu Jingji) and his staff at FSE who provided financial, social, and intellectual sustenance throughout the year. The Institute of Taiwan History of Academia Sinica provided me with an academic home and research facilities; its director, Huang Fusan, was an excellent guide and friend in that early research. The Center for Chinese

Studies of the National Library offered convenient facilities and rich materials for the work in 1999, including a study space that overlooked the Chiang Kai-shek Memorial.

The College of Liberal Arts of the University of Minnesota provided critical support in many ways. In addition to generous research funds, Deans Steven Rosenstone and James Parente offered excellent administrative direction and collegial understanding, enabling me to negotiate the demands of being department chair while pursuing this research. I also must thank Ramona French, whose guidance, advice, and friendship kept me from getting completely lost in the bureaucratic and political woods of the university.

In Taiwan, I was fortunate to receive the help of many institutions and individuals over the years. Early on, I had the opportunity to meet with the well-known writer and public intellectual Long Yingtai, when she was commissioner of the Cultural Affairs Office of Taipei City. Her encouragement at the very beginning of my work was especially important to me. Later, I would also have similar conversations with her successor, Liao Xianhao, a professor of comparative literature whom I have known for years. As the research progressed, I worked at the Taiwan Research Materials Center of the National Taiwan Library in Zhonghe, which not only provided excellent facilities and materials (including the entire Japanese colonial library collection) but also wonderful service by Chen Limei and her staff. In addition, the staff at the Taipei City Archives, especially Zhang Zhonghe, helped me over the years in numerous ways, including allowing me access to many original maps from the Japanese period.

Closer to home, I benefited from the support of a number of academic institutions. First was the East Asian Library of the University of Minnesota, where the help and goodwill of the head librarian, Chen Su, have been invaluable throughout the project. The East Asian Studies Program at Washington University in St. Louis hosted me as a visiting scholar twice during this time; I not only benefited from their facilities but also from the input I received from my colleagues there. Over the years, I had the opportunity to present parts of this work at a number of institutions, including Columbia University, Harvard University, National Cheng-chi University, National Taiwan University, University of California at Los Angeles, University of Illinois at Urbana Champaign, University of Texas at Austin, and Washington University in St. Louis.

Numerous individuals contributed directly and indirectly to this work. Wei Dewen, owner of SMC Publishing and well-known scholar and collector, provided me with a great deal of material and good advice. One of the most important conversations I had was with Peter Kang (Kang Peide) of National Donghwa University in the fall of 1999; it was he who suggested I concentrate on Taipei Park. Long-time friend Lo Ching (Luo Qing) provided much help over the years, especially introducing me to Long Yingtai and coordinating my visits and interviews in Daxi. Li Zi'ning of the National Taiwan Museum shared his insights and stories on the history and curatorial work of the museum; he also introduced me to his colleague He Xunyao in my search for the bronze horse. C. J. Hsia (Xia Zhujiu) of National Taiwan University introduced me to his students who had studied Taipei Park, one of whom, Lai Zhengzhe (A'zhe), spent an afternoon sharing his work and thoughts. Chen Yijun, graduate student at National Yilan Technical College, shared his thesis and thoughts with me in another memorable conversation.

Of many others who helped over the years, I also want to thank Yomi Braester, Cynthia Chennault, Leo Ching, Chen Fangming, Ted Farmer, Douglas Fix, Todd Henry, Huang Ruiyu, Huang Wuda, Maki Isaka, Jou Sue-Ching, William Kirby, Anru Lee, Li Qianlang, Sylvia Li-chun Lin, Robert and Sachiko Morrell, Andrew Morris, Marco Moskowitz, Stephen Riep, John Shepherd, David Schak, Bert Scruggs, James Shih, Stephen Phillips, Su Shuobin, Jeremy Taylor, Caroline Tsai, David Tucker, and David Wang. In addition, I want to thank my students in "Maps, Stories, and Pictures: Representations of Taiwan," who over the years have provided me with feedback and insights about this work.

I also thank those individuals who saw this book through the winding paths of preparation and production. In the spring of 2007, I received a warm and enthusiastic note from a friend, colleague, and now my sponsoring editor at the University of Washington Press, Lorri Hagman, who has advised, encouraged, and cajoled me through many moments of panic and doubt to get the job done. At a critical juncture, copyeditor Laura Iwasaki gave the work a much-needed editorial overall. Then at the Press, Ashley Saleeba, Marilyn Trueblood, and Timothy Zimmermann shepherded it through the labyrinth of textual and graphic details with insight, care, and kindness. My gratitude to all of you.

Finally, from the days of our early sojourn in the little town of Danshui to the last few very peripatetic years, Lauren has been my constant support and companion.

Note to Readers

This study is in three parts, which can be read together or in different subsets. The Prologue is a brief overview of Taiwan for the reader unfamiliar with the cultural history of the island; it provides a backdrop against which to read the specifics of the core chapters. The Postface describes the theoretical underpinnings and scholarship that inform the study, especially the key term of "displacement"; this can be read before or after the core chapters, or not at all. The seven core chapters work their way through a set of chronologically and spatially interrelated materials, although not in a particularly linear fashion. The first two chapters consider representations of the city in various visual media over a period of a hundred years; the third chapter sketches patterns of traffic in the city, and the final four chapters focus on a set of increasingly smaller spaces and emplacements in the downtown area, in both their historical and contemporary conditions.

TAIPEI

Naming the Island

*The Island of Formosa lies off the east coast of China, opposite the Fu-kien prov-
ince. It is separated from the mainland by the Formosa Channel, which varies in
breadth from eighty to two hundred miles.*

—GEORGE LESLIE MACKAY, D.D., 1895

*The Taiwan Strait, ranging in width from 100 to 150 miles, separates the main
island [of Taiwan] from the coast of Fujian Province on the Chinese mainland.*

—DENNY ROY, 2000

To refer to Taiwan as "off the coast of China" may seem self-evident, but
this is a historically contingent and profoundly ideological statement,
especially given current geopolitical conditions. This positioning is
also found in almost every modern map of the island: the frame of these
maps is shifted just enough to allow the Fujian coast to intrude from the
west, but not the Philippines from the south or the Ryukus (to say nothing
of Japan) from the north.

In these discursive and cartographic renderings, Taiwan is attached to
China, both geographically and culturally. That attachment is geologically
inaccurate, however. The island is not an extension of the continental shelf,
as are, for example, the Penghu/Pescadore Islands, but rather a volcanic
uplift from the sea, like the other islands in the archipelagos along the western Pacific Rim, from Japan to Indonesia. Moreover, for most of its history
as an inhabited island, Taiwan was not culturally attached to China; its orientation was insular, and if there were an outward gaze at all, it would have
been toward the Austronesian islands of the South Pacific, with which the

indigenous people of Taiwan share origins.[1] Chinese contact with the island before the seventeenth century was haphazard at best, even though China's imperial reach was notoriously extensive many centuries before that. As late as 1697, Yu Yonghe wrote, upon the eve of his journey to the island, "Taiwan is far off in the eastern seas and has lived in an uncivilized state. There is no record that it has ever sent tribute or had any contact with China."[2] Thus, until very recently, Taiwan was not "off the coast of China" but rather off its map entirely.[3]

Ironically, Europeans were the first to appreciate Taiwan's strategic relationship with the continent, although they were just as interested in its position between Japan and their colonies in Southeast Asia.[4] The island enters the European vocabulary and imagination as "Ilha Formosa" (beautiful island) when named so by Portuguese traders sailing past on a voyage between Malaysia and Japan in the early 1540s.[5] This name, and its abbreviation (Formosa), "so euphonious and yet appropriate, replaced all others in the European literature."[6] A 1662 European map of the island, for example, contains the dual label "Pakan ô Ilha Formosa," wherein an indigenous term is joined with the new European usage.[7] Except in some residual contexts, during the twentieth century the name Formosa was gradually displaced by the Chinese/Japanese term "Taiwan" as the island's common designation.[8] Yet, in the late 1970s, the old European name reemerged in a most peculiar fashion: it was translated into Chinese as *meilidao* (beautiful island) and used by oppositional political forces on the island to name their magazine and movement. The 1979 "Meilidao Incident" was a defining moment in the emergence of a new political and social structure for the island. Since that time, *meilidao*/Formosa has taken on a cultural cachet that projects an alternative to the "China attached" narrative.

While the Portuguese gave the Europeans a name for the island, the Dutch were first to begin its colonization, as part of their efforts to challenge the Portuguese and Spanish in the emerging China-Japan trade. When the Dutch built their Fort Zeelandia on the southwest coast in 1624 (near the present-day city of Tainan), they were not alone, however there was already a population of approximately one hundred thousand indigenous "Formosans" living in small villages scattered throughout the island, particularly on the plains of the west coast.[9] There were also Chinese and Japanese traders who worked and lived in these villages, as well as seasonal fishermen from the continent. The colonial work of the Dutch was effective but short-lived. They made substantial trade and missionary inroads on the plains around Zeelandia and even drove the Spanish out of northern Taiwan in 1642. Their most lasting legacy was the beginning of settled rice and sugar farming using emigrant Chinese workers, at first temporary and later settled, from the continent's southeast coast, particularly the Fujian area. This is what Tonio Andrade describes as a type of "co-colonization" of the island.

The Fujian connection begins with the Dutch, but the Dutch were driven off the island in 1661 by the Ming dynasty loyalist Zheng Chenggong (known as Koxinga in European and Japanese literatures), who was fighting a deteriorating resistance against the new Manchu Qing dynasty. Zheng's retreat to Taiwan may now seem inevitable, since his base of power had been "just across the strait" in Fujian, but he may have been drawn there primarily by the Dutch presence, which had established the island in the trade and military configuration of China and Japan—Zheng's father had been a well-known profiteer (some would say pirate) once aligned with the Dutch; he was from Fujian, his wife was Japanese, and Zheng junior was born in Japan.

The Zheng government-in-exile was short-lived and its colonial occupation of the island limited, although it did bring a denser Chinese settlement pattern to the western plain as its troops, some twenty-five thousand, established farming communities both within and outside of the Dutch area. There are still many towns in this area that are named "such-and-such *ying*" (barracks), a linguistic remnant of the period. The most significant legacy of Zheng rule was the solidification of the island's connection with the Chinese southeast coastal cultures. Qing imperial forces finally took the island as their own in 1683, and Taiwan was claimed—after some hesitancy and debate—as Chinese and designated as a prefecture (Taiwanfu) of Fujian province. It then officially "entered the Chinese map," and the name Taiwan was firmly established in the Chinese (and Japanese) records. This early prefectural territory was limited to the western plain, especially the southern portion—the north, the towering central mountains, and the narrow eastern seaboard that faced a blue-water ocean were not part of the Chinese purview.

The years of Qing rule, officially from 1683 to 1895, are generally called the Chinese period of Taiwan's history,[10] although those two centuries were hardly fully Chinese. The dynastic government in Beijing continued to view the island as a site for potential trouble rather than a resource for the continent.[11] There was no government policy to open up the new territory for a Chinese population, as might be expected; in fact, for most of the Qing period, there were restrictions on immigration and other barriers to development of the island. Given the distance from the Chinese capital in the far north and local conditions on the southeast coast, those restrictions were not very effective. Immigration to the island, which accelerated over the following hundred years, was driven primarily by population and economic pressures on the southern Fujian-Guangdong coast, and over time the island attracted the entrepreneurial attention for which the people of that region are known. In the early phases, this immigrant population was composed largely of unattached males from the rural communities of Fujian and Guangdong provinces. That, along with the thin official presence, gave the island a frontier mentality of lawlessness and violence, with strongmen organizing and controlling economic and social developments. Subsequently, the island was wracked with conflict and rebellions, including battles between Chinese settlers and the indigenous population. This reputation for warfare and toughness still remains in some aspects of contemporary Taiwanese society: witness the fistfights and chair throwing that were common in the legislature of the early post–martial law period.

During the Qing period, the majority of settlers came from three areas along the coast: the Fujian towns of Quanzhou and Zhangzhou and various sites in Guandong province. These three emigrating groups form the ancestral base of the oldest Chinese population currently on the island. In the literature, the people from the two Fujian areas are typically called Hoklo (Heluo) or Fukienese, and most families still recognize their Quanzhou or Zhangzhou origins. The people from the Guangdong area, who speak a different dialect and have distinctive cultural forms, are called Hakka (Kejia). Often the Hoklo and Hakka are lumped together as "Taiwanese," usually in distinction to a colonizing elite.

Immigrating populations tended to arrive in successive waves, settle in certain areas, and fill select occupations. Once on the island, they established strong social ties based on places of origin that came to inform much of the island's social structure and fuel its ethnic tensions. The conflict between the Quanzhou and Zhangzhou peoples was particularly prevalent, even though they had emigrated from the same province and shared language, religion, and other cultural formations.

Over the two hundred years of nominal Qing rule, Chinese settlement of Taiwan spread northward, filling the western plain and reaching into the Taipei basin area. At the same time, Taiwan was drawn more and more into China's political and cultural spheres. In part, this was a reaction to foreign interest in the island: first from the Japanese, who threatened occupation in 1874, and then from the French, who attacked the island in 1884, with their own colonial designs. With the increasing perceived strategic importance of the island, the Chinese dynastic government moved to strengthen the island's political position, first by establishing another prefecture in the north (Taibeifu, in 1876) and then by making the island its own province (Taiwansheng, in 1887). Under the influence of these different forces, political and cultural power on the island shifted from the older communities in the southern part of the island to the newly settled and contested north. Thus, when the province was established, the northern prefectural capital of Taipei was designated as the provincial capital as well.

This belated Qing interest and investment in the island did not last long. In 1895 Taiwan was ceded in perpetuity to the Meiji government of Japan as part of the settlement of the Sino-Japanese War, in which China was soundly defeated by the modernized Japanese navy. In this way, Taiwan became the first in Japan's colonial collection. There was some hesitancy and confusion in the early years, but by 1898 Japan embarked on an extensive and calculated colonial remaking of the island. The Japanese rulers were determined to "outcolonize" the Western colonial powers, which they studied and often emulated.[12] The reach of those colonial efforts was far and deep, especially for the Chinese population, and included education and language reforms, sanitation and hygiene regimens, detailed census taking and map making, modern police and military controls, extensive development of rice and sugar production, promotion of the recreational and tourist industries, and, most important for our purposes, urban planning and development that transformed the cities of Taiwan into models of colonial modernity.

For the populations of Taiwan, both indigenous and Chinese, the changes in the lives of individuals were dramatic and oftentimes traumatic. The indigenous peoples were treated in a typically colonial way: they were both oppressed and patronized, depending on the particular circumstances of the moment and the parties involved. In all cases, they were seen as uncivilized and inferior, and this had distinct racist constructions. The situation for the Chinese population was markedly different. First, the separate Chinese communities were all called Islanders (Hontōjin) or Taiwanese (Taiwanjin), thus the ethnic and subethnic distinctions that were so important in the Qing period were officially displaced by the external, generalizing point of view of the Japanese colonialists, although they certainly were cognizant of the distinction between Hoklo and Hakka.[13] These Islanders were distinguished from both the Japanese Homelanders (Naichijin) and the indigenous peoples, first called *banjin* and *seiban* (savages) and later *takasago zoku* (original people of the island of Taiwan), a more culturally neutral term.[14]

For complex historical and cultural reasons, the Taiwanese, especially the elite population, were considered more closely aligned with their Japanese colonial rulers than with the colonized indigenous peoples (and this seemed to be a view shared to some extent by both the Japanese and Taiwanese). This certainly was true in social policy. Although the so-called principles of *dōka* (shared culture) and *dōbun* (shared writing), which were meant to emphasize the similarities between the Japanese and the Chinese, never amounted to anything close to equality or even parity, the underlying logic did lead to a relatively integrated elite colonial society in which Japanese and Taiwanese worked together, especially in the cities. For example, while always holding subordinate positions, Taiwanese were employed extensively in the colonial police force; and at the upper end of the social spectrum, there emerged a large cohort of Taiwanese physicians, many of whom trained in Japan, although they could not hold the most privileged positions in the state hospitals of the island. [15]

These elite colonial subjects, who held an in-between position in the system, became more and more implicated in colonial power and its resistance as the colony went through its transformations, heading toward the final period of the *kōminka* (creating imperial subjects) policy. In his short story "The Doctor's Mother," Wu Zhuoliu parodied the position of the "in-between subject" in the late colonial period:

> When Japanese was being promoted as the "all-family" language, Qian Xinfa [the doctor] lied to the investigators that his mother was able to handle at least some conversational Japanese. For this reason, the Qians met the requirements for the "all Japanese" family, and he considered this the highest honor ever bestowed on him. He immediately remodeled his house in Japanese style, installing new tatami mats and rice paper sliding doors. The lighting was good and everyone who saw it expressed approval. But before ten days had passed, this kind of genuine Japanese style of living had made his mother angry. She didn't like Japanese miso soup for breakfast for one thing, and she couldn't bear the pain of sitting cross-legged on the straw mats. When his mother ate her meals, she had to force her stiffened legs to bend to sit down. In less than ten minutes, her legs became so numb that not only wasn't she able to swallow her food, she couldn't even stand up.[16]

Clearly the doctor and his mother are allegorical figures for extreme subjective positions under colonial rule. She is the model of "Taiwaneseness" in her resistance to that rule (she cannot even bend her legs), while he represents the groveling desire to "be one of them," although the reader knows he never really can be, similar to what Homi Bhabba calls the state of mimicry: "almost the same but not quite."[17]

Colonial rule in Taiwan finally fell victim to the overreaching imperialism of the Japanese state when World War II brought an abrupt end to Japanese military expansion into East and Southeast Asia. In those final years of the war, the people of Taiwan were called upon to support and suffer for Japan: they endured domestic shortages, they served in the Japanese imperial army, and they were bombed by Allied forces. While a planned invasion of the island was in the end diverted to other islands in the Pacific, Taipei City was still bombed extensively, as were other cities. Despite that, the infrastructure of the island was relatively intact when the Japanese surrendered the island in 1945.

In 1943 the Allied Powers had agreed that Taiwan would be placed under Chinese rule with victory in the Pacific; at the time, Chinese rule meant the Republic of China, led by Chiang Kai-shek (Jiang Jieshi) and his Nationalist (Guomingdang or KMT) party. The story of that handover is one of the most tragic in the history of the island. What began in relative optimism and goodwill on both sides ended in violence and brutality a few years later. At the end of the war, the Nationalist government was preoccupied with its problems on the continent, especially the looming civil war with communist forces, and the resources and efforts it expended in Taiwan were minimal and marginal. Moreover, in policy and personality, the Chinese government regarded the Taiwanese, especially the Japanese-educated elite, with deep suspicion and distrust—as a people who had a "slave mentality" (*nuhua jiaoyu*). The Taiwanese, on the other hand, came to see the new Chinese rulers, especially the army and police, as uncivilized boors and brutes. While the Nationalist forces expected to be seen as comrades who had suffered through a horrendous war on the continent against the Japanese, the Taiwanese elites expected to be treated as an educated class who had gained experience and insight into the modern world during fifty years of Japanese rule. These worldviews were on a collision course.[18]

The incidents and aftermath of events beginning on February 28, 1947, fully manifested that collision.[19] The initial public protest over police brutality, which included large-scale vandalism, beatings, and even murder on the part of the protesters, was quickly commandeered by the Taiwanese elite and turned into a formal and escalating confrontation with Nationalist authorities. When the Chinese military moved in to put down the protest, they proceeded to punish the representative elite very severely: an estimated twenty thousand Taiwanese, primarily from the elite class, were brutally and often publicly executed or disappeared in the following months. Before the massacre, Governor Chen Yi had assured the local population, "As for those who participated in this incident and were arrested by the officials or the military police, the government will be lenient and send them to the military police headquarters, where they will be released to their families and relatives."[20] The subsequent duplicity and violence not only hollowed out the Taiwanese leadership on the island; it precipitated the long period of "White Terror" that silenced for decades any public protest against the Nationalist government or any discussion of this February 28th Incident (Ererba Shijian). In every aspect of public life, the Nationalist government sought to erase signs of that brutality, but certainly private memories remained and festered; these memories and resentments became the central markers of Taiwanese ethnic consciousness, which saw public light again in the post–martial law period beginning in the late 1980s.

When the Nationalists lost the civil war to the communists and, like the Ming loyalist Zheng Chenggong, retreated to the island to set up their Republic of China in exile, the political and social division between the Taiwanese and the newly arrived Chinese grew significantly larger. First, there were the sheer numbers: in just a few months during 1949 and 1950, two million mainland refugees fled to the island, which theretofore had a population of approximately six million. This tsunami of displaced Chinese included the Nationalist leadership and middle management as well as thousands of impoverished foot soldiers. Most of this new population settled in the city of Taipei, which was designated the temporary national capital—the leadership moved into the posh, formerly Japanese neighborhoods, but the lower echelon found refuge only in crowded military housing (juancun) and makeshift hovels. Although these displaced people were commonly lumped into one group of Mainlanders (Waishengren), they were actually an extremely diverse population, regionally, ethnically, and in social class. In the official media we often hear of and from the Nationalist leadership, but there were many Mainlanders who remained displaced and disenfranchised for decades. At the lower levels of society, there was a great deal of intermingling, even marriage, between Mainlanders and Taiwanese, although the ideological divide remained strong.

In addition to the hardship caused by the sheer numbers, governmental policies exacerbated the rift between Taiwanese and Mainlanders, especially in the mechanisms that imposed a new Chinese nationalism on the island, overshadowing local concerns and issues. In Taipei, the central government occupied all major buildings and proceeded to focus its attention and resources, including a huge standing army, on the goal of regaining the mainland. At the local level, officials developed cultural policies that centered on Sinicization (Zhongguohua) of the island, clearly projecting the attitude that Taiwanese culture, with its Japanese overlay, was not authentically "Chinese" and needed to be restored to its lost roots.

Over time, the Taiwanese dialect, along with Japanese, was banned from public life; cultural practices, including the study of geography and history, focused exclusively on the mainland. The Taiwanese literally lost their voice, and many writers lost their ability to write until they could learn the new national language (guoyu), this time Mandarin, not Japanese. These policies, collectively called a "cultural renaissance," also promoted mainland cultural forms in public life, such as the Peking Opera and the northern "palace" style architecture that featured red-pillared buildings with intricately (but nonfunctioning) bracketed and cantilevered roofs. In this way, the Nationalists claimed to possess authentic Chinese culture, which they said was being destroyed in the People's Republic and was not readily available to the local population. The famed National Palace Museum collection of Chinese art, which the Nationalists brought to Taiwan, became the emblem of that ownership. The Taiwanese, along with their history and culture, were once again displaced by these policies. What is more, anyone criticizing such policies and practices, even Mainlanders, was severely punished, typically by being sent to the gulag on Green Island. To implement punishment, the Chiang regime maintained a secret police force and citizen surveillance programs that were ruthlessly efficient, extending to Chinese communities living abroad, especially in the United States. At that time, any opposition politics that did exist was carried out by the exiled Taiwanese population, especially in Japan. It is for these reasons, among many others, that the martial law period under the Nationalists (1949–87) is sometimes called "neocolonial." [21]

Ironically, the Korean War was what assured the survival of the Nationalist government and its neocolonial agenda. After the Nationalist loss in the civil war, which was largely regarded as a manifestation of the incompetence and corruption of the Chiang regime, the United States began to remove its support for the government. With the outbreak of the Korean War in 1951, that course was reversed, and the U.S. government recruited Chiang Kai-shek and his government as allies in the Cold War. With the Chiang government and the United States joined again at the hip, substantial financial and strategic support for the government in Taiwan was assured for the next fifteen years. While this kept the communists at bay and maintained the Nationalists' hegemony over the island, it also led to substantial reforms, especially in agriculture and education. During the 1960s, these policies and practices helped foster the economic recovery that has been called the "Taiwan miracle." While the Nationalist government maintained control over major industries and utilities, it allowed the expansion of small and medium-sized manufacturing, beginning in fabrics and moving on to electronics, which drove the new economic engine. These small companies were largely Taiwanese owned and operated in a social-business system below the radar of the Mainlanders, who dominated government and education; the small firms have sometimes been called agents of guerrilla capitalism. Under this system, large segments of the Taiwanese population began to move into the middle class, with income disparities remaining very low by world standards.[22]

The Nationalists' protection by the United States and their isolated position on the island allowed the fiction that the Republic of China's government was "in exile" to remain on the books long after anyone seriously believed the Nationalists would retake the mainland—in fact, that fiction remains in place today, but largely because the Chinese government on the mainland will not allow its logical alternative, an independent island, to be considered. In 1971 the United Nations recognized the People's Republic of China, as did the United States in 1978; this effectively pulled the plug on Taiwan's international status. The government in Taiwan was forced to take a hard look at its tenuous geopolitical position and contemplate new strategies for bringing stability to the island, moving toward policies of "cultural reconstruction" associated with the post–Chiang Kai-shek government.[23] The motivation for these changes may have been entirely self-serving, but the results were ultimately revolutionary. Strategies included an aggressive campaign to promote Taiwan's reputation in the international community, especially in arts and culture. For example, Taipei became a venue for tier-one international performances, especially in classical music; at the same time, Taiwan exported its own cultural productions. While many of these exports remained in the "authentic Chinese" mode, others were more local in flavor, such as the international success of the Cloud Gate Dance Theatre (Yunmen Wuji). Moreover, the now largely middle-class and highly educated society began to bring social change from within; these were often activities associated with quality of life issues that were not too politically sensitive. For example, an emerging environmental movement, driven in part by a concerned citizenry who had international experience with environmental issues, made substantial inroads into the pollution politics of Taiwan's economic miracle. Robert Weller writes:

> Taiwan had discovered "nature" sometime in the mid-1980s. I could hardly pick up a newspaper without seeing reports of environmental demonstrations, although I had never heard about one in the 1970s. Some cities had enormous, ongoing movements against factory construction. In the most famous case, the multinational giant DuPont had been forced to cancel plans for a titanium dioxide plant in Lugang in 1986. Smaller skirmishes popped up all over the island, and fights over landfills were so numerous that the newspapers dubbed them the "garbage wars."[24]

In addition to these concerns for the physical environment, identity and minority issues began to find a foothold in the social discourse. For example, a strong feminist movement and the subsequent first steps in gay rights activities date from this period. Nonetheless, the hot-button issue of Taiwanese-versus-Mainlander relations remained off the public agenda—but not for long.

The emerging civil society, combined with the "Taiwanization" of the Nationalist party, laid the foundation for the startling transformation of Taiwan beginning in the late 1980s. In 1987 President Chiang Ching-kuo (Jiang Jingguo), son of Chiang Kai-shek and instrumental in the brutal policies of the early regime, announced the lifting of martial law that had been continuously in place since 1949. In doing so, he set in motion one of the most successful reforms of authoritarian rule of the late twentieth century. Chiang's death a few months later (he had been in ill health for years) brought his vice president, Lee Teng-hui (Li Denghui), to the presidency. Lee, a longtime Nationalist bureaucrat and politician, is Taiwanese, in fact, Hakka. He had been raised during the Japanese period (he reads and speaks Japanese regularly), went to college in Japan, and received a PhD from Cornell University. Later in his rule, Lee would say that when he was growing up he thought of himself as Japanese.[25] In an earlier time, such a statement might have landed him in prison. In 1990 Lee was elected president by the National Assembly and then reelected in 1996 in the first direct election of a national leader in Taiwan—some would say, in China. Then, even more dramatically, in 2000 Chen Shuibian from the opposition Democratic Progressive Party (Minzhu Jinbu Dang, or DPP) was elected president, with the out-spoken Annette Lu (Lü Xiulian or Lu Hsiu-lian) as vice president. Both Chen and Lu had come to public prominence as members of the Meilidao (Formosa) opposition movement of the late 1970s, which the Nationalist government, in its last gasp of authoritarian rule, punished in a public military trial. Lu was one of the defendants (serving five years of a twelve-year sentence) and Chen was their lawyer. Chen made his political reputation as the first popularly elected mayor of Taipei, serving from 1994 to 1998, during which time he instituted a series of public reforms that focused on local, rather than national issues, including renaming Taipei Park "February 28th Peace Park."

In these changing times, Taiwanese identity was constantly invoked; there was open and vigorous debate about what it meant to be Taiwanese or from Taiwan, with Lee Teng-hui calling for the recognition of a "new Taiwanese person" (*xin Taiwanren*) to bridge the old divisions of Mainlander and Taiwanese.[26] Politically, the early twenty-first century witnessed a reversal of the power relationships of the previous hundred years. Through the emergence of democratic politics, the Taiwanese people were no longer the subject of a ruling minority, either Japanese or Mainlander. In fact, the Nationalists became the "opposition" party, with the Democratic Progressive Party capturing the national leadership under Chen Shuibian in 2000. In the ensuing eight years, there emerged a new hegemony of the DPP, with the expected accompanying issues of corruption and abuse—in a cruel twist of fate, Chen and others are now in jail, convicted of embezzlement. At the same time, there was a new Nationalist leadership under Taipei mayor Ma Ying-jeou (Ma Yingjiu) that focused more on local issues and promoted clean politics, which made the Nationalists an effective alternative in the new multiparty system of Taiwan, as Ma's election as president in 2008 firmly attests.

The election of the president by popular vote in 1996 had been preceded by many new avenues of public life in Taiwan after 1988. These included removing restrictions on the formation of political parties, uncensored and expanded media, popular protests on a variety of issues, open discussion of formerly taboo topics such as the February 28th Incident, and the infamous fistfights that broke out regularly in the national legislature. Taiwan quickly emerged as the center of its own attention, and its dramatic move to a full and dynamic democratic state attracted the notice of the rest of the world and dramatically improved its international status.

This localization of culture (*bentuhua*) meshed with an increasingly open and globalized society that permeated all aspects of life in Taiwan, from the political to the private, creating complex mixtures of taste and consciousness. The international decor of Starbucks and Japanese gourmet coffee shops now vie with upscale Taiwanese teahouses, which often display materials and images that recollect Taiwan's own history—local, folk, and nostalgic—of the Qing and Japanese periods, what June Yip calls the "ambiance of the island's pre-KMT [Nationalist] past."[27] Gucci stores, now with authentic rather than knock-off goods, are intermixed with small dress shops that offer chic, updated versions of "Taiwanese" clothes. The Gin Gin Bookstore offers gay pornography from around the world, while new museums focus on Taiwanese folk and indigenous cultures. We also sense that change in some of the most symbolic public spaces in the city. The Chiang Kai-shek Memorial, built in the late 1970s, for example, represents (or, one might even say, unintentionally parodies) the extremes of the architecture style that the Nationalists promoted in their policy of Sinicization in the 1960s. The current tourist brochure still reads like something from a much earlier time:

> The Chiang Kai-shek Memorial is located in downtown Taipei. Its majestic architectural design is fully based on the beauty of Chinese culture while incorporating features of memorial halls in other countries. The vibrant design of the palace roof of the National Theater, the hip-and-gable roof of the National Concert Hall, and the octagon-shaped twin roof of the Memorial Hall complement one another in a "3-mountain standing" layout that exhibits the spirit of Chinese culture.[28]

This memorial space continues to function in its official capacity as a site for national holiday celebrations or for reviewing the troops when the occasional head of state comes to town, but it is also an important site for opposition rallies, sit-ins, and other protests against the government. This latter use was established early on, when, in March 1990, thousands of students occupied part of the grounds for nearly a week to protest the antiquated political structures of the central government. In the spirit of the new era,

1 Dance routines in front of the plate glass windows of the Concert Hall, with reflections of the National Theater, Chiang Kai-shek Memorial, 2010

President Lee Teng-hui visited the students, promising to bring their concerns to the appropriate governmental bodies—in fact, those reforms were instituted in the following years. At the other end of social action, on the weekends young people gather on the wide porches of the memorial's theater and concert halls and use the massive plate-glass doors as informal dance studio mirrors with which to practice their moves, which range from quaint folk dances to flailing hip-hop (fig. 1). These are two uses of public space, both representative of current social life in Taiwan, that the designers of the memorial never had in mind.

For over three hundred and fifty years Taiwan has been in a "conditional" state, never complete on its own terms but always contingent on another framework for its definition. Always colonized, always named by another: Formosa, Taiwan (in Chinese and Japanese), the Republic of China, Chinese Taipei, and an unrecovered province of the People's Republic of China. Yet, resisting that official, externally generated nomenclature were the indigenes, the natives, the insiders who wanted to claim the island as their own on their own terms: Pakan, Ban'ka, Meilidao, and even the Republic of Taiwan.

ONE

Mapping the City

I n the fall of 1999 the Taipei City government sponsored the exhibition Old Maps of Taipei, which brought together approximately thirty-five different types of maps, dating from 1654 to 1995.[1] The exhibition was held in the old Qing dynasty administrative office (*yamen*) that had been recently restored and opened to the public. According to the official brochure, these maps were produced by the "different ethnic groups" that have "lived on Taiwan over the last four hundred years," and the purpose of the exhibition was to demonstrate how "Westerners, Chinese, Japanese, and Taiwanese have all used cartography to record the Taiwan that they knew." For practical as well as ideological purposes, the exhibit was dominated by maps from the Japanese period, a graphic manifestation of the emerging interest in describing the island as "multicultural" (*duoyuanhua*) in the post–martial law period.[2]

That sanctioned narrative of multiculturalism was further developed in 2004, when the Taipei City Cultural Affairs Bureau sponsored a second exhibition as part of the celebration of the 120th anniversary of the building of the city wall. The exhibition, held this time at the February 28th Museum, included maps, photographs, and other materials from the past hundred years. The full title of the exhibition says much: Viewing Taipei through Time and Space: The 120th Anniversary of the Taipei City Wall: An Exhibition of

Maps, Images, Documents, and Historical Relics.[3] Not only was the range of materials displayed in this exhibition wider than in Old Maps of Taipei, but the supporting paraphernalia were also far richer and the exhibition itself technically more sophisticated. In his preface to the substantial and well-designed catalogue, Taipei mayor Ma Ying-jeou (Ma Yingjiu) said that the purpose of the exhibition was "to recover lost remains, restore original conditions distorted by the historical record, deepen cultural understanding of Taipei City, and build a new consciousness of the people of Taipei."[4] Liao Xianhao, commissioner of cultural affairs, said that there was "a need to promote the foundational work that had been long neglected" in order to "restore the memory of the wall."[5] The promotional nature of this exhibition required Ma and Liao to speak in these positive terms, under the assumption that there is a physical reality that these materials (especially maps and photographs) can recover.

There is, indeed, much to be recovered through those images, but that recovery is necessarily conditioned by the ideological grounding of the materials, both in their construction and in their re-presentation. We note that the presence of images from the Japanese colonial period in Viewing Taipei is exceptionally strong, even stronger than in Old Maps of Taipei. For example, of the approximately thirty-seven maps (or details) that appear in the catalogue, twenty-nine are from the Japanese period; even more startling, only *one* map is from the postwar period. This penchant is clearly seen in the other types of media as well, especially the photographs, which are predominantly from the Japanese period. Why is this? Again, it is partly dictated by what is available: the Japanese colonial government is well known for its detailed cartographic and photographic record; in contrast, during the early years of Nationalist rule, records of the city were poorly maintained and promotional materials more haphazard. This discrepancy in management reflects the ruling authorities' respective visions of the city: for the Japanese, Taihoku was their first and most important colonial capital; while for the Chinese rulers, Taipei was a temporary capital of a government-in-exile, not worthy of their full attention. On the other hand, there are contemporary social and political conditions surrounding these exhibitions that bring prominence to the Japanese materials, and it appears that those conditions intensified over the five years between the first and second exhibitions.

These two displays may be read as part of a new narrative that is being written about the meaning of Taipei City (and Taiwan in general), in which its specific historic conditions have become a leitmotif for a unique cultural identity. This narration, which includes statements about a multicultural society, is very much an argument against Chinese nationalism. The Japanese visual materials in these exhibitions bring the long-displaced Japanese cultural experience back into the public discourse. The new narrative strikes at two agents of Chinese political domination: (1) the oppressive postwar Nationalist regime, with its strongly anti-Japanese rhetoric; and (2) the looming Chinese Communist government, which claims Taiwan as an integral part of *its* nation. It strikes against the Nationalists by performing what Ma Ying-jeou called the recovery of "lost remains" and the restoration of "original conditions" that were "distorted" (we could also say "displaced") in the postwar years. It strikes at the Communist policy by celebrating the "new consciousness of the people of Taipei," which makes them fully aware of not just how different they are from their contemporaries on the mainland but also *in what ways* they are different. Although Ma is from Hong Kong and a leader of the Nationalist Party, here he is adopting, perhaps for practical political purposes, a much more "Taiwanese" narration of the island. The second exhibition's extensive silence on the postwar period tempers the ideology of Chinese nationalism that is shared by standard Nationalist, Communist, and American rhetoric—the so-called one-China policy. In its place, Viewing Taipei offered a more local nationalism, determined by the postcolonial argument that citizens of Taipei are "less Chinese" and—because of their Japanese and American experiences—more cosmopolitan.

It is no coincidence that the promotion of these ideological views manifests itself in a review of the cartographic and photographic records. Despite their deeply ideological constructions, maps and photographs offer a visualization of the past that *seems* immediate, concrete, and unambiguous. Thus, the Japanese visual materials are ideally suited to the "recovery and restoration" of a Taiwan consciousness. For example, Japanese maps often sever the geographic link between island and continent, replacing it with depictions of the island alone in the sea, sometimes with the Japanese home islands looming on the horizon.[6] In one such map, an insert of the home islands is placed exactly where the Fujian coast should appear: a very clear form of graphic displacement.[7] The photographs, in contrast, present specific local indices of this new relationship, especially as Viewing Taipei tends to focus on the architecture and administrative organs of the colonial project in the city.[8] Together, these images promote the island as a site of early modernization—city planning, railways, and industry being extensively mapped and photographed—at a time when the Chinese continent was slogging through decades of devastation and mismanagement (principally at the hands of the Nationalists). Finally, these images represent the very materials and thoughts that were hidden from public view and closed off from debate by the shroud of martial law and its accompanying White Terror. What had been in the 1950s, 1960s, and 1970s the "dirty laundry" of colonial collaboration and servitude has become in the 1990s the celebration of the island's early modernization.[9]

Looking at these exhibitions, especially the 2004 Viewing Taipei, the city of the fifty-year postwar, martial law period seems to have disappeared from the public consciousness, as it has from the photographs and maps. This is, of course, a condition not of disappearance, but rather merely of another displacement, as the new narrative of localized cultural celebration (*bentuhua*) pushed aside the former one of "national" unity. This celebration of the local creates new conditions in which a pathology of avoidance continues.

The Earliest Maps

The detailed cartography of the Taipei basin began on a European note with maps by Spanish and Dutch colonialists of the seventeenth century.[10] This was a time when Holland was at the center of modern European cartography,[11] and because of their control over northern Taiwan, the Dutch produced maps that are particularly revealing. If Chinese maps prior to the seventeenth century recorded Taiwan at all, they did so in a perfunctory way, reflecting the common view that the island was "just a mud ball in the sea."[12] For the Dutch, however, Taiwan was indeed "off the coast of China," a location from which they could engage in the China trade; just as importantly, it was along the ocean trade routes from colonial Batavia (Jakarta) to Japan.[13] They saw the island as an entrepôt for trade with and within East Asia, and their maps clearly display that interest.[14] Among the many and varied maps of Taiwan coming from the Dutch period (1624–61), there is, for example, a relatively detailed coastal map of the entire island, dating from 1638.[15] Yet, since the Dutch concentrated their occupation in the southwestern part of the island, with Fort Zeelandia situated on the coast near present-day Tainan City, most maps are of that harbor and the surrounding area.[16] That limited view changed somewhat toward the end of the brief period of Dutch occupation.

In 1642 the Dutch took possession of the Spanish installations at Danshui (Tamsui) and Jilong (Keelong), which stood at the coastal edge of the Taipei basin area. A 1654 map not only provides a substantially detailed description of the Taipei basin but also demonstrates the official nature of the Dutch presence there.[17] The map hints at modern maritime navigation, with a compass rose and abbreviated rhumb lines ending at the coast. Along with illustrations of the harbors and the Spanish coastal forts of San Salvador and Santo Domingo, we find full representation of the basin as well. This includes details of major rivers (as far south as the middle reaches of present-day Xindian Xi and Dahan Xi), with the settlements and forested areas that line those waterways. This is not a map of Dutch or Chinese settlement, however; rather, it depicts the villages of the indigenous Ketagalan people with whom the Dutch traded, primarily through licensed Chinese agents.[18] In a very graphic projection of European concepts of landownership, the basin in this map is also divided into regular rectangles of what appear to be plot lines, similar to those found in the Dutch cadastral maps of the time. This implies Dutch plans far beyond trading local products with the native population: agricultural development based on Chinese immigration, which the Dutch had promoted successfully in the south, seems to have been on their minds.

The 1654 Dutch map is prominently placed in almost all recent reviews and narratives of the development of Taipei City. It is an exceedingly satisfying map for those, like me, who want to construct a narrative of the city; it is an illuminating beginning because it is detailed in those areas that allow us to "envision" the city, such as its accurate depiction of the course of rivers through the basin, making identifiable each site-to-be. Most recently, a full-color reproduction of the map was accompanied by this note from Gao Chuanqi: "This is the earliest known map presenting a detailed description of conditions of greater Taipei"; there was, of course, no Taipei (prefecture or city) at that time.[19] Likewise, a monograph with the telling title, *Greater Taipei: Investigations of an Old Map*, is concerned primarily with tracing the development of given sites on the map through the Ketagalan, Dutch, and Chinese names to the present.[20]

The 1654 map is also satisfying to critics who want to project the multicultural nature of Taiwan, given its European and aboriginal orientation, although in reality the legacies of Dutch and aboriginal cultures in present-day Taipei are very limited. The attention the map brings to the river settlements of the aboriginal people does remind us of what is missing from early descriptions of the basin (and Taiwan in general): the mapping (if not the maps), though ephemeral and strategic, that must have been a significant part of the lives of the Ketagalan people. We can now only imagine what and how such mapping was represented—certainly not as a penetration from the coast into the basin, as does the Dutch map, but rather something more interior and interconnected, village to village.

Early Chinese Mapping

With the fall of the Dutch to Zheng Chenggong in 1661, followed by the Manchus' victory over the Zheng house in 1683, Taiwan became nominally part of the Qing dynastic empire. In 1684 administrative control of the island was given to Fujian province; an account of that process in the *Fujian tongzhi* (Gazetteer of Fujian Province) includes the earliest Qing map with a representation of Taipei basin.[21] Since that map is concerned primarily with military emplacements, Taipei basin, at the very edge of the map and outside of the area of military contention, is represented only by a vague depiction of the Tamsui (Danshui) River in an exaggeratedly large plain with just three settlements: the Danshui Fort (Danshui Cheng) of the Spanish and Dutch settlers, and two aboriginal villages named in Chinese, Qiguishe and Shouhuangshe.[22]

Given the Qing government's lack of attention to, even suspicion of, the island, settlement proceeded by fits and starts during the two hundred years of Chinese purview, and the Taipei basin was occupied late and haphazardly by ripples of Chinese agricultural settlers.[23] Official mapping of the island continued in a similarly random and limited way, but, again, we must recognize that local mapping, this time by Chinese settlers, would have been extensive and based on a set of assumptions and purposes that differed sharply from those that characterized the maps issued by various authorities.[24]

During the eighteenth century, Taipei basin appears at the terminal end of several scroll maps of the island, which unroll, as did settlement, south to north, along the west coast. These maps, which blend traditional cartographic systems with landscape painting, have been described in detail by Emma Teng in terms of the emerging gaze that imperial China directed toward the island. Of the early Qing maps, she writes:

> Seventeenth- and eighteenth-century scroll maps of Taiwan conventionally depicted the island face-on from the perspective of the China coast rather than from a bird's-eye perspective. Taiwan is thus shown in isolation and

not part of the larger Qing Empire. The Taiwan Strait is pictured in the foreground, standing between the viewer and the island.[25]

Over time, there is, however, a progressive change in the maps as they chart
the evolution of Qing colonialist policies that began to draw the island into
the empire. It was also during this period that Taipei basin slowly became
part of Chinese-occupied Taiwan.

The most commonly cited Taiwan scroll maps from the eighteenth century are the *Map of Taiwan from the Qianlong Period* (Qianlong Taiwan
yutu), dating from 1759, and the *Map of the Savage Settlement Border* (Taiwan fanjie tu) of 1760. The formal quality and widespread reproduction of
these two maps have drawn the attention of many scholars.[26] If we focus on
the maps' depictions of the Taipei basin, which had only recently recovered
from massive flooding, we note an emerging vision of that space. [27] The representative detail in the 1759 map is quite remarkable: in addition to many
aboriginal villages dispersed throughout the plain, there are signs of the very
beginnings of Chinese settlement.[28] In the Taipei City area, clearly marked
are Mengjia Ferry (Mengjia Zhoudutoujie) and Guting Village (Guting
Cun). Mengjia (currently the Wanhua neighborhood) is the name of the earliest settlement in the Taipei City core area; Guting is now an area just east
of the city center. Elsewhere throughout the basin are iconic depictions of
Chinese farms (*zhuang*), their tiled roofs interspersed among the thatched-
roof buildings of the aboriginal villages (*she*). Similarly, cultivation of the
area is marked with "crop fields" (*tian*) and "gardens" (*yuan*), although it is
not clear whether these belong to the new Chinese settlers or the aboriginal
villagers, or both. The primary representational goal of the second, 1760,
map is, as its title suggests, to delineate space "available" for Chinese settlement. A red/blue line nominally marks the division between land "reserved"
for aboriginal occupation (primarily foothills and mountains) and the plains
area, which was open for development, even though both areas were inhabited by the aboriginal peoples.[29] Taipei basin falls completely within the
"available" space.

These maps offer a relatively idealized view of early Chinese settlement
in Taipei basin, yet if we compare them with the area around Tainan in the
south, it is clear that Taipei basin was still at the edge of Chinese imagination and control. The southern part of the island depicted in these maps is
filled with both formal Chinese settlement areas (numerous walled towns)
and imperial presence (marked by the banners of military encampments)

and is almost devoid of aboriginal villages. Conversely, the northern part of the island is still represented as a space primarily for the aboriginal "other," with Chinese settlement a growing infringement. Over the next hundred years, the Qing vision of Taiwan and the position that the Taipei basin held in that vision would undergo radical change. Chinese infringement would become displacement and then, for the Ketagalan people, nearly complete erasure.

The New North

The strategic importance of northern Taiwan emerges partly in response to new "foreign" (non-Chinese) threats to the island, coming this time from Japan in 1874 and from France in 1884, as well as in response to the development of natural resources for emerging technology, especially coal for steam vessels.

In 1874 the Japanese government sent a large military force to the island, ostensibly to respond to an aboriginal attack on shipwrecked Ryukyu sailors along the southeast coast. Negotiations over this conflict induced the Qing government to revise its political rationale and claim the entire island (not just the west coast) as its territory, sending Shen Baozhen to shore up the island's defenses against Japanese incursions in preparation for the impending war.[30] Following Beijing's completion of negotiations with the Japanese, Shen issued a series of memorials, proposing widespread reform on the island. He recommended incorporation of the entire island, including the interior mountains, into active rule by the Qing, as well as the establishment of a northern prefecture (Taibeifu) to manage the emerging northern third of the island, especially the Taipei basin area, of which he said: "Mengjia lies between Jilong (Keelong) and the twin peaks of Guilun, in a fertile plain encompassed by two rivers, with towns and villages, highways and markets, constituting a grand sight . . . therefore we should organize the establishment of what would be called Taibei Prefecture."[31] Following the submission of this memorial, the new prefecture was established by imperial decree in 1876, and the first prefect, Lin Daquan, was appointed by Shen in 1877.[32] At this time, restrictions on Chinese immigration to the island were finally lifted.[33]

This new emphasis on the northern part of the island, which culminates with the establishment of the province and its northern capital in 1887, represents a dramatic displacement of political power. The former imperial presence in the south, represented by the prefectural city of Taiwanfu (present-day Tainan), was superseded by the new political and economic importance of the north. This is, in fact, a displacement that largely remains in effect to the present day, although one could argue that in recent years it has been somewhat reversed by the reemergence of the economic and political power of the southern part of the island, particularly the deep-water port and politically vibrant city of Gaoxiong.[34]

Taipei City in Colonial Transition

The sequence of events by which Taipei, the Qing provincial capital, suddenly became Taihoku, the colonial capital of the Japanese Meiji government, have been well documented, but ruptures from this change cannot be overstated.[35] The Sino-Japanese War of 1894–95 announced a new balance of power in the region, with Japan emerging not only as dominant over China but also as a challenge to European and American imperialists. In the treaty conditions that concluded the war, the presentation of Taiwan to Japan was in many ways a consolation prize; in geopolitical terms, the control of northeast Asia was far more important. The Qing quickly abandoned any claim to the island, which fell into chaos and internal bickering.[36] The attempt by some local elite figures to establish a Republic of Taiwan (Taiwan Minzhuguo), although often celebrated in recent social-political rhetoric of independence, was really a belated and rather equivocal response to the swiftly changing conditions. When the Qing governor and erstwhile president of the Republic, Tang Jinggsong, abandoned the new state after twelve days and fled to the mainland, the city fell into Japanese hands.

Although it took months, even years, to gain full control of the island, Taihoku was occupied within a few days. Upon the invitation of the local elite, Japanese armies entered the city on horseback through Northgate on June 8, 1895, with little local resistance and some welcoming crowds.[37] This moment is represented in one of the earliest Japanese images of the city: a painting that depicts Japanese military forces, elegant and commanding on their high-stepping horses, parading through Northgate and down a street lined with welcoming Chinese residents. While it is unclear just how optimistic (at the very least) this representation of events might be, it became an iconic image of early Japanese colonial rule.[38] Given the sequence of events leading up to the parade, if Qing officials were surprised by the military rise of Japan, the residents of the Taipei area must have been dumbfounded by the troops' arrival.

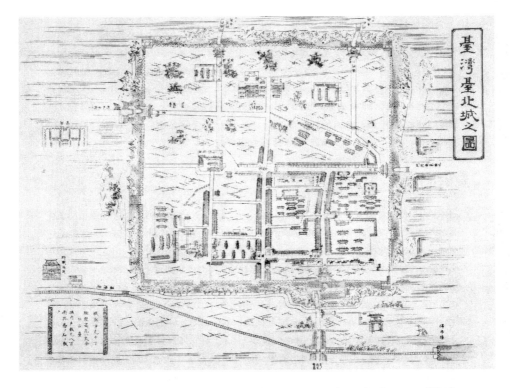

1.1 1896 *Map of Taipei, Taiwan*, in traditional Chinese cartographic style. Courtesy of SMC Publishing, Taipei, Taiwan

Several important maps of Taipei City cluster around these events in 1895. First, a block-printed map of the city from 1896 depicts, I believe, a Chinese conception of the city prior to 1895, despite its date and slight Japanese overlay.[39] I say this since the map draws principally from the conventions of traditional Chinese cartography and gazetteer illustration, not Japanese forms of representation (fig. 1.1).[40] For example, much of the architecture is labeled and represented by diagrammatic depictions of rooflines, conventions shared with both the gazetteer and early landscape maps. Moreover, the city wall is mapped as a conventionalized square oriented toward the south (Northgate is at the bottom of the map) with radically changing perspectives throughout.[41] This change in perspective is most clearly seen in the way each gate is viewed from outside the wall looking in. The gate and its representation are important and complicated elements in the Chinese urban semiotic system; chapter 3 considers their shifting symbolic value over time.

As conventional and conservative as the map is, hints of the new modernizing city are present, seen in the railroad line that crosses the bottom of the map, passing by the European-style building outside the wall and terminating at the Taipei train station.[42] The railroad was a strong index of modernization efforts initiated by Governor Liu Mingchuan, who first came to the island in 1884 to defend it against the French. In addition to building the railroad from Jilong to Taipei, his innovations included electrification, schools of Western learning, rickshaws, and other material changes that propelled the city toward the leading edge of change in China. Although Liu was removed from power in 1891 before he could make much more than surface changes to the city, these were changes that Japanese colonialists embraced and deepened. Nothing would become more emblematic of colonial development of the island than the early and extensive Japanese railroad system, which is celebrated in colonial and postcolonial materials.[43]

Other maps from this transitional period present a different, complementary view of the city, especially the *Outline Map of Taipei, Dadaocheng, and Mengjia* (Taihoku oyobi Daitotei Mōkō ryakuzu), in two versions dated from 1895 and 1897 (fig. 1.2).[44] In specific content, these Japanese maps differ little from the Chinese map, but they offer an entirely new system of representation of those details.

Following modern European cartographic conventions of a ground-plan design, which the Japanese embraced as part of their Meiji reforms, the orientation of the map is the reverse of the Chinese map (north is now at the top), uniform in its point of view, and planimetric (two-dimensional) in design, with standards of scale and topo-

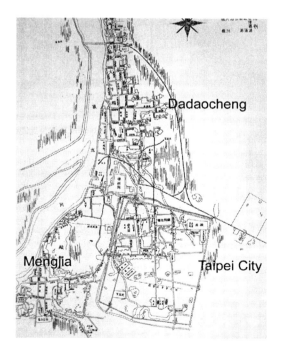

1.2 1897 *Outline Map of Taipei, Dadaocheng, and Mengjia* in modern cartographic style. Courtesy of National Taiwan Library; labeling by author

graphic representations formally stated in an accompanying legend.[45] The conventions of these maps were as if to say: we don't quite know what we are going to do with this space, but clearly it will be part of a vision that leans more toward Tokyo and Europe than toward the city's imperial or local origins. Indeed, at the beginning of the colonization period, the Meiji government had no clear policy on the future of the island; Japanese authorities, new to the colonial enterprise, were occupied with debates on fundamental issues, including whether to keep the colony at all. Then for the first few years of the occupation, the colonial government was concerned primarily with pacifying the island, not with developing a coherent colonial plan.[46] These early Japanese maps of Taihoku reflect that moment of distraction and indecision.

Over the coming decades, the cartographic representations of Taihoku (and of the island as a whole) moved ever closer to an alignment with the modern metropole of Tokyo. There were concerted efforts to produce large-scale, topographical survey maps for the entire island, as part of the scientific accounting of the new colonial possession.[47] These topographic maps were accompanied by progressively detailed urban-planning maps for Taihoku and other important cities, each filled with graphic statements of ideological intent.

Urban Planning Maps of Taihoku

The vacillation in early colonial policy began to be resolved in 1898, with the arrival of the new governor-general, Kodama Gentarō, and his celebrated civil administrator, Gotō Shimpei. These two men, informed by deep exposure to European colonialism and "Western learning," brought with them a progressive agenda for the island. This was especially so for Gotō, who would go on to become mayor of Tokyo and then urban planner for that city after the 1923 earthquake; later he would have substantial influence on the construction of the colonial capital of Manchukuo in the 1930s.[48] His early experience in Taipei undoubtedly informed both of those later projects. Mark Peattie writes:

> With the arrival of Kodama Gentarō and his civil administrator Gotō Shimpei, the Japanese presence in Taiwan at last found a policy and a purpose. Superbly trained in the medical profession in Germany, widely read in the contemporary literature of colonialism, Gotō combined outstanding organi-

zational talent with a quick and searching mind. Working under an influential and trusting superior and reinforced by important political connections at home, moreover, he had the benefit of operating in an undeveloped territory with a broad latitude of authority.[49]

Gotō's vision created the fundamental direction for many aspects of the development of the colony, not the least in city planning and architecture: "Taking his cue from the role of the public edifice in British India," Peattie writes, "[Gotō] undertook the transformation of the decaying jumble of Chinese Taipei into the stately European-style capital of Taihoku."[50] The transformative nature of Gotō's urban planning is clear, but I would argue that at that time intramural Taipei was less a "decaying jumble" and more a vacant lot.

That vacancy is evident in the 1897 map (fig. 1.2) suggesting that at least 50 percent of the land between the walls was undeveloped at that time, still primarily agricultural fields.[51] This urban emptiness is striking, especially by late imperial Chinese standards, and presented opportunities for Japanese urban planners, upon which they clearly seized in their first urban planning map, issued in August 1900.[52] In subsequent chapters, I will return to the intramural details of that plan, but here we should note that the space within the wall was primarily reconfigured with a series of new streets that extended and complemented the original Qing streets, creating a more extensive grid and piercing the city wall with nine new gates. The map is most revealing, however, in what it fails to include in its early vision: the extramural settlements of Mengjia and Dadaocheng, the oldest settlements in the area, where the large majority of Taiwanese lived and worked. It seems that in 1900, Japanese planners chose to focus their attention solely on the relatively neutral intramural space that they saw available for occupation and worthy of their colonial aspirations. When the planners did turn their gaze to areas beyond the wall, they first looked toward the south and east, away from these older Chinese settlements. This is seen, for example, in the 1901 *Planning Map for South of the City Wall* that sketched out the new Japanese residential area there.[53] This suburban plan was then incorporated into the first new comprehensive city map (1901), *Complete Map of Remodeled Taipei* (Taihoku shigai kaisei zenzu), which echoed the general shape of the 1895–97 transition maps. Here Mengjia and Dadaocheng stay largely untouched, while the Qing contents of the intramural city are almost completely written over by detailed Japanese projections (fig. 1.3).[54] This was a bold new plan for downtown Taihoku, but much more was soon to come.

1.3 1901 *Complete Map of Remodeled Taipei*. Courtesy of SMC Publishing, Taipei, Taiwan

In 1905 a new Taihoku planning map cast the die that would project the colonial vision out through the Japanese colonial period and beyond, reaching its full form in the 1932 plan for greater Taipei. The 1905 map is a concrete manifestation of Gotō Shimpei's progressive and expansive urban policy.[55] The map's most immediate innovation is its integration of the Japanese and Chinese sections of the city. Su Shuobin says that "with this 1905

Taipei City Area Remodeling Plan (Taihokushiku kaisei kaikagu), Mengjia and Dadaocheng are finally drawn into the whole design and the concept of Taipei as 'one city' enters a new phase."[56] Japan's attitude toward the colonial status of the "islanders" (*hontōjin*) was ambivalent at best, yet over time there emerged a professed policy of "assimilation" (*dōka*) that captured the imagination of both the rulers and the ruled elite, especially during the 1920s.[57] That attitude of potential inclusion, as illusory and one-sided as it might have been, seems to have begun with the cosmopolitan vision of the Kodama-Gotō rule and this map.

The insularity that was by definition the natural condition of the intramural city is here dissolved into a state of porousness and integration. The city wall, that mechanism and emblem of exclusion, disappears and is replaced by large boulevards encircling the city core. This circulation reaches into the Chinese communities, with major streets fanning out from the central business and administrative areas of the city, extending deep into settlement areas and drawing them into the matrix of different economies, both financial and symbolic. In the case of Mengjia, the oldest Chinese section, this includes the recovery of a major section of marshland on which the planned streets were to be built—that marshland is clearly visible in the 1901 map (see fig. 1.3).[58] As significant as those integrative steps were for the formation of Taipei City, it was the extension of the city grid out into the eastern suburbs that signaled its Japanese future. Here would develop the extensive neighborhoods of Japanese residential housing that completed the full architectural imprint of the city, wherein Japanese domestic construction combined with the European colonial buildings of downtown and the older Chinese residential/commercial architecture to the west and north. To some extent, that tripartite city remains with us today, although the Japanese suburbs have sprawled far out across the basin, climbing the foothills and filling the river valleys with various forms of postwar architecture, largely (but not entirely) displacing the vernacular Japanese forms. For economic, geographic, and social reasons, the two older Chinese sections of the city have remained relatively intact and circumscribed.

The 1905 urban plan that envisioned the integrated city was projected out twenty-five years to a city of 150,000 people (beginning with a population of 86,775 in 1905). When those twenty-five years concluded, the population of the city had already grown to nearly 250,000, and a new plan was needed.[59] There are intervening maps of the city during this period (such as those of 1914 and 1920), but they represent only the infilling of

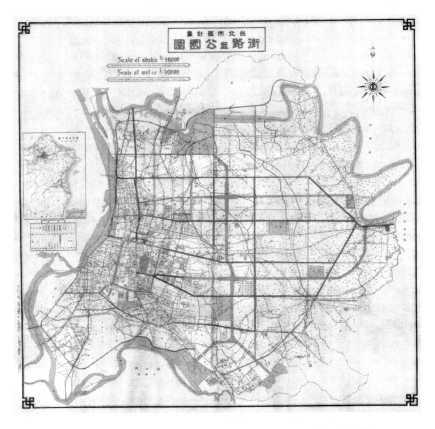

1.4 1932 *Map of Streets and Parks: Plan for Taipei Area.* Courtesy of SMC Publishing, Taipei, Taiwan

the 1905 map plans, not a new vision for the city. Then, in 1932, the central government issued a new urban development plan projected to 1955 for a city of 600,000.[60] That plan has several accompanying maps, but the most revealing is the *Map of Streets and Parks: Plan for Taipei Area* (Taihoku shiku keikaku: Gairo yo kōen zu), which presents an expansive vision of the city (fig. 1.4). This map might be viewed as a local articulation of the imperialist plans that were then dominating Japan's geopolitical agenda. Moving from the downtown area toward the eastern hills, the map plots out a grid of arterials deep into the agricultural land surrounding the city. The ruler-straight lines, with their 90-degree intersections, suggest that no local accommodations needed to be made in these plans, as urban modernity displaces the rural economy. Along with the aggressiveness of this design is the articulation of a public park system for the city, expanded to include sixteen parks, all numbered and most linked by wide parkways (*kōen michi*) in the eastern and northern suburbs.

This optimistic plan, in which an efficient transportation system joins sites of civic leisure, is a statement of progressive modernity that was the logical extension of Japan's rising prominence in the world and Taihoku's symbolic value within it. In the end, these plans were derailed by the international military entanglements that emerged with that rising prominence. As Japan and its colony moved through the 1930s, less and less attention and resources could go toward the luxuries of modern life; thus, these plans for the city, including the park system, were never fully implemented, although they remained "on the books."[61]

Photographing the City

Along with progressively detailed mapping of Taipei and other cities throughout the colonial period, we also have a colonial photographic record that offers a similarly rich, optimistic representation of the city. As with the colonial cartography, the photographs live on in the postwar period, playing a part in the ideological work of different political and cultural powers over the last fifty years. When Su Shuobin examines the "visible Taipei" (kandejian de Taibei), this photography is implicated in his arguments, not just as part of the record of the colony but also in its construction of social space.

Photography in early colonial Taiwan became a primary medium for providing "evidence" of the realities promoted by disciplinary and social institutions, similar to that identified by John Tagg in Europe and the United States at a slightly earlier time; in this case, the social institutions were the urban planning and renovation projects of the colonial state. This photography had several well-established genres; of them, the celebration of colonial architecture is central to our concerns here. We have a continual and complex visual record of the construction of the colonial edifice in the downtown area. The earliest colonial institution to receive extensive photographic celebration was the governor-general's residence, which was constructed in 1901, modeled on German-style architecture. The residence represents the earliest phase of the insertion of European-style built space into the intramural area, a project inherited from the Japanese experiments in the Meiji capital of Tokyo (a topic to which I will return in

1.5 Photographs of Taihoku architecture, 1926: (a) Sōtokufu; (b) Governor General Residence, with Sōtokufu in the distance; (c) Taihoku District Office; (d) three-lane downtown boulevard (*sansenro*), with East Gate in the distance. Source: *Taiwan Shashinchō*; courtesy of National Taiwan Library

later chapters). This visualization of the colonial presence becomes nearly obsessive with the completion of the new Sōtokufu (Colonial Administration Building) in 1919. Everything about the Sōtokufu—its size, ornamentation, and shape—declared the commanding presence of the Japanese in the city and colony (fig. 1.5). Visualization of the building merges with the urban mapping project in numerous ways, but none is so telling as the way its footprint was designed to inscribe the word *ni* 日 of Nihon (Japan) onto the city space. Since this design is visible only from the air and in planimetric maps, it privileges an elite and commanding view. The Sōtokufu building, along with others, was repeatedly photographed and the images circulated throughout the colonial media and public space, carefully reiterating the Japanese reformulation of the city.

At the end of World War II, these were the very buildings that the Chinese national government adopted for its own. When the Japanese evacuated the downtown and suburban areas at the end of the war, the new Chinese governmental organs and personnel quickly filled the vacuum. They disparaged the Japanese influence on the island yet seemingly accepted its colonialist project. This was especially evident when, in 1949, the Republic of China's government-in-exile established its national headquarters in the central colonial buildings that anchored the downtown; by switching one Chinese character, the Sōtokufu became the Zongtongfu (presidential palace). The obsessive visuality of this building was sustained throughout the postwar period, as it became the primary site of pomp and ritual for the Chinese government and its Nationalist party but with a studied avoidance of references to its Japanese origins. During this period, the provenance of these buildings was displaced by a new level of malfeasance, when the colonial legacy was shrouded by the neocolonial machinery and its White Terror. That shroud was lifted with the end of martial law. The public celebration of the buildings' Japanese legacy became part of the wave of cultural recovery and refractive nostalgia that characterized the 1990s; a hobbyist could even buy a paper model of the Sōtokufu/Zongtongfu building.[62] This embrace of the colonial is a particular quality of postcoloniality in Taiwan.[63]

During the Japanese period, there was also a photographic celebration of the new commercial streets in the downtown area—although retail buildings maintained the plot and storefront dimensions established in the Qing period, they took facade ornamentation to new heights. To intensify the evidence of these designs, the photographs typically take an oblique angle on the facades, projecting a dense layering of elaborate ornamentation as one gazes down the street. In August 1911, Taipei suffered a major typhoon that destroyed much of its old housing and structures. In the spirit of a growing colonial confidence, the Japanese government turned the destruction into an opportunity to rebuild parts of the intramural city, especially the Kyō ward, into a modern commercial district. The results of this renovation project are documented in a photo album that compares the old and new in a series of excellent black-and-white photographs that "prove" the progressive nature of the colony.[64]

In the 1960s and 1970s, the new Chinese government made similar photographic claims for *its* modernization efforts. But it typically made comparisons only with the pre-Japanese city and elided the intervening fifty years of colonial changes, since in many ways the renovations of the 1960s would not have compared so well with the Japanese city at its height. After the lifting of martial law and the widespread availability of historical materials, both commercial and government publications made the comparisons again. In those materials, one often finds a multilayered comparison ranging from Qing through contemporary conditions, with the Japanese period fully and positively represented.[65] In a new form of displacement, these contemporary narratives of the city often play down, or even ridicule, the modernization efforts of the early Nationalist period.

Thus, it is clear that, in the sense John Tagg has argued, any given photograph is not an index of a prior reality but rather produces a specific meaning depending on the discursive system in which it is embedded. In the examples we have been considering here, these discursive systems have changed from the Japanese colonialist to the Chinese nationalist to that of Taiwan localization. Yet, there *is* some indexical quality of the photograph that cannot be unwritten or completely rewritten; that is why ideological narratives have to be illustrated very carefully, for fear that another reality will show through. We will return to those ideological choices and their inherent dangers in subsequent chapters.

Maps for Consumption

Contemporaneous with the celebrated 1911 renovation project in downtown Taihoku is a map that offers the city in near-photographic three-dimensionality. This map, dating from October 1911, translates the planning maps of that project period, along with on-site investigations and photographs, into a new visuality of the city.[66] In his accompanying note, the map's editor, Iwahashi Shōzan, writes:

> This map is based on the Revised Map of Taipei City, made from a survey directed by the Department of Public Works of the Taiwan Governor-General's Office, with additional changes based on a recent survey. My main purpose for having this made is to provide a map of the city that is popular in style and comprehensible to all. For that reason we have drawn the buildings and vegetation as if viewed from the side, giving the impression of the actual scenery projected from an elevated position, thereby allowing viewers without special cartographic training, such as women and children, to comprehend easily the layout of the whole city. We hope this will lead them to pursue the formal study of maps. I understand that some might not approve of this type of illustrative, three-dimensional cartography. I ask your indul-

gence: my sole purpose here is to make the general outlines of the city easier to visualize.[67]

As this note makes clear, the map's intended function was not for planning or even navigating the city but rather for making the city an object of contemplation and admiration, making it visible even to "women and children."

In that bid for visibility, the 1911 map's title, *The New Comprehensive Bird's Eye Map of Taipei* (Saishin Taihoku shigai chōmoku zenzu), seems to claim a new avian perspective, prefiguring the arrival of aerial photography in modern cartography. Yet the map's continuation of the shifting perspectives of earlier three-dimensional maps is an indication that the actual technology of aerial photography had yet to penetrate the cartographic world (this would not happen until the 1920s).[68] The neologism *chōmoku*, which normally might be translated as "bird's eye," perhaps should really be translated as "birds' eyes"[69] These multiple "bird views" are reinforced by the extensive labeling of architectural pieces in the form of standing cartouches, each oriented with its architectural referent.

In the 1930s, another type of colonial mapmaking emerged in which this project of visualization conjoined new photographic technology with Japanese pictorialism: these are the panoramic "bird's-eye-view maps" (*chōkanzu/niaokantu*) of the island.[70] These maps present the island and selected localities as picturesque places in three-dimensional, full-color representations; but this time the point of view has been unified and elevated as the bird/airplane seems to approach the site at shadowless noon, thousands of feet off the ground. These maps are a graphic celebration of the island in both its natural and its colonized beauty, combining stunning landscapes with significant signs of modern progress (including airplanes overhead, but under our gaze). They help document the transformation of the island into a postcard destination inviting the tourist's gaze: the island of rebels and headhunters had become one of tropical fruit and hot springs.[71] While the audiences for earlier maps may have been primarily the urban planner and the administrator, here they are clearly the actual or imagined tourist.

The lush renderings of the island in these panoramic maps of the 1930s are in a consistent pictorial style, with conventionalized points of view, in both elevation and direction.[72] Views of the entire island are almost always from the west side looking east, just as in the Qing maps, but the new technology invites views from "twenty thousand feet" so that the east side of the island is also partly visible "beyond the mountains." Views of specific sites along the coasts are consistently backed by the barrier of central mountains (as we shall see, Taipei presents an interesting variation on this orientation). The maps are no doubt derivative of aerial photography of the time, yielding horizons and perspective not found in the early Japanese and Chinese maps. In this case, the new technology is enhanced by the old, as landscape painting techniques increase the depth of field and the width of the lens, creating "encompassability, partial exaggeration, and density of composition" not available in the photographic medium.[73]

There are several *chōkanzu* maps of the greater Taipei area, but none is as celebrated as the one issued on the eve of the 1935 Taiwan Exposition (discussed in chapter 5).[74] This map can be viewed as a full complement to the 1932 comprehensive planning map of the city: iconic versus symbolic, isometric versus planimetric, and pictorial versus engineered. Both maps present an entirely optimistic view of the city; the *chōkanzu* map celebrates what "is," while the 1932 maps project what is to come. In the 1935 map, we find all the conventions of the *chōkanzu*: the wide, unified view; the detailed rendering of architecture; cartouche labeling; and even airplanes casting their noon shadows on the airfield south of the city. However, instead of the conventional onshore view, the gaze here is from southwest of the city, looking north down the Danshui River. This perspective does several things: it foregrounds the newer, Japanese sections of the city in favor of the older Chinese sections and it affords a view out to sea, where, through artistic license taken with both distance and direction, Japan's emblematic Mount Fuji stands, along with a necklace of other colonies (Korea and Manchukuo) and coastal temptations (Shanghai, Fuzhou, Xiamen, Shantou, Hong Kong, and Guangzhou) (fig. 1.6). The view is fully one of colonial possession and desire. In the foreground, Taihoku is laid out as a teeming but orderly city, its multicolor cartouches reminding us of all its civic activity, although its streets are nearly without traffic. Celebration of colonial success fills the map: the bottom left-hand corner of the map is pushed down and the Xindian River bent sharply enough to allow for the depiction of the new Taihoku Imperial University (1928). And in the upper right-hand corner, just beyond the city, rise the great Taiwan Shinto Shrine and mountain spas of Yangming Mountain and Hoto/Beitou. The rail line down the river valley leads finally to picturesque Guanyin Mountain, beyond which modern ships cruise along the coast. Unlike the 1932 planning map, however, the new eastern suburbs are cropped from view, although there are trains, buses, and cars headed in that direction.

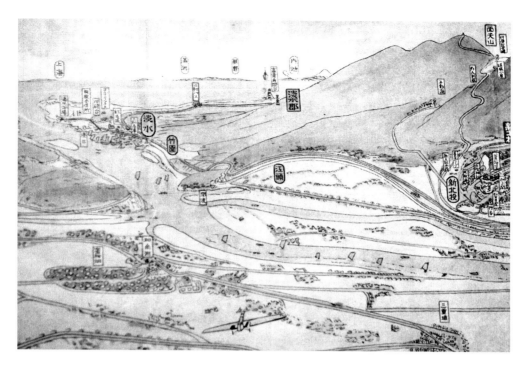

1.6 Detail of 1935 panorama map of Taipei, *Bird's Eye Map of Greater Taipei,* Danshui harbor, Mount Fuji on the horizon. Courtesy of Taipei City Archives

Viewed through the lens of current cultural debates on the island, this map seems to embody the now often posited qualities of the Japanese period, which is said to have produced a well-run society, where order, discipline, and fairness prevailed (at least in hindsight) as it progressed steadily toward the future. When young urban professionals of Taipei today speak of the need for a "quality of life" (*shenghuo pinzhi*), that may be what they can see in this utopian map of 1935.

The U.S. bombing of Taiwan began in October 1944, coordinated with the Allied approach to the Philippines. Bombing intensified once U.S. forces had control of Luzon (March 1945) and reached Taipei City in earnest in May—on May 31, downtown Taipei endured 124 sorties by B-29 bombers.[75] In the beginning, those attacks were in preparation for an assumed deadly invasion; later, they were in support of military actions in the region, especially the battle of Okinawa. When the U.S. military designed its bombing maps of Taipei, it drew on Japanese maps as well as its own aerial photography; this time, however, the "bird's-eye view" was that from a military reconnaissance plane.[76] On these maps, downtown Taipei (using the Japanese term, Jonai District) was designated as bombing target number 47.[77] The labels are all there, including those of the celebrated colonial sites (Residence of Governor General, Taihoku Park, Museum, Medical College, and Shinto Shrine), yet there is also labeling for the soft underbelly of the city (Prison, Freight Yard, Ice Plant, and Officer Barracks). The details of the core city, with its central government buildings, are especially dense—even the winding pathways in Taipei Park are clearly delineated.[78]

TWO

Picturing the City

Maps continued to be part of the vision of postwar Taipei (and I consider some of them in subsequent chapters), but the power of cartographic projection faded in comparison to the dominant visual medium of photography. In part, this is because postwar maps of the city merely reiterated the 1932 Japanese plans, although there was a growing disparity between what the maps were projecting and what changes were actually occurring on the ground.[1] That disparity was exacerbated by the conflicted nature of the city as defined by the new Nationalist government: Taipei was seen both as a temporary outpost and as a bastion of authentic "Chineseness." Moreover, with the increasing influence of cold war politics, Taipei also acquired the trappings of an "international" city, which trans-lated into a facade of international materials and capitalist modernity.

As part of the ideological apparatus of the state, official photography from this period presents a view of the city dominated by architecture of either modernity or the Chinese tradition—the skyscraper or the temple. When remnants of Japanese-period material culture, such as colonial archi-tecture, do appear in these photographs, they are often unlabeled, relabeled, or reformulated by anti-colonial discourse. Perhaps the most representative of this official visualization of the city is the early *Taipei Pictorial* (Taibei huakan), which began publication in 1968, a year after the city was raised to the status of special metropolitan district directly under the jurisdiction of the national government. In the early issues of the *Pictorial*, we can easily see the duality that had defined the city. The city had to be "free China" as well as international, and it had to be presented to both local and international audiences. An index of that duality is that *Pictorial* featured both Chinese and English captions (although they were not entirely equivalent in content or tone).

The first issue of *Taipei Pictorial* opens with a two-page fold-out of downtown Taipei, where "in celebration of the 80th birthday anniversary of President Chiang Kai-shek, a chorus of one hundred thousand cheering people sing[s] out their sincere respect to the national leader."[2] This grainy photograph is layered with signs of displaced power: in the center the "hundred thousand people" line up in military formation, facing down the street toward the renamed Presidential Palace (Zongtongfu), where, presumably, the president stands in review. Over head fly military planes; below is the newly constructed Jieshou Park, with its requisite traditional Chinese pavilion and bridge.[3] Behind the chorus stand the emblematic Japanese colonial constructions of the guesthouse and museum. Then, finally, on the horizon rise the reinforced concrete office and government buildings of downtown.

The modern city, which the new buildings in the background of this inaugural photograph represent, is celebrated throughout the pages of *Taipei Pictorial*. For example, we see a comparison of this new built space and the old city in the 1972 photo essay "Taipei . . . Then and Now" (captioned in Chinese, "The Twenty-seventh Anniversary of Taiwan after Retrocession" [Taiwan guangfu nianqi zhounian]). The essay opens with a series of early colonial photographs. While the English-language captions cast the Japanese presence in a negative relationship to the architecture, the Chinese-language captions are completely silent about the Japanese presence. For example, the caption for a picture of the Qing dynasty *yamen* reads in English: "This was the Ching [Qing] Dynasty Administration Center, which the Japanese tore down to build what [was] called Old City Hall on Yanping S. Rd"; but the Chinese reads: "The *yamen* for the Taiwan imperial government, which was established by Governor Liu Mingchuan during the Guangxu reign period [1875–1908], is now the location of the Sun Yat-sen Hall of Taipei." Here the levels of displacement, if not denial, are remarkable. The Chinese caption elides the Japanese colonial presence, while the one in English suggests that the photograph is somehow pre-Japanese. In fact, the central human figure in the image is a mounted Japanese military officer who is approaching the building that functioned as the colonial administration building (*Sōtokufu*) for the colony during its first twenty years. And, yes, the Japanese did indeed raze the *yamen* in 1931 to build the Old City Hall (Kōkaidō, Civic Hall, which is now Sun Yat-sen Hall), but the Japanese preserved the central buildings of the *yamen* and rebuilt them as public monuments in the Botanical Garden. Ironically, in 1972, when this essay appeared, those old *yamen* buildings had been relegated to use by the city forestry department and had been filled with junk and forgotten. They would not be restored again until the mid-1990s.

The remainder of the photographs in "Then and Now" are the other side of this traditional/modern coin: five scenes featuring new office and government buildings, a bank, a plaza, and a newly developed boulevard. This is the "pseudo Western" architecture that Yi-wen Wang and Tim Heath describe as central to the construction of a modern national identity in Taiwan.[4] Here the architectural progress of Taipei is celebrated in conventional terms of modernization: one caption reads (in Chinese) "Multicolored fountains have been installed in the grassy median of the tree-lined Ren'ai Road; these are particularly striking at night. During the summer, citizens go for walks in this area." The focus of the modern elements in this photographic essay is on the former Japanese areas: the intramural sector, its encircling boulevards, and the suburban areas featured in the 1932 urban plans. This Japanese focus is not merely a penchant of *Taipei Pictorial*, however; it reflects quite closely the way the city was treated by urban planners. The colonial center and its arterials reaching out into the suburbs were the symbolic spaces worthy of attention, rendering other parts of the city invisible. The gaze diverted away from the older, densely populated Taiwanese neighborhoods created conditions of neglect. That neglect, in turn, kept the official gaze averted for decades.

Despite the photographic and material attention to these islands and ribbons of renewal, most of the people of Taipei pursued their mundane lives in neighborhoods in which the city infrastructure was overtaxed, antiquated, or broken down, and often just a street or block away from an officially sanctioned, fully supported site. These neighborhoods were often constructed and maintained with the shortsighted logic of petty capitalism, which the government encouraged. Crudely poured concrete adorned with a wild assortment of "bathroom tile" (both materials produced locally in great abundance) began to cover structures in major portions of the city that tried to absorb the displaced and mushrooming population. In his typology of Hong Kong architecture, Akbar Abbas describes this "anonymous" architecture, where "nondescript commercial and residential blocks . . . seem to replicate themselves endlessly."[5] Felix Tardio, a professor of architecture living in Taipei during the late 1960s, wrote a scathing critique of its built environment. With both prejudice and insight, he described those anonymous "in-between" neighborhoods:

> Take a bus ride out from the city of Taipei to Ban Jowl [Banqiao] sometime. For practically the whole distance, except going over the one-way bridge, both sides of the road are completely built-up and cluttered. Built-up with cheap, ugly, crudely built shacks and concrete buildings. And in those buildings and in front of them can only be seen oil drums, old tires, motorcycle factories, metal and welding shops, oil, grease, mud, puddles, sugar cane spittings, melon rinds, piles of garbage, refuse; everywhere dirt and filth. Amongst it all run little half-naked children urinating everywhere. . . .
> The exact amount of dangerous and harmful [construction] practices going on in Taiwan could be the subject of a long and interesting study.[6]

Even allowing for exaggeration, Tardio seems to be describing a city of a completely different time and place from that projected in *Taipei Pictorial*. This is, in part, the geography of economics and ethnicity. Banqiao is a relatively poor Taiwanese suburb just south of Taipei; to get there, you travel through local neighborhoods (such as Wanhua) that had fallen completely outside the attention of city planners. As the debris in Tardio's description suggests, these are the very neighborhoods that provided the cheap labor and petty entrepreneurs that drove the "economic miracle" engine in these early years.

Over the decades, even official propaganda organs and their products necessarily reflect and contribute to the subtle evolution of attitudes and conditions in the city. Those changes were most marked in the mid-1990s, when the first directly elected mayor, Chen Shuibian (1994–98), brought new attention to the city's human services and physical plant.[7] Changes are visible in any number of registers, but in official publications, they find their instantiation most clearly in *Discover Taipei*, a magazine launched in 1997 in English-language format by the Taipei City Information Office. The mission of *Discover Taipei* is to celebrate the city of Taipei, especially its new global status. Although it never exposes the neglected underside of the city,

Discover has developed a more self-reflective and critical eye toward the city's built environment. For example, in the second issue (November 1997), a feature article and photo essay, "The Political Architecture of the 1960's: The Architecture of the 'Chinese Cultural Renaissance,'" criticizes the early Nationalist agenda of Sinicization. In a sidebar it asks, "What does the Sun Yat-sen building represent?" Its answer, in part, is:

> These Ming and Ching [Qing] style buildings have found their way thousands of kilometers from northern China by an accident of history. Their presence is due only to the political needs and sentiments of a dictator [Chiang Kai-shek] and his cronies from a faraway place; they have no local roots or context. They are as alien as the Western-style [colonial] structures built by the Japanese around the Po-Ai [Bo'ai] area. . . . As symbols of the ruling regime, these structures were a comfort to the army that had come along with it, and helped flesh out their ideology of representing the true China.[8]

This is certainly a long way from "one hundred thousand cheering people singing out their sincere respect to the national leader," but this new view of the city is just as ideologically driven. "Cultural renaissance" has been replaced with "cultural diversity."

Alternative Views

While photography of the city as a site of progress and optimism dominated official postwar media, of which *Taipei Pictorial* and *Discover Taipei* are particularly visible forms, work by some professional and amateur photographers included representations of the local, unsung sections of the city. The first-generation of these professional photographers were all trained during the Japanese period, and their work carries on many of the visual genres of that time, including ethnographic photographs, portraits of pretty girls, and the picturesque vision of "local customs." Deng Nanguang (1907–1971), Zhang Cai (1916–1994), and Li Mingdiao (b. 1921), the so-called Three Musketeers (San Jianke), are the most celebrated of these photographers. All three were interested in the pictorial quality of everyday life, both in urban and rural settings, especially Li, whose celebrated pastoral portrait "Shepherd Boys" (Muyangtong, 1947) is the archetypal elegant portrayal of working people. Yet from their work also emerges a vein of "straight photography" that captures images of the city far removed from those in *Taipei Pictorial*, such as Deng Nanguang's 1950 photograph of homes along a back alley of Dadaocheng, where the small huts along the river levee are a reminder of that older part of the city forgotten by the official photographers (fig. 2.1). Yet, even here, the low morning light that illuminates the drying clothes suggests an air of domestic tranquility and simple pleasure—imagine the same scene under the sheets of cold rain that haunt the city during the winter months. Only occasionally does this photography offer truly subversive views of the city in which the official vision might be exposed as idealized and the narrative of tradition and progress might be challenged. Many of Zhang Cai's portraits, especially of the aboriginal people, are as picturesque as those of Li and Deng, but he also occasionally captures the darker side of everyday life in his candid photographs of the city, which tend to be grainier and more muted. His 1949 scene in Dadaocheng, in which he turns his camera toward the densely layered crowd of the city's poor, who stare back at us, framed by torn concrete and old brick buildings, is such a moment (fig. 2.2). The primary ideology of this photography remains embedded in the aesthetics of the medium, rather than in any overt social commentary, but each of these

2.1 Deng Nanguang, 1950. "Dadaocheng: Living on the Levee at No. 9 Watergate." Courtesy of Deng Nanguang Estate, Deng Shiguang

photographers knew well the Taiwanese burden during the early Nationalist period and that burden occasionally shows through, intended or not, in
these candid portraits of the people and the city.

2.2 Zhang Cai, 1949. "Dadaocheng." Courtesy of Zhang Cai Estate, Jiang Yongbin

Huang Boji (Pai-Chi Hwang, 1931–), an amateur photographer self-trained in the 1960s, is a member of a second generation of photographers who began to move toward photography of urban social commentary. Huang, who transitioned into the postwar educational system to become a successful pediatrician, worked very much in the genre of candid portraiture, nearly of the Cartier-Bresson mode. His photographs of poor children are particularly noteworthy in their avoidance of sentimentality. Some of his work challenges directly the narrative of progress in the city. Here we consider three photographs that offer increasingly critical comments on the built environment of Taipei in the 1960s and 1970s. A 1966 photograph focuses on one of the officially touted, modern tourist hotels rising along the arterials of the eastern suburbs, yet Huang's view is of the *back* of the hotel, featuring a full-length fire escape, which looms as a backdrop not only to the rice paddy in the foreground but also to a makeshift residence in the middle ground, with a young woman and her child caught mid-stride—very much *not* part of the economic miracle (fig. 2.3). The caption is flat, "The scene surrounding the Mandarina Crown Hotel after completion of construction" (Zhongtai binguan jungonghou de zhouwei jingguan), but the silent comment about whose backs (and land) supported the economic miracle seems clear, at least in retrospect.

Another photograph, from 1968, is stripped almost completely of the picturesque, providing a stark, slightly confusing portrait of a young father and his children on an outing in the middle of a narrow, bedraggled median strip. The wide-angle lens creates a vast stretch of concrete that seems to envelop the little family gathering, suggesting its vulnerability in this inexplicable setting (fig. 2.4). Behind their abandoned baby carriage, a taxi and a motorcycle (the new vehicles of the 1960s) speed by. As if to explain away these incongruities in euphemistic political rhetoric, the label reads "People's Democracy East Road, Safety [traffic] Island" (Minquan donglu, anquandao). We are ironically reminded of the *Taipei Pictorial* photo of the grassy median with colored lights in Ren'ai Road, captioned in English "During the summer, citizens go for walks in this area."

The social critique presented by a 1977 Huang Boji photograph is lower in key, but perhaps more poignant. Captioned simply "West Gate District" (Ximending), the photograph shows gigantic billboards, looming over the bustling crowd in downtown Taipei, that are dramatically emblematic of the America presence in Taiwan. The 1976 movies *The Enforcer* (with Clint Eastwood) and *King Kong* (with Jessica Lange) seem to parody what the

2.3 Huang Boji, 1966. "The Scene Surrounding the Mandarina Crown Hotel after Completion of Construction." Courtesy of Huang Boji

United States meant to Taiwan at the time: military might and sensational entertainment. The low angle of the shot not only accentuates the towering billboards but also foregrounds the backs of two boys who seem to be drawn through the crowd toward these Hollywood icons of American popular cul-

2.4 Huang Boji, 1968. "People's Democracy East Road, Safety [traffic] Island." Courtesy of Huang Boji

2.5 Huang Boji, 1977. "West Gate District." Courtesy of Huang Boji

ture (fig. 2.5). The boys' military-style crewcuts mark them as students in the authoritarian school system that dominated the island at the time, suggesting that they are new recruits into the cold war metaphorically reenacted by Dirty Harry and King Kong.

In Retrospect

In recent years there have been a number of retrospective photographic exhibitions in Taiwan on the subject of this alternative photography. "In retrospect" (huigu/huishou/jinian) may indeed be to the key concept in appreciating these first- and second-generation postwar photographers. As successful as they were after the war, their vision of the city could not have seriously challenged the ubiquitous and powerful narrative in the official media. Given the economics and politics of the time, the photographic culture during the 1960s, 1970s, and 1980s was characterized primarily by salon aesthetics.[9] Deng Nanguang, a well-known postwar photographer and entrepreneur, owned a photo supply store in the downtown commercial district; established an annual photography exhibition, Free Images (Ziyou yingzhan) in 1952 and the Taiwan Photographic Association (Taiwansheng Sheying Xuehui) in 1963; and published a textbook, Introduction to Photographic Art (Sheyingshu rumen) in 1962.[10] Yet, after his death in 1971, there was not a single exhibition of his works until 1990. Since 1990, however, Deng and other postwar photographers have been celebrated in a series of publications and exhibits, several held at the National Museum of History, a former bastion of the Nationalist agenda that pointedly ignored the local. This belated recognition culminated in 2003 with an exhibition at the museum, A Retrospective of One Hundred Years of Taiwan Photography (Huishou Taiwan Bainian Sheying Youguang). Although this exhibition was steeped in the assumptions of pictorial photography, with little representation of alternative or contemporary trends, it is enfolded into the 1990s' ideology celebrating local culture and conditions.

This retrospective strategy in photography is also seen in the activities of the Taipei City government, and there it embraces a much richer range of the medium's representational modes. In 1996 the Taipei City Information Office inaugurated a series of photography albums dedicated to portrayals of the city and its people, under the series title Images in Taipei History (Taibei Lishi Yingxiang Xilie): to date this includes Young Taipei (Nianqing Taibei) in 1996, Old Taipei People (LaoTaibeiren) in 1998, and Hardworking

Taipei People (Renzhen Taibeiren) in 1999. These three albums all draw on photography from the 1940s to the 1990s, presented together as an informal but official portrait of the city. Mayors Chen Shuibian and Ma Ying-jeou wrote requisite prefaces extolling the albums for allowing "all the citizens of Taipei to find in these vibrant images a common history," making it possible for them "to see the many transformations that have taken place in the city until now," and illustrating "the hard work and devotion of the masses that has initiated a new era 'free in body and tolerant in spirit.'"[11] This optimistic narrative is both reinforced and undermined by the complexity of the photography presented in these albums, and one essayist warns us off the simplistic mayoral rhetoric. In his essay "Hardworking Taipei People" (Renzhende Taibeiren), Wu Yongyi begins on a sardonic note:

> And who are the people of Taipei? Those who live in the city and go to work on city buses in their special traffic lanes? Or those who live there but drive to work, and become so excited when they actually find a parking space that the next day they can't bear to leave such a good parking spot, so they get a cab to work? Or are they environmentalists who bravely ride their bikes to work? [12]

But Wu ends on a more sober note when he speaks about the social reality of the photography itself, here directly challenging Mayor Ma's post–martial law optimism of freedom and tolerance for the people of Taiwan.

> Finding high-quality photographs for the *Hardworking People of Taipei* collection was probably more difficult than for other types of collections. This is because, on the one hand, society has not valued the deep and multifaceted significance of daily work and hard labor, so there has been no record made of it; on the other hand, although the Taiwan government has lifted martial law, in the workplace (be it the factory, office, or retail store), we are still stuck in the attitudes of the old martial law period. In the past, every factory's security office posted the warning issued by the Central Garrison Command: "Secure Factory Area; No Unauthorized Entry." Now the police have become public safety personnel, there are 24-hour surveillance cameras, and the new warning reads "Industrial Secrets: Observation Prohibited." In the domain of production, the amount of one's freedom has not increased; in fact it may have declined.[13]

Like the views of the mayor and this critic, these photo collections present complex, even contradictory, representations of the city. In part this is because there is no single view being expressed, as in *Taipei Pictorial* or *Discover Taipei* or in the collections of individual photographers, but rather the gaze here is multilensed, creating a kaleidoscope of images brought retrospectively into one consideration. Driven by the ideology of multiculturalism, these collections seek to establish an authorized view of the city, just as did the monocular vision presented by both the authorities and the auteurs.

This new, more multifaceted vision of the city results in part from purposeful acts of displacement that bring it together. Photographs from a variety of contexts and intentions—few, if any, were meant to be a portrait of the city—are brought into a new order (this includes the photographs used in this chapter). The diverse portraits, both self-conscious and candid, of the people of Taipei are now given new meaning in the frame and title of the album. These photographs were undoubtedly available in other venues prior to these collections, but it is fair to say that those venues could not have been as public and sanctioned as they are here.

In these three albums we are asked to see the city on the human scales of young, old, and hardworking inhabitants, as myriad people move through its built spaces. Given the inherent conditions of the media, that movement is, of course, always arrested: waiting for the next step, turn of the head, or blow of the hammer. Below we will consider representations of the city that capture or construct some of that lost movement.

Filming Taipei

There are numerous important studies of Taipei City and film, including those by Yomi Braester, Whitney Crothers Dilley, Carlos Rojas, Ban Wang, and June Yip, as well as the essays in the *Xunzhao dianyingzhong de Taipei*. Even Fredric Jameson weighed in. These critics most often discuss the films identified as New and Second Generation Taiwanese Cinema, typically by the directors Hou Hsiao-hsien (Hou Xiaoxian), Edward Yang (Yang Dechang), and Tsai Ming-liang (Cai Mingliang). Although the studies cover a wide range of issues, they tend toward a consideration of the socio/psychopolitics and ideology of the media (for example, identity formation, cultural politics, and/or economic globalization). Yomi Braester's remarks set this tone:

The particular economy of space and memory in Taipei in the 1980s and 1990s is captured in the cinematic poetics of demolition. The film camera reveals construction sites as spaces of the erasure of memory and destruction of identity. Whether by choice or through an inevitable process of economic development, Taipei becomes—at least according to the films at hand—its own grave, burying its past under itself. Although well-regulated city spaces have at times served as memory palaces, visual aids to remembering one's mental makeup, urban ruin is a monument to forgetting.[14]

The studies by Braester and others inform my work here, yet my intent is to discuss films that are generally more mainstream and in which the depiction of urban space is relatively mundane and incidental to the thematic thrust of the film. From this mundaneness, I hope to identify a level of representation of the city that is more broadly embedded in the media and, therefore, I would argue, more ideologically profound: profound because it comes to the film relatively unbidden, not as its "main character."[15] For my purposes here, I will focus on representations of urban spaces that harbor a sense of displacement, both physical and cultural. In discussing Edward Yang's *Terrorizer* (Kongbu fenzi) of 1986, Jameson has claimed a special status for Taipei as an urban space in East Asia, in part because of the "rapid construction of buildings along both sides of great linear arteries, which are somehow its central formal category."[16] One point of my study is to explore that "somehow" of Taipei spatiality, which is a function not just of late capitalism and postmodernism but also of the deeply layered cultural substructure upon which that economy has been built. For every city, despite the leveling effect of globalization, is also modern/postmodern in its own way.

Allegory of Space: *The Taste of Apples*

Huang Chunming's 1974 short story "The Taste of Apples" (Pingguo de ciwei) is one of three that were translated into film at the very beginning of the Taiwanese New Cinema, in the trilogy *Son's Big Doll* (Erzi de da wan'ou), released in 1983. Huang was a seminal writer in the Nativist Literature Movement (Xiangtu Wenxue Yundong) of the 1970s, which challenged modernist and Nationalist sentiments with a new emphasis on local conditions. This trilogy featured three young directors very much under the influence of Nativist thinking.[17]

In brief, the story and film describe a Taiwanese laborer (Afa) who is run down by a U.S. military officer's car early one morning in Taipei as he bikes to work—in the film, the opening set of long shots shows the tiny bicycle passing through landmarks of the city (including old East Gate) in the early morning light. This is abruptly interrupted by an extreme close-up of a huge, black American sedan careening around a corner—what the short story describes as "like a wild animal."[18] The rest of the narrative entails the roundup and transport of Afa's family to the U.S. military hospital where he has been taken, whereupon they are all "rescued" from their meager lives by American largesse, including the gift of apples. The sarcastic conclusion is pronounced by the police officer toward the end of the story: "This has been a stroke of luck for you [Afa] . . . being run down by an American's car. If it had been anyone else, you would probably still be lying in the road, covered with a grass mat."[19]

The story is larded with heavy-handed symbolism that is graphically enhanced in the film, functioning primarily as a commentary on the cold-war relations between the Americans, Chinese, and Taiwanese on the island. June Yip has said that the "comic and fantastical story" raises "serious questions about the American military presence in Taiwan and the degree to which the penetration of American culture has led to a blind admiration of all things Western."[20] Yip has also noted the central importance of the "communication gaps between the Chinese authorities and the Taiwanese people," wherein "multiple layers of translation" entwine the narrative: English into Mandarin (by the Chinese police officer), Mandarin into Taiwanese (by the elder daughter), English into Taiwanese (by the American nun/nurse), and all back again.[21] The film performs these linguistic transformations much more effortlessly than can be accomplished in print: in the film, everyone speaks in his or her own language or dialect (including the American colonel), with all the accompanying frustrations and translations.[22] Among all of these, the vocalizations and gestures of the deaf-mute younger daughter stand as an index of the communication difficulties.

Both of the film's overt ideological thrusts, American cultural hegemony and identity formation through language and translation, involve multilayered displacements. In the most straightforward manner, American power has pushed aside that of the Nationalist government, which pushed aside the Japanese, which had pushed aside the Qing; all the while, the Taiwanese populations have remained submerged below the surface. In the film, aspects of this displacement are captured spatially in the representation of the two localities that bookend the narrative: the "maze" (*mihunzhen*) of the shantytown where the family lives, and the "White House" (*Baigong*) of the U.S. military hospital where they are gathered.[23] In the first, we see the submerged life of the family in the dark, rain-drenched squalor of their shantytown home; the second site is defined by the overwhelming whiteness of the hospital interior, emphasized by suffused lighting, in which the family is finally embraced/devoured.

In the film, these diametrically opposed sites are connected by a long sequence that follows the American's vehicle across the city, with the family drama being performed in the back seat. This passage is one of the film's most innovative interjections into the narrative. It is composed of a vast array of shots and techniques that give a strong presence to both the vehicle and the connection between the passengers, including two complex dissolves that carry the narrative into and out of an important flashback. In many ways, the representation of the family's passage "from hovel to heaven" mimics the transformativity of the layers of translation that also define the film: transportation and translation are functionally the same, dragging the family from their subaltern world to one of dominant power. At the end of the film, transportation and translation converge when the deaf-mute daughter is sent off to the United States to learn to speak (presumably, English). The film closes with a scene in which the camera, to a classical piano sound track, pans a room and then zooms in on a family portrait hanging on the perfectly white wall; all are dressed anew in Western suits and dresses (the deaf-mute daughter is missing). Everyone has been "translated" into a cold-war success story.

The early sequence wherein the American colonel and the foreign affairs police officer go in search of the family is established with a dissolve from an extreme close-up of the bloody stain on the street to an overhead shot of the shantytown in all its disorder (*lingluan*).[24] This is followed by a series of shots of the two men wandering through the bewildering maze of illegal buildings, coming toward us, moving away, in and out of the frame—the contrast between the two men in their smart uniforms and the people of this maze, including old men walking around in their boxer shorts, provides overt commentary on the socioeconomic disparities that define the city. Finally, almost inadvertently, the two men find the family's dank and dingy home, wherein the complex translations begin.

While the original short story does not name the shantytown, in the film the policeman's comments clearly identify it as the one off Xinsheng North

Road in Taipei's Zhongshan Ward, currently the location of Lin Sen Park (or Park No. 14).[25] This is the type of construction site that Braester describes in his "poetics of destruction," but it is also an important site in "the politics of displacement," in fact, a series of displacements over the last hundred years. Of course, there must have been an original displacement (either physical or by assimilation) of the indigenous inhabitants of the area by Chinese settlers during the eighteenth and nineteenth centuries—by the time Taibeifu was built, this Chinese agricultural area, known as Sanbanqiao, was also the site of a small public cemetery. During the colonial period, the cemetery became one designated for the Japanese population—its most famous occupant was the seventh governor-general, Akashi Motojirō. Then in 1932 the area was designated as Park No. 14; although the park was never built, it implied a displacement of function if not actual residents. In 1997 the site was finally restored as Lin Sen Park; at that time the Japanese remains were recovered and removed and a commemoration stone was placed at the site of Akashi's grave. The displacement that the film captures is, however, the one that defined the site and the political conditions of the island in the postwar period. Following the flood of Mainlanders who accompanied the Nationalists' defeat on the mainland, housing projects (*juancun*) were constructed specifically to accommodate the middle ranks of the military; these sites were often on public lands formerly owned by the Japanese government. Many of these areas also included surrounding squatter villages, which the lowest echelon of the immigrant population came to occupy. At this site, the first Mayor of Taipei recalls that "the comrades who came from the mainland to Taiwan leveled all the grave stones, creating an open area where they set up their homes and businesses"[26]—a dramatic and morbid type of displacement. Although these residences were technically illegal, they were allowed by the central government as a necessary condition of its strategy to retake the mainland (*fangong dalu*). In the film, this semi-legal condition is signaled by the official postal plates that hang throughout the squatter village and which the policeman reads as the two men search.

These squatter villages also became sites for a secondary, internal displacement. With the transformation of the economy of the island into one based primarily on light industry, there was an internal migration of workers from the rural areas into the cities to fill the low-end factory jobs and services that surrounded them. Given the massive influx of the Mainlander population in 1949–50, housing in Taipei City was extremely scarce, and squatter villages became primary sites for the new urban population. These internal migrants were either Taiwanese or aborigine. In the film, the move of Afa's family from the countryside to the city is enacted in the elaborate flashback that occurs as the family is being transported to the hospital.[27] In the wife's recollection, the back seat of the car dissolves into a train car—the visual flashback is also matched by the transformation of digetic traffic sounds between the train and the automobile. In the train scene, Afa is trying to convince his wife (this is her "memory") that the move to the city will be a good one; she does not speak but she and the children clearly are worried. The implication is that the move was ill-advised, but the viewer can already sense that material fortunes will be reversed in the second move, across the city in the colonel's car.

Eat Drink Man Woman: Alternative Spaces

Ang Lee's (Li An) critically acclaimed and commercially successful "father knows best" comedy *Eat Drink Man Woman* (Yinshi nannü) of 1994 is his only film set entirely in Taiwan, specifically Taipei City.[28] The film has drawn a good deal of critical attention regarding family dynamics, identity formation, and challenges to social convention, especially in its "patriarchal flexibility."[29] Whitney Crothers Dilley reviews the film primarily in terms of the impact of globalization on traditional Chinese culture. June Yip has discussed members of this family, a father and three daughters, in terms of their "cultural hybridity." She says that "nearly all the characters in Lee's film defy easy categorization, illustrating not only the variety of cultural influences that shape today's Taiwanese but also the slipperiness of identity."[30] Here I want to turn our attention to the spaces that the father and daughters occupy as a gestalt of the *city's* hybridity. The film presents the city far beyond its cold-war dyad of hovel and heaven, as a place of multiple, differentiating sites.

The members of the Zhu family all live in the same house but carry on their lives independently. They are drawn together only for the elaborate Sunday dinners that the father prepares. He is a celebrated chef and a widower who has become his grown daughters' caretaker: cooking their food, doing their laundry, and waking them up in the morning. The preparation of these family dinners, filmed with dramatic lighting and details, are some of the film's most celebrated scenes. For example, in the long opening sequence (four minutes without dialogue), Chef Zhu performs a battle and a dance of culinary preparations, sending fish and chickens to their ends while slicing and dicing to the beat of the traditional Chinese music that is the scene's sonic background. There is a great deal of spectacle, almost pornography, in the lighting and detailed attention to this "body" of the foodstuffs—every preparation and dish basks in luminescence.[31] Despite their lavishness and mouth-watering beauty, the dinners have become (as the middle daughter says) a "Sunday dinner torture ritual" for everyone.[32] They are torture because, in their intended intimacy, they amplify the alienation of the family members: literally, no one knows what the others are doing. The dinners are characterized by silence, abrupt pronouncements, and nasty exchanges about the father's declining taste buds. What is less noted is the "torture" of the house itself. The house is looming and claustrophobic, tempting its inhabitants to escape to someplace where they can become more than part of this fragmented family. Except for the kitchen scenes, the interior house is almost always shot down corridors and through doorways that emphasize the cluttered, cramped interior. For everyone, even the father, there is the enticement of other spaces. The tension between those alternative spaces and the anchoring home is central to the urban spatiality of the film.

The primary alternative spaces in which the family members seek refuge are culturally much "flatter" than the family home and thus much less fraught. The father has his gigantic restaurant in the Grand Hotel (Yuanshan Dafandian), where he is the master chef; the oldest daughter has the technical college, where she teaches chemistry; the middle daughter has her high-rise office, with its corner window; and the youngest daughter has the counter and kitchen at the local Wendy's. While each of these spaces is predicable in its own cultural shape, they come together as a gestalt to plot the sociopolitical spatiality of the city over time.

First, let us consider the family house. June Yip has suggested that the house, which she describes as formal courtyard-style, is part of the representation of the father as "traditional Chinese gentleman."[33] Architecturally speaking, that is not quite accurate. The house, which we learn in an early exchange between the oldest daughter and her to-be boyfriend, is located on Heping East Road and is in one of the few remaining Japanese residencies that once filled this eastern section of the city.[34] These are the empty houses that were filled with the displaced Mainlanders who came with the Nationalists in the postwar period—in some ways, they were the upscale equivalent of the military housing projects depicted in *Taste of Apples*. Thus, Chef Zhu may be a Chinese gentleman, but he is one who has taken up long-term residence in a house that is very much part of Taiwan's postwar spatial constructions. The house has been modified by the presence of the family, especially by the insertion of a large kitchen that is featured in the celebrated opening sequence. Clearly, what the father has tried to do is to bring his work and prestige home, but that has largely failed, at least as indexed by his Sunday dinners.

When Chef Zhu is summoned to rescue an important banquet gone bad, we see just how his work is supposed to proceed. With one intervening distant shot of the Grand Hotel glistening in the dark night, Zhu is transported from the front of his old house to the front of the elegant hotel with its looming red facade. The Grand Hotel represents the height, perhaps the overstatement, of Nationalist nostalgia for "Chinese" architecture. Under the direction of President and Madame Chiang Kai-shek, the hotel was built on the grounds of the former Taiwan Shinto Shrine, designed to entertain important guests and diplomats during the cold war: it is implied that Zhu was a chef for those important evenings, thus affirming his mainland connections. In this passage, Zhu's status in the wings of power is quickly established in a sequence of shots in which he hurriedly makes his way through the hotel, acknowledged by everyone he passes. His sense of command is most dramatically represented in the long, hand-held take that follows him through the massive, mazelike kitchen, where scores of cooks and assistants are working frantically among steaming cauldrons and flaming gas burners. Like a beloved general passing through the front lines, he is warmly and respectfully greeted—"Master Chef Zhu" (Zhu shifu); in turn, he speaks to the "troops" by name and pats a few on the back as he passes. He is completely in his element—and, of course, he saves the banquet with an innovative battle plan (with what Crothers Dilley calls "military precision").[35] Later, at night's end, he sits in the back of the restaurant with his old comrade-in-arms, Chef (Uncle) Wen, sharing a quiet drunken moment of gratitude and affection, just what he is not getting at home. The whole sequence, from the abrupt summoning phone call to the tipsy end, exudes the power of that first generation of elite Mainlanders on the island. In this sense, his three daughters represent a series of different accommodations to his fundamentally displaced condition.

In the spaces where the three daughters work, we find a map of the changing social conditions on the island during the postwar period. The deeply religious eldest daughter, Jiazhen, teaches chemistry in a large technical college of the sort that helped provide the educated personnel for the economic transformation of Taiwan as it moved from an agricultural economy to textile and plastic factory assembly-line work, and finally on to electronics and software production. In many ways, the spaces of the school imply the residual power of the martial law period, exuding disciplinary control over the young students—in fact, the school is spatially identical to the primary school seen in *Taste of Apples*. It is prisonlike: pseudo-military uniforms, desks in rigid order, an authoritarian teacher (who lectures with a microphone), Nationalist flags and portraits everywhere, and a massive central courtyard where the school regimens are performed. While the city has moved on, the school is caught in an earlier time. One shot of the school courtyard shows students and staff assembled for their morning routines, as luxury high-rise apartment buildings loom above them: a new architecture that surrounds the old "prison." Nonetheless, for Jiazhen, this is the space where she has authority and where she finds love and escape. Higher education was one of the social institutions dominated by the Mainlanders in the early Nationalist period, and it was also one of the few professional fields open to a woman of Jiazhen's age. In this world, she has found the safest haven she can from the claustrophobic conditions of her family home.

The two younger daughters occupy very different but similarly signifying work spaces: the fast-food restaurant and the corporate office. The character of youngest daughter, Jianing, nominally a college student, is defined largely by the Wendy's restaurant where she works and finds her boyfriend, who provides her escape from the family home (in the form of a premarital pregnancy). Like the food she serves, Jianing's life and ambitions seem fluid and undefined: in the introductory scene of her working the counter, a shot crammed with customers, a large Caucasian guy reaches over the crowd with his sandwich in hand and says (in badly accented Chinese) "I wanted chicken" (*wo yao ji*). To which her coworker replies, "That *is* chicken" (*na jiushi ji*). The young man walks away staring perplexedly at his sandwich. There is an obvious filmic dialogue here between the father's kitchen and Jianing's. His is over-determined by culinary care and zeal, while hers is characterized by chaos and detachment: no one is too concerned whether the meat is chicken or beef. Her pregnancy, which is the event that starts the unraveling of the family unit, is similarly casual and perplexing. After she blurts out her announcement at one of the Sunday dinners, the family stares in disbelief as the youngest and least-driven daughter makes a hasty departure from the old home to her boyfriend's apartment—it, too, an unfinished, undefined space.

The middle daughter, Jiaqian, is very much her father's child: they not only share success in their respective professional worlds but also share complex, interlinking psychologies, ripe for Freudian analysis.[36] As she says, "Neither of us can sneeze without starting a fight." Like her father's kitchen and its knives, Jiaqian's large, smartly decorated corner office, filled with all the latest technological gizmos (and a hidden bottle of scotch), is the primary index of her professional success. In her introductory scene, we first see a close-up of her hands and a display screen as she rattles through a spreadsheet; the shot parallel to that of her father killing the fish. In the narrative, we quickly learn that she has broken through the glass ceiling of international business and finance (the defining economic sphere of Taiwan in the 1990s) because of her intelligence, sophistication, and drive. In this alternative world, she operates with authority and autonomy, and her sense of command and competence is given full play, especially marked by her interactions with the suave, jet-setting Li Kai. Yet, over the length of the film, we also learn that *that* is exactly the problem: she wants the kitchen and knives, not the office and spreadsheets. For her, the well-appointed office is a complex physical and psychological displacement: she has been pushed into that corporate space and waits, full of tension, to return to her father's kitchen. That, in the end, is the basis of the squabbling between father and daughter. The old disagreement is played out with Uncle Wen officiating:

Old Wen: It seems like only yesterday you [Jiaqian] were a little girl following me around the kitchen. How quickly you learned everything! What a talent, eh, Zhu?

Mr. Zhu (*uncomfortable*): Yes, of course.

Jiaqian: Until you banished me from the kitchen.

Mr. Zhu: Until you learned to do something serious with your life!

Jiaqian: You know you just couldn't conceive of a woman being a real chef!

Old Wen: Don't start that again, you two. (*speaking softly to Jiaqian, taking her hand, as Mr. Zhu walks over to a window*) Yes, you could have become one of the greats. But your father was right to encourage you in your studies. And you, such a success! You owe it all to your father for throwing you out of our smelly old kitchen and keeping you on the right path.

Jiaqian. No one asked me if I wanted such a favor![37]

Jiaqian prefigures her return to the kitchen when she goes off to her lover's house to prepare an elaborate dinner. She shows up at the front door unannounced, saying only, "I felt like cooking."[38] The lighting and photography of the following sequence, as she takes over Raymond's small kitchen, is a diminished version of the cinematography of her father's performances in his grand kitchen. She is clearly having a delightful time, as she accompanies her work with a commentary on culinary philosophy and aesthetics for the food philistine Raymond. Her enthusiasm then leads to a revelry that reveals her lost position; she says, "He [her father] used to let me play around so much in that big kitchen. Jiazhen was so jealous!"[39]

The final sequence of the film provides a somewhat overwrought resolution of the family tensions, with Jiaqian playing the commanding role. The house has been sold and packed up. Jiaqian is leaving for a job in Amsterdam, Jianing has a baby, Jiazhen's husband is being baptized, and the father's young new wife (his escape) is also pregnant. But for now, Jiaqian is back in the kitchen, preparing one last Sunday night dinner. While she makes the thin tortilla-like *baobing* with one deft hand (again, the culinary choreography has returned), she handles phone calls from family members one after the other. The tension and resentment have all disappeared. In the end, only Dad comes. The piano music is slow and nostalgic as are his gazes on the old house. It is a sweet reunion in which Jiaqian prepares dinner for him, taking over his space and at the same time being a "wife"—she prepares soup by her mother's recipe. In the last sequence, what appears to begin as one of their spats (about the soup) suddenly turns into the resolution of his highly symbolic loss: his sense of taste returns. Stunned, he says, "Your soup, Jiaqian, I can taste it." In the final freeze frame, they hold hands and gaze at each other, saying only "My little girl" (*nü'er*), "Dad" (*ba*).[40] Their lost affection, even to some extent their missing mother/wife, rushes back into the kitchen and house that have been the central architecture of its earlier loss.

Twenty-something Taipei: City of Light

The 2002 film *Twenty-something Taipei* (Taibei wanjiu chaowu) has received little critical attention, and deservedly so. The plot is paper thin, the acting spotty, and the movie's messages are written in very large letters. The greatest draw of the movie, and the reason for its modest commercial success, was undoubtedly the voyeuristic presentation of gorgeous young bodies that populate the film. Yet, in terms of a filmic presentation of Taipei City at the turn of the millennium, it is well worth our attention, not so much because it is "true" but because it is so ideologically fraught. In some ways,

the film is all about light falling on surfaces in such as way as to create a utopia of consumption: objects bathed in "boutique lighting."[41]

The opening sequence of the film establishes the geoeconomic conditions of the city: the chirpy voice of a flight attendant announces the arrival
of a plane into Chiang Kai-shek (soon to be renamed Taoyuan) International
Airport, speaking over the noisy approach of a 747, with the standardized
spiel, including the ironic "According to the laws of the Republic of China,
smuggling of weapons or drugs into Taiwan is a serious criminal offense
punishable by the death penalty." After a shot of a taxiing plane, there is
a series of quick tracking shots of Eva striding confidently and amused
through the airport: she is impeccably dressed, her clothes without a wrin-
kle after her a twelve-hour flight from the States. Then we cut to her step-
ping up to the taxi stand and a pristine yellow cab gleaming in the flood of
light; she slides in and speaks for the first time, "Taipei, Eastside, thanks"
(*Taibei, Dongqu, xiexie*). *That* says it all. We are headed for the hip eastern
part of Taipei that Sue-Ching Jou calls a "newly emerged consumption and
entertainment centre [that] distinguished itself from centres in other districts, because costumers were willing to travel and pay higher prices."[42] As
if to make that point, the image of the departing taxi cab is wiped over with
the film's first "body shot."

As the new image slides onto the screen, the camera slowly pans the
side of a black Alfa Romeo Spider convertible in extreme close-up: bum-
per, headlight, fender, windshield, all capturing the reflections of the night
lights of the city in the car's perfect gleaming finish. The shot caresses the
smooth, highlighted curves of the car, just as it will the young naked bodies
that are the focus of the film. In this case, the camera comes to rest on the
outstretched arm of our handsome anti-hero, Ma'ge, then to the interior of
the car, where his other hand taps out the details of an Internet drug sale on
his Sony VAIO Netbook, one of the several serious product placements of
the film. Cut, and the sale goes down. Over his shoulder, we see a woman's
slim firm torso, naked between a halter top and low-cut micro-skirt (perfect
navel and discreet tattoo), saunter toward him with a fashion-model gait;
she leans deliberately over the passenger door to shows him/us her gorgeous
face and upper body, and again the light is full and flattering. There follows
a rapid series of shots of the completely open pass-off and pay—so much for
the threat of the death penalty. The car speeds off, and the woman stands
staring at the disappearing taillights; shot from near to the ground, she is
all legs and almost no skirt. The implication is that she is more interested in

Ma'ge than her little blue pills—and he has not said a word yet. The scene is a metonym for the entire film: a lifestyle filled with the surfaces of sophistication and hedonistic pleasure.

Taipei Eastside (also known as the Xinyi District [Xinyi Qu]) emerged in the 1990s as an alternative downtown area, built around the bubble economy and new political conditions of the city. As Sue-Ching Jou says: "new downtown [Eastside] has been shaped through the intertwining forces of globalization, state transformation, the real estate market and the evolution of a new consumption society."[43] Jou argues that this establishes a "bi-nuclei spatial structure" for the city—the other nucleus is the old downtown area. These two areas are anchored by the iconic skyscrapers towering over their respective parts of town—the Shin Kong Mitsukoshi Tower (51 stories, 1993) in downtown, and Taipei 101 (101 stories, 2004) in the Xinyi District.[44] At one level, the Eastside represents a displacement of political power from the downtown area and the central government. During the late 1980s and 1990s, the Taipei City government emerged as a political entity to challenge the old guard of the Nationalist government, which occupied that other famously towered structure in the downtown, the colonial Sōtokufu/Zongtongfu. When the new City Hall opened in the Xinyi area in 1994, it drew dramatic attention to the fact that the city government was moving away from downtown and into a new spatiality, variously called "global," "cyber," and even "Manhattan." In some ways, the city, under the leadership of the opposition party, was becoming the "state" for the people of Taipei. A state that did not have to deal directly with the "one China policy" and thus could represent a "new citizen of Taiwan" (*xin Taiwan ren*). This new status of the city as nation-state is emblematically captured in the title used by athletic teams from Taiwan participating in the Olympics and other world games: Chinese Taipei. Be that as it may, it is the other face of the "Manhattan of Taipei" that is represented in the film: conspicuous consumption in a globalized world.

There are a number of Eastside urban spaces in which the group of eight young professionals in *Twenty-something* carry out their lives of desire and consumption.[45] Centrally, there is their "home": the dance club Deep, where the pulsating lights and music are a loud backdrop for sex and drugs. The dance scenes are practically the only ones in the film shot to available light and imitate the fast-cutting style popularized by MTV and its derivatives.[46] We see some of that frenzied desire transferred to other sites in the new city center as well—the club's backrooms, karaoke joints, vans, apartments, and the street. The street scenes feature signature Eastside buildings such as Warner Village, Neo 19 Department Stores, Mitsukoshi AB Store: those "placeless" constructions of the globalized city.[47]

In contrast, scenes in domestic interiors of their ultra-modern lives are often slower and bathed in full, suffused light, turning every object, especially the young bodies, into fully contemplated material. In the earliest such scene, Hitomi, alone in the condo of a movie producer after a night of couch casting, strolls and poses naked (only for us) as she makes cell phone calls to her friends. The final shot is doubly voyeuristic: we gaze through the glass walls of the bathroom (an oddly chic architectural detail of the time) as the camera pans across her sitting elegantly on the edge of the bathtub, porcelain skin on porcelain tub. She is daffy but beautifully self-displayed. Another scene of similar slow sensuality is the lesbian love scene that comes toward the end of the film. One of the most aesthetically rendered sequences, this scene certainly is meant to stand in contrast to the much more frantic desire of the other (heterosexual) sex scenes. To the music of a slow ballad, close-ups and extreme close-ups show the two women's intertwined bodies; the camera moves slowly, and one shot dissolves smoothly into the next. The last lingering kiss is seen through the internal frame of an open bookcase— here we are given the point of view of Vivi's erstwhile boyfriend, who walks away dejectedly in the face of such obvious affection. The overt message is clear and conservative: love, not lust, is the basis for happiness.

Despite all the nudity, compared to *The Taste of Apples* and *Eat Drink Man Woman, Twenty-something Taipei* is a more ideologically conservative, even prudish film; it argues for romantic love, family values, and being "true to oneself." The personal tensions between couples that are the principal plot of the film all come to sweet or corny resolutions in the final scenes: Eva finally offers Ben her virginity but ends up keeping it, and the two say a weepy good-bye; the two high-school girlfriends fall in bed/love and get married in "Taiwan's first lesbian marriage"; philandering Cola goes home to the south and speaks the only Taiwanese heard in the whole film (finding his sexual, social, and linguistic self); and, finally, after an angst-filled, torrid meeting in which Cindy seduces Ma'ge via the Internet and the Howard Plaza Hotel, Ma'ge finally seems resolved to accept her affection but, in a drug-induced daze, gets run over by a truck!

Throughout the movie, there is one domestic interior where a deeper, more interesting connection is made: the hospital room where Ma'ge's father lies in near-vegetative state and where Ma'ge goes every morning to take up his daily vigil and get some sleep. Despite the obvious solemnity of the place, it too is presented in a cheerful light: the room full of large windows with a view, the latest in medical equipment, and plenty of stylish nurses (who have obvious crushes on Ma'ge). If the Alfa Romeo is Ma'ge's office and the VAIO Netbook is his partner, then the hospital room seems to be his home. Emotionally disconnected from the other characters in the film, here he can display the affection that is missing elsewhere in his life. Affection that is sometimes performed in very twenty-first-century ways, such as getting his comatose father stoned on marijuana after the nurses say Dad has had a restless night: the filial piety of a transcultural son.

THREE

Traffic in the City

In classical Chinese, "to erect a wall" (*jian cheng*) is to build a city, and even in the contemporary language, the general term for "city "(*cheng-shi*) retains that essential sense of the wall-cum-city, something akin to a "walled market." In traditional China, the walled city was closely associated with the bureaucratic centers of the imperial state, including its principal and many regional capitals. The old walled administrative centers were of diverse types and contingencies, but to some extent all "symboliz[ed] state authority and the Chinese moral order."[1] These included large planned imperial capitals, especially of the Han and Tang dynasties in Chang'an (present-day Xi'an) and of the Yuan, Ming, and Qing dynasties in Beijing, which were elaborately gridded urban areas projecting the "magic square" that Alfred Schinz has suggested as a general model for all early architectural constructions in China, including the city. This ideal city was first described in the late classical period.[2] Nonetheless, most walled cities in China were smaller, less planned, and much contingent on the coincidences of history and location. Instead of structures that projected the regulated geometry of the "magic square," these cities were more likely to be circular or particularly irregular in shape.[3]

The circular or irregular walled city was especially prevalent in the latter part of China's imperial period, when population centers were fully formed and densely packed; this was even more so in the southern parts of the empire, where topography was far more articulated with mountains and waterways than in the relatively open plains of the north. The dual significance of population density and topography is clearly manifested in the walled cities that were built in Taiwan throughout the evolution of the Chinese occupation of the island, with the significant exception of Taipei.[4] While other walled cities on the island exhibit irregular shapes that reflect local settlement patterns and specific topography, the wall of the late-developing Taipei Prefecture (Taibeifu) was so rectangular that it approached being a "magic square."

The Prefectural Wall

When in the early 1880s the Chinese imperial government began, rather belatedly, building the wall for its new prefectural city, it was responding to territorial threats from the Japanese and French and the new strategic prominence of the island's northern region.[5] This shift in political and cultural power on the island during the late Qing period had both regional and local implications, including the shape of Taipei's wall.

After Shen Baozhen recommended in 1875 that a new prefecture be established in the north, local power brokers, especially in the form of city elders and regional landowning families, began to negotiate for the capital to be placed in their city or settlement area.[6] Conventional logic would have argued that the prefecture be located in the urban center of Xinzhu, on the northwest coast. Xinzhu was established in 1723 (as Zhuqian) and, beginning in 1733, functioned as the site of Danshui Subprefecture (Danshuiting), which included most of the northern part of the island. By the 1880s, Xinzhu was firmly established as an administrative center that had been extensively developed and elaborately walled.[7] In fact, during the early months of his rule, Lin Daquan, the first Taipei prefect, was stationed in Xinzhu, although he spent most of his time in the northern port of Jilong tending to military affairs.[8] In early 1878, Lin formally relocated the prefectural office north to the Taipei basin area, further acknowledging that the base of power and attention was shifting northward. By this time, the seaport of Danshui and the river ports of Mengjia and Dadaocheng, had emerged as centers of foreign export trade for the island, based principally on tea and camphor. Mengjia had also become a base of military operations and had functioned as an informal governmental center for the region for some time.

Once the decision was made to establish the prefectural city in the "Mengjia area," local sociopolitical dynamics entered the picture. As Harry Lamley and others have discussed, Taiwan at this time was still rife with ethnic and subethnic tensions, with rival parties often coalescing in delimited locales. In the Taipei basin, the twin settlements of Mengjia and Dadaocheng had gone through a series of armed conflicts in the latter half of the nineteenth century and emerged as principal rivals, with Mengjia representing the Quanzhou and Sanyi group of Fukienese (Hoklo) immigrants, and Dadaocheng representing the Zhangzhou and Tong'an (also Hoklo) groups. Lamley writes, "Memories of those two severe 'armed conflicts' were still vivid in the minds of those Hoklo leaders who supported the construction of Taibeifu some twenty years after the second disturbance had subsided."[9] Thus, when it came time to choose a specific location for the new city, the second prefect, Chen Xingju, split the difference, situating the new city wall in the open agricultural land *between* the two settlements (see chapter 1 and fig. 1.2). While we will never know the exact rationale for the decision, one can assume that it was in part a practical negotiation of subethnic tensions between those two communities. By choosing this location, the Qing imperial government, represented by Prefect Chen, would not alienate either group and could call on leaders in both communities to contribute to the building of the wall nearest their settlements. In defying the common practice of constructing new bureaucratic centers in established settlement areas, the construction of Taibeifu represented a fundamental form of cultural displacement, which would contribute to the particular spatiality of the city over the next one hundred years.

The details of the construction of the Taibeifu wall are complex and somewhat shrouded in mystery.[10] Nonetheless, Japanese and Chinese researchers have pieced together a good deal of the details, and their work, especially that of Yin Zhangyi, shapes the arguments below.[11] We know that construction of the wall was done under the direction of Prefect Chen Xingju, with a board of fourteen managers (*zongli*) representing the most important families in the area. The fourteen managers were the primary source of funding for the wall, with the wealthiest adopting parts of the construction project closest to their communities.[12] One of these managers was Lin Weiyuan of the wealthy Lin family of Banqiao, a town that lies south of the city. Lin's presence on the board allowed the authorities to pressure him to take responsibility for building the south wall. Lin at first resisted this appeal, but when he finally did acquiesce, he made certain to put his family's mark on the construction by building the distinctive "extra" Small South Gate (Xiao Nanmen). This was more than a symbolic gesture; the new gate, oriented toward Banqiao, allowed Lin access to the city without going through the West Gate in Mengjia, an area dominated by the rival Quanzhou subethnic group (Lin's family was from Zhangzhou).[13]

The city was planned in 1879, although wall construction did not begin until 1882 (the delay was for both financial and practical reasons) and was then rushed to completion in 1884 under the threat of the French invasion.[14] In March 1879, Prefect Chen announced plans for the city, including a design for the streets and city plots. Shortly afterward, several merchants from Mengjia set up establishments on the newly designed street, Fuhoujie (Prefecture Back Street), long before construction of the wall began.[15] Not only did these early streets determine the spatiality of the city but the commercial plot size established by Chen would be used thereafter, continuing to define the configuration of establishments in the old downtown area even today.[16] Thus, most of the current shops in this area, including the three-story Starbucks at the corner of Hengyang and Chongqing South Roads, still basically fit into Chen's standard plot (fig. 3.1;).[17]

3.1   Starbucks Coffee, downtown Taipei, 2010

One anomaly of the Taibeifu plan was the nonalignment of the wall and its intramural streets. One might expect a city planned with such freedom of design to take full advantage of the opportunity to align the intramural streets with the walls, as is the standard treatment (Beijing being the prime example).[18] That expectation is manifested in the 1896 idealized map of the city, which portrayed Taibeifu as a square, with streets basically parallel with the walls (see fig. 1.1). The reality was much different, however. While the bisecting intramural streets were primarily at right angles to each other, they were not aligned with the direction of the walls: specifically, the north-south walls align thirteen degrees to the east of the streets. Alfred Schinz has suggested that this deflection was intentional, related to complicated *fengshui* theory and derived from "an interesting line of thought that was very typical for the world concept of imperial China."[19] Schinz first made this argument in 1976, and several Chinese critics have adopted his general ideas, often reproducing his map.[20] Yet, their interpretations of the discrepancy, while also related to geomancy and city planning, are far more practical and historically contingent. According to these critics, the pattern of the streets and the layout of the wall were designed by two separate individuals representing contending schools of geomancy.[21] Given the political machinations and shifting personnel involved in the building of the wall, I am inclined to agree with this more coincidental rationale. In fact, what matters here is not how this anomaly developed, but rather how it affected the configuration of intramural space, especially as the city developed through the decades. As Shih-wei Lo has stated: "A large, linear form, the wall nevertheless continued to act as a structuring element for the city. It left morphological traces that conditioned later developments, among them the coexistence of two inconsistent orientation systems."[22] One of those specific morphological traces is the very shape of Taipei Park (discussed in chapter 4).

The Empty City

The placement of the Taipei city in open paddy lands between the two settlement areas contributed to an even more important spatiality that both reflected and impacted the physical, social, and political environment of the time. The primary result of this placement was the creation of the "empty city" phenomenon; that is, a large percentage of the intramural area was vacant at the time of the construction of the wall (see chapter 1). That emptiness constituted a special if not unique condition of the city, one that created a distinct trajectory in urban development over the next century. Given that the West and North Gates lay closest to the established commercial areas of Mengjia and Dadaocheng, almost all early settlement and establishments were brought into this corner of the intramural area, leaving the southern and eastern portions still in paddy lands surrounding a few scattered buildings. Both maps and photographs attest to this distribution (see fig. 1.2).[23]

The Chinese prefectural and provincial governments had important plans for these vacant areas that lay between the projected arterials, but most of that late imperial architecture would never be built. In its place, the Japanese brought in colonial architecture that almost completely displaced the Chinese architecture over the next fifty years. Sometimes that displacement was literal, as in the dismantling of the Qing dynasty provincial *yamen* in 1931 so they would have space to build their Civic Hall (Kōkaidō) in the downtown area.[24] But much of the new colonial construction was in the empty spaces: a displacement of intended, not actual, structures. In this sense, there was not the degree of contestation over land that occurred in building colonial Seoul a decade later.[25]

The Japanese city planners arrived in Taiwan with a good deal of experience in building according to European models of architecture. The modernization of Tokyo that began in the first few decades of the Meiji period involved the insertion of classical European and modern architecture into the cityscape. Su Shuobin has said specifically that Hausmann's reconfigured Paris was the model for Meiji reforms in Tokyo, and, as we shall see, Paris lies behind the plans for Taihoku as well. There were, however, significant differences in the urban planning efforts in Tokyo and Taihoku, both structurally and conceptually. First, at the end of the nineteenth century, Tokyo was a dense and crowded city offering few open areas for urban development, especially in the core areas of the Low City. With the establishment of Meiji rule, the spaces that did become available were the *daimyō* feudal estates located throughout the High City but rendered masterless with Meiji reforms. This is where most modern construction took place in the earlier period.[26] But these estates remained relatively isolated from the rest of the city, with no larger plan to bring them together through some "massive urban surgery."[27] As Jinnai Hidenobu notes, this new architecture functioned as Western landmarks in a sea of indigenous buildings—these spaces, in fact, became modern "estates," often retaining the separate, gated surroundings that they inherited from the *daimyō* grounds. Even when modernizing efforts moved to the more street-oriented urban areas, there still was little integration of these architectural monuments, which Jinnai calls "self contained little worlds in which the dramas of modernization were performed."[28]

While some construction similar to the former *daimyō* estates of Tokyo was represented in the colonial city of Taihoku, such as in the walled and gated governor-general's residence (built in 1901), the distinct histories of the two cities also produced striking structural differences. Jinnai remarks that it was only after the earthquake of 1923 that Tokyo was "opened up" for centralized city planning such as seen in Paris. In Taihoku, on the other hand, the undeveloped intramural space offered an opportunity for a small, Haussmann-like plan to be implemented—and with little "surgery." In other words, Taipei was a much more suitable area for the Japanese city planners to work out their modernization project. In the early phases of urban planning, this meant the construction of large integrated buildings in the southern and eastern sections of the city, where we find not only the governor-general's residence but also the home of the civil administrator, its accompanying large athletic facilities, the public park, and the nearby Taihoku Hospital. By 1935 the southern and eastern sections of the city were filled with colonial and metropolitan establishments: added were the signature Sōtokufu (Colonial Administration Building), museums, libraries, courthouses, the Bank of Taiwan, offices for public utilities, the radio station, military barracks, and several important schools. These institutions and public spaces, which were both the face and the actual organs of colonial power, were built on a scale that defied anything the Qing architects might have planned.[29] Thus, while the northern and western sections of the intramural city remained on the scale established by Prefect Chen Yingju's plans, with narrow storefronts concealing extensive living and working quarters, the newer sections of town were populated by large modern, renaissance, and neoclassical buildings surrounded by open spaces. All of these just screamed "colonialism."

When older parts of the intramural city were drawn into the colonization efforts, this sometimes meant, in Tokyo fashion, the insertion of large institutional buildings over existing spaces, such as the Post Office on the corner across from North Gate. For the most part, modernization projects in this area were limited to the building's facades and facilities, with little change to overall structures or spaces. This can be seen, for example, in the major renovations following the 1911 typhoon and flood of the city in which large swaths of the old commercial district of the intramural city were rebuilt to modern standards and styles using an elaborate blend of renaissance, art deco, and modernist facades; the major structural changes were limited to raising the buildings to three stories.[30] The spatial differences between these two parts of the intramural city remain to this day. Most of the contemporary northern half of the intramural area is still defined by the narrow, cheek-by-jowl type of architecture, with some old facades still in place. In fact, in a recent renovation project, a new set of arcade fronts was built not only to scale but also in imitation of the colonial renovation work.[31] In the southern section of the city, the monuments to colonialism or their contemporary counterparts still stand. Even after all the construction that was done during the late twentieth century, a walk down Chongqing South Road still brings one quickly through these two architectural environments, from cramped late Qing commercial plots to early twentieth-century colonial excess. In many ways, it is a walk from Prefecture Front Street (Fuqianjie) of the Qing city to Splendor Ward (Eichō) of the Japanese colonial capital.

The Boulevards

Of the many changes that the Japanese brought to the city in the early years of the colony, none was as dramatic and lasting as their decision on how to deal with the city wall. As mentioned in chapter 1, the first intramural plan of 1900 proposed several changes, but central to all of them was a design in which the wall was penetrated by all the main intramural arterials passing through accompanying gates—nine new gates were proposed, for a total of fourteen. While this would have significantly altered the intramural city, it would not, as Su Shuobin notes, have changed its essential dynamic: the wall and its gates still would have functioned in the role, albeit diminished, of control and protection, and all traffic would have flowed from the center toward the periphery.[32]

Perhaps it was the practical problems involved in building nine new gates that halted this plan, but more likely it was the experience and vision of Gotō Shimpei that offered a more innovative and yet functional plan in its stead: to raze the wall and replace it with boulevards that encircled the city. A foreshadowing of that decision can actually be seen in the 1900 plan: the new railroad line that was to go south from the station along the west wall needed to cut through the northwest corner of the wall in order to make its initial, 90-degree turn out of the station (see fig. 1.3).[33] Thus, it may have occurred to the planners that if a small section of the wall could be removed, why not the whole thing? That was indeed the solution introduced in the 1905 urban plan, which set the direction for the development of the city. The planning map published in 1905 highlighted these boulevards in bolded graphics, clearly marking this as the new "center" of the city—a center displaced to its periphery, as it were. The old walls of exclusion and limitation were replaced by avenues of circulation allowing easy and multiple entries into the city; traffic no longer ritually penetrated the city at its gates, moving toward a stationary center, but rather circumnavigated the open modern city.

What may now seem a logical treatment of the old wall was at its time quite radical. During the twentieth century, many old city walls in China, including the iconic walls of Beijing, were to be razed to make way for the machinery of modernization; but at the turn of the century, city walls in China were all still intact and functioning in their traditional manner. The Taipei city wall may have been the last wall built by the Qing government, but it was the first one razed as part of the modernization of urban space in East Asia. This East Asian innovation did not come from whole cloth, however. It was inspired, at least in part, by European examples in which medieval walls had been transformed into the promenades and wide boulevards that were implicated in the modernization of those cities in the mid-nineteenth century. Before coming to Taiwan, Gotō Shimpei spent two years (1890–92) studying in Berlin, a city marked by such razed walls and inserted boulevards; his experience in the German city must have been very much on his mind as he contemplated the modernization of Taihoku.[34]

In Taihoku, the boulevards were elaborately designed as thoroughfares with three traffic lanes (*sansenro*) divided by tree-lined islands, a design that seems to have been based on models derived from Haussmann's Paris (fig. 3.2, compare 1.6d).[35] Similar to the effect of Hausmann's *grandes boulevards* on Paris, but on a much smaller scale, the *sansenro* of Taihoku transformed the city from a traditional bureaucratic center, walled and imperial, into a site of colonial modernism. They replaced the wall symbolically as well as physically: the *sansenro* thoroughfares became the sign of the modern city.

At the end of the Japanese period, these signature boulevards were fully embraced by the Chinese Nationalist government, and they continue to dominate the downtown area. Shih-wei Lo has discussed the special role played by the west-side boulevard (present-day Zhonghualu), where displaced Mainlanders of 1949 took up temporary residence, which then morphed into a vital retail and restaurant district in the 1960s.[36] On the

3.2 Sansenro (three-lane) boulevard, ca. 1930. Source: *Taiwan shashi taikan*; courtesy of National Taiwan Library

north and east side of the city, the two boulevards were renamed Chiang Kai-shek (Zhongzheng) and Sun Yat-sen (Zhongshan) roads, and their elaborate intersection marked the center of the city—this is the point where street numbers and the quadrants of the city begin. Of particular interest is the short Sun Yat-sen South Road (approximately three-quarters of a mile, formerly the east wall), which has developed particular cultural weight over the years; alongside it now stands the Freedom (formerly Chiang Kai-shek) Plaza, the National Central Library, the Ministry of Foreign Affairs, the Nationalist Party headquarters, the diplomatic guest house (the former Japanese governor-general's residence), the National Taiwan University Hospital (both its Japanese-era buildings and its new high-rises), the Ministry of Education, the Legislative Yuan, and the Control Yuan. In the center of all this stands the old East Gate, often festooned and dramatically lighted at night. This gate draws our attention in many ways.

The Gates

The building of the Taipei prefectural wall also included the strategic placement and construction of its five city gates. Reflecting traditional Chinese conventions, South Gate (Da Nanmen) was nominally the principal gate for the whole city; yet, given the positioning of the city between the two settlement areas, West Gate and North Gate were the actual "front doors" of the new city, giving on to Mengjia and Dadaocheng, respectively.[37] In contrast, the gates on the east and south opened onto relatively unpopulated spaces— we have already noted the "extra" gate in the south wall resulting from Lin Weiyuan's special contribution to the construction of the wall.[38] While the wall is the nominal marker of the Chinese city, the gates are the centerpieces of architectural and strategic attention: they provide the wall's permeability necessary to its function of control, while at the same time they represent a breach in its defenses. No matter their intended use and original stature, the Taipei gates, each in its own way, have maintained a presence (in one case through a telling absence) in the everyday life of the city. Even after they lost all functional value as gates, their symbolic value remains, although its implications have changed.

When the Japanese began to raze the wall in 1904 in preparation for building the boulevards, they apparently had planned to include the gates in that demolition. That is what happened with West Gate; it went with the wall and became a presence in name only.[39] Li Qianlang suggests that the destruction of West Gate was a colonial strike against Chinese sentiments associated with the gates, but if so, it was short-lived.[40] Before the demolition work could proceed to the other walls, a controversy arose regarding the fate of the remaining gates. The Chinese elite may have had a strong voice in this debate, but the conservation effort was officially led by the head of the Sōtokufu Library, Yamanaka Shō, later joined by Gotō Shimpei, resulting in the preservation of the remaining four gates, as reflected in the 1905 planning map.[41] Although Li Qianlang is correct that the colonial government did engage in purges of traditional Taiwanese culture, there were also efforts to preserve institutions and monuments of elite culture; the decision to preserve the city gates was one of the first of those efforts. For Gotō Shimpei, the preservation of the gates may have had particular appeal; he had personally seen the grand monument of Berlin, the Brandenburg Gate.

With the Taipei city wall gone, the remaining four gates became fully and blatantly impractical. No longer marking the liminal space between the outside and inside of the wall, the gates came to reify the missing wall itself: they stand witness to its absence, but instead of being a mechanism for channeling urban traffic, they are an obstruction to it. Since the gates stand dead center in the new boulevards, sideways to the flow of traffic, they create a need for rotaries to funnel the traffic around them. These rotaries are still an important part of the city's traffic patterns. In the beginning, the traffic of the city (bicycles, rickshaws, and the occasional motor vehicle) must have made its way around these rotaries with relative ease, but now, with the density and speed of traffic in the modern-day city, one witnesses the hair-raising surge of boulevard traffic suddenly forced to negotiate the multiple swirling lanes and traffic lights of the elaborate circles. Heaven help the bicyclist these days.

Each of the Taipei gates has played a part in this transformation of the city, but none more than East Gate, which has evolved into one of the city's most gazed upon and circumnavigated public monuments of the twentieth century (fig. 3.3, compare fig. 1.6d). Originally, this gate was the back door of the Chinese city, outside of which stretched an open plain of sparsely settled agricultural land, with one small road leading through the hills to far-off Jilong harbor. But for the Japanese city, East Gate became its *front* door. With the construction of the colonial institutions in the southern and eastern sections of the city, beginning in 1901, with the governor-general's residence just inside of East Gate, the orientation of the entire city slowly turned away from the old Chinese settlements outside West and North

3.3 Aerial view of East Gate, rotary, and boulevards, 2011

Gates, toward the south and, especially, the east. This reorientation was set in stone when the new signature Sōtokufu was built (1912–19) on the site of the former athletic grounds.[42] The tallest building in the colony, Sōtokufu looked out directly onto East Gate. From that moment onward, the city's gaze is emphatically eastward, a gaze that is reinforced by the 1932 planning map (see fig. 1.4) and its elaborate designs on the eastern suburbs, and a gaze that some see as ideologically motivated. [43]

The city's eastward gaze was also adopted by the postwar Chinese government, especially after the exiled Republic of China set itself up in the old Sōtokufu building. As I noted in chapter 2, in the end, this gaze reached far beyond the intramural area and out into the suburbs, where, at the end of the twentieth century, the new Taipei City Hall was built in celebration of the globalized status of the city: its so-called Manhattan. But the first object of that gaze was and is always East Gate. For the Nationalist government, the Qing gates were an especially poignant reminder of the island's Chinese heritage, which they wanted to emphasize and exploit in their ideological battles with both the People's Republic of China and the Taiwanese residents. In this way, East Gate became the billboard for the Chinese project—used to display various "signs" of the Nationalist party, most notably large portraits of Sun Yat-sen and Chiang Kai-shek during the Double-Ten Festivities (October 10, the Founding Day of the Republic of China). Yet, like other aspects of indigenous Chinese/Taiwanese culture, in the 1960s the gates were deemed "not Chinese enough" by the standards of the Nationalist Party's Sinicization (Zhongguohua) Project. At that time, three of the four gates were remodeled in the "northern palace style" (*beifang gongdianshi*) that was the neoclassical rage of the time—the stone bases and passages were left in place, but the distinctive "fortress" (*diaobao*) superstructures were removed and replaced with the orthodox pillar-and-bracket pavilions.[44] Just to make the point overly clear, the Nationalist party symbol (a white sunburst on a blue background) was also embedded into the decorative materials on the roofs of the renovated gates.[45] The architectural historian Li Qianlang later called these renovations "especially regrettable," and it has been said that this kind of architectural work represents "the political needs and sentiments of a dictator."[46]

Ironically, only North Gate was spared this "renovation" fate, and that was simply because the government intended to dismantle it to make way for an elevated highway: a latter-day West Gate, to be destroyed in the name of public works. In the end, a civil protest led by students in 1977 saved

3.4 North Gate and adjacent highway ramp, viewed from the east, 1994

the gate, so that it now stands as the only gate of original "fortress" design. Yet the legacy of the government's former disregard remains: unable to dismantle the gate, the Department of Public Works proceeded to insult it by placing the highway entrance ramp within inches of its upper level (fig. 3.4). Nonetheless, in 1983 North Gate was declared a Grade One National Historic Monument, and now *it* is the symbol of the city.

Naming the Streets

Streets in Taibeifu were named in the conventional Chinese manner with directional or locational designations—West Gate Street (Ximenjie), Prefecture Back Street (Fuhoujie), and so on. In the earliest Japanese maps, these Qing names were adapted to the Japanese-style *chō* (district) postal system of the new colonial city: a hybrid system whereby the old street names were used to designate districts of several city blocks (*chōme*), numbered accordingly. Thus, the block where the Tianhougong temple stood is labeled "Block 7 of Fukōkai (Prefecture Back Street)." It would not be until the 1920s that the *chō* system would largely displace the Qing street names with more colonial names, for example, "Splendor District" (Eichō).[47]

When Taiwan fell abruptly back into the hands of the Chinese at the end of the war, there was a period of uncertainty regarding policy toward the island, with a debate about the status of the former Japanese colony in the Nationalist Government agenda.[48] Some sense of this is seen in a tourist map from April 1946 in which the Japanese, Chinese, and American elements meet to map a new city.[49] There are new Chinese street names, but there is also a finding list between the Japanese and Chinese names; the Chinese governmental organs are already ensconced in the Japanese colonial buildings, but there is a label that points out "the old Sōtokofu"; and although the "Places of Interest" list emphasizes things Chinese (Confucius, City God, and Sun Yat-sen), they also allow for older Japanese sites, including a handwritten cartouche that says, in English, "Many cosy restaurants a la Japanaise located here." In this map, the Chinese street names in the downtown area have been largely resurrected from the Qing nomenclature: Back Prefectural Street, East Gate Street (Dongmenjie), Civil-Martial Street (Wenwujie), and the like.[50] The original displacement of the Qing nomenclature by the Japanese was here reversed, with the old Chinese names flooding back when the Japanese departed. This was not a resurrection that lasted long, however; soon another level of displacement took place.

In November 1945, the new Taiwan Provincial Government announced its intention to change the postal system and street names "in order to erase all thoughts of Japanese rule."[51] It declared that within two months of setting up the metropolitan government, they would purge all references to names of Japanese people, terms that glorify Japanese nationalism, and any term that is clearly Japanese. This wholesale purging of the Japanese nomenclature created something equivalent to the "empty city" phenomenon we saw in the 1895 transition; but this time, the city was empty of names, not architecture. In this purged space, the Chinese government declared it would use the following:

1. Terms related to the national spirit, such as China Road (Zhonghualu), Sincerity Road (Xinyilu) and Peace Road (Hepinglu);
2. Terms that promoted the Three Principles of the People (Sanmin Zhuyi), such as Three Principles Road (Sanminlu), Peoples Power Road (Minquanlu), and People's Livelihood Road (Mingshenglu) ;
3. Names of important national figures, such as Sun Yat-sen Road (Zhongshanlu) and Chiang Kai-shek Road (Zhongzhenglu);
4. Terms that have local geographic or common usages.[52]

The ideological work of this announcement is obvious, and its mandates are evident in our 1946 tourist map. But for anyone who knows the postwar map of Taipei, there is a type of nomenclature completely missing from this list: the naming of the city streets with mainland place names, such as Chongqing Road and Kaifeng Street. This is, in fact, the primary nomenclature for the entire city as we now know it. Many have noted that this "implantation" of mainland China onto the city was one of the most ideologically fraught acts of the early postwar period, and it was assumed to have come with the Nationalists in 1945, as claimed by official sources.[53] Yet, apparently that policy was not implemented until a later date, as the 1946 map suggests. Let's take a closer look at this transition period.

Two maps dating from March and April of 1949 record the transition to the Nationalist street-naming policy with its mainland-based nomenclature. While both maps employ the new nomenclature, the map from March also includes an elaborate legend that echoes the 1946 accommodations.[54] The legend includes three registers: (1) the new street name (*xinjieluming*), (2) the original name (*yuanyou luming*), and (3) the place-name before retrocession (*guangfuqian diming*), that is, before 1945. Between the Japanese *chō* system (register 3) and the mainland-oriented names (register 1) is the nomenclature of the 1946 map, largely but not wholly of resurrected Qing names.[55]

By 1949, as preparations began for an evacuation of the central government to the island, the Nationalist street-naming policy was being fully implemented. In terms of official policy, these maps confirm the "at least" dates of street system conversions (1946 and 1949, respectively). Yet, if we look at life usage, we find a more ambiguous process at work for the period. The *Taiwan New Life News* (Taiwan Xinsheng Ribao), a newspaper sponsored by the Nationalist Party, began publishing in Taiwan on October 25, 1945, Retrocession Day (Guangfujie). The news of the day is all about the arrival of the new governor, the infamous Chen Yi, presented in both Chinese and Japanese. As we would expect, at that time all street addresses in the newspaper were in Japanese—the address for the newspaper is given on the front page as Eichō, Block 4, Number 22. On February 1, 1946, the newspaper's address was changed to Civil-Martial Street, 4th Section, Number 32 (reflecting the November 1945 decree). From this point on, the new Chinese names are slowly integrated, but the Japanese terms remain continually in use, both by themselves and in a series of hybridizations. A year later, on February 2, 1947, addresses in front-page advertisements for the Chinese New Year are still primarily in Japanese only—one for a hotel does include a basic new hybridization in which the new Chinese address is followed by the Japanese address and some clarification: "Taipei City, Retrocession Road (originally Kyō District, Block 1, No. 2, behind the Matsui Dry Goods Store) 臺北市光復路(元京町一丁目二番/松井呉服店後進)—these addresses defy romanization.

Even after the implementation of the second Nationalist street-naming project, the Japanese addresses do not disappear. The second conversion is registered in the newspaper on April 10, 1947, when it changes its address to Hengyang Street, Section 4, Number 32.[56] After this, most Japanese usage is incorporated into the new addresses, typically with the Japanese address labeled "the old" (*kyū* or *jiu*) one. For example, on September 25, an advertisement on page 1 for Mid-autumn Festival moon cakes directs us to Taipei City, Hengyang Street (old Ei District)" 臺北市衡陽街 (舊榮町). Sometimes the Japanese address is still given priority, such as in an October 31, 1948, obituary for Jing Caifeng, wife of Yan Bicong, in which the address is given as "Taihoku City, Nishin District, Block One (Chaoyang Street)" 台北市日新町一丁目 (潮陽街). At other times, bizarre mixtures emerge, such as on the front page of the October 7, 1947, issue, where the address for a chemical company appears to begin in Japanese and end in Chinese 西門町三段四號, leading one to "read" the address in mixed form: "Seimonchō, sanduan, sihao."[57] Over time, the use of Japanese addresses decreases in the face of the Nationalist government's anti-Japanese and pro-Chinese cultural agenda, yet even as late as December 30, 1950, an obituary includes the old, fully Japanese designation Taiheichō, long after Japanese references have been dropped from official maps of the city. In the end, the Japanese name for the West Gate District, Seimonchō (or Ximending, in its Chinese reading) is what fails to fall: as of summer 2010, a restaurant that is nominally at 101 Hanzhong Street brandished the name/address, "101 西門町," however one wants to read it (fig. 3.5)

Nonetheless, by the early 1950s, the mainland-oriented nomenclature fully claimed the city as a displaced "Republic of China," what Steven Riep calls "a simulacrum of the China mainland."[58] This was a political position rendered fully in cartographic terms, such as manifested in the city street map of 1957, *Taibeishi jiedaotu*. Riep and others provide an extended discussion of this ideological work, including the systematic manner in which street names and place-names were spread over the city so as to mimic the map of China (i.e., the southwestern part of the city dominated by place-

3.5 101 Ximending Restaurant in West Gate entertainment district, 2010

names from southwest China), with the main arterials carrying more open ideological weight—either reflecting traditional "Confucian" values (e.g., Loyalty and Filial Piety Street, Zhongxiaolu) or close associations with the work of the Republic of China (e.g., New Life Road, Xinshenglu). Such street names are not unique to Taipei, yet the extensive and systematic use of such place-names in the city is of a much higher order than anywhere else.

Given the current political climate in Taiwan, where the promotion and celebration of all things Taiwanese are much in the air, we might expect a movement toward another displacement: replacing Nationalist nomenclature with one more in line with the spirit of "localization." That may come and, if it does, I would expect to see the emergence (once again) of the Qing names. So far there has been only one significant change to this Taipei-cum-China street system since its implementation, and it strikes at the heart of the Nationalist nomenclature.

This change involves a street dedicated to Chiang Kai-shek, the short but highly symbolic boulevard that leads from the Presidential Palace to East Gate, which was named Long Live [Chiang] Kai[-shek] Road (Jieshoulu) in October 1946 on the occasion of Chiang's first visit to Taiwan. This was one of several new "Jieshou" institutions established during this time, including renaming the old Sōtokufu as Long Live Kai Hall (Jieshouguan) and later its neighboring Long Live Kai Park (Jieshou Gongyuan).[59] One sign of the exclusive condition of this space was that all bicycles and motorcycles were banned from the boulevard. In a slight bid for modesty, Long Live Kai Hall was renamed the Presidential Palace (Zongtongfu) in 1950 with the arrival of the central government.[60] Jieshou Street was also recently renamed, although this certainly was not in a bid for discretion or modesty. On March 21, 1996, the mayor of Taipei City, Chen Shuibian, announced the renaming of Jieshou Road as Ketagalan Boulevard (Gaidagelan Dadao) as part of the localization efforts sweeping his administration and the island. The nearly panegyric account in the left-leaning *Liberty Times* (Ziyou shibao) reads:

> Amidst the celebratory singing and dancing of aboriginal people, the name Long Live Kai Road that has been used for fifty years was yesterday officially relegated to history, and chosen to replace it was the new name full of the spirit of the aboriginal people, Ketagalan Boulevard.[61]

In a more mundane acknowledgment of the new status of this renamed space, the city government also declared that you could ride your bicycle or motorcycle down the boulevard if you so desired.[62]

Renaming this highly symbolic street with the name of the original indigenous people of the Taipei basin was a displacement of a very high order, leaping over the multiple displacements that had been enacted there since the original one of the Ketagalan people. One can hardly argue that the indigenous people somehow reclaimed their land in this renaming, but the act was a small element in the celebration of post–martial law "multiculturalism." Testimony to the tentative new status of the indigenous people signaled by this renaming came later when Mayor Hao Longbin of the Nationalist Party wanted to rename the boulevard as the (hard-to-believe) "Anticorruption Democracy Boulevard." Because of protests by indigenous groups and their supporters, the "Anticorruption" name was restricted to one block of the boulevard, the so-called Anticorruption Democracy Square

(Fantanfu Minzhu Guangchang). As the mayor explained, "the new establishment is not changing the name of Ketagalan Boulevard, since the city government is only naming a portion of the boulevard."[63] In his defensiveness was a modicum of cultural sensitivity.

While Mayor Hao may have had one demonstration in mind (the September 15, 2006, protests against President Chen Shuibian), since 1996 this twice-renamed space has, in fact, become the principal area for the demonstration of dissent and opposition politics of various types. Nearly every weekend, one group or another holds (generally) lawful and peaceful rallies in the space between the Presidential Palace and East Gate. The space once reserved for the pomp and circumstance of official power, where "one hundred thousand people [sang] out their sincere respect to the national leader," has become the space of public challenges to that power.[64]

The Wall and the Subway

The unearthing of a remnant of the Taipei City wall in November 1993, during excavation for the Blue Line of the Metropolitan Rapid Transit System (Taibei Dazhong Jieyun Xitong, or MRT), was not an archaeological coincidence. The transit line was being built at that site *because* of the wall, both geographically and historically. Nor was the archaeological rescue of the discovered remnants (the substructure of the wall's base in two places along its northern side) merely a scientific act or simple cultural preservation; it was a political statement that could be read in different ways from different ideological perspectives.

When the first lines of the Taipei MRT system were planned through the downtown area, they largely reenacted the building of the *sansenro* by the Japanese government, except this time, in subterranean terms. Segments of the Blue and the Light Green lines trace almost exactly the footprint of the wall; just as the wall's footprint provided the space for the boulevards, the boulevards provided access to the subterranean space for the subway.[65] That pattern is seen in other parts of the system as well, such as where the Red Line follows the old railroad bed (built by the Japanese in 1901) to the old port town of Danshui.

The progress of the MRT system over the last twenty years has acted as a barometer of changes in governmentality.[66] Discussed as early as the 1960s, construction on the MRT finally began in the 1980s when Taiwan was at the height of its economic strength, just before the lifting of martial law. Its early phases were mired in corruption and controversy as it performed the last stages of "old politics" and plummeted the city into the "dark age of traffic" (*jiaotong heianqi*), during which subway construction severely disrupted surface traffic patterns along these arterials. The apparent shoddiness of the early construction became an emblem of the city in collapse: Yomi Braester writes, "The train fire, on the [MRT's] Mucha Line's first trial run in October 1994, became a symbol of Taiwan's social and political shortcomings."[67] Yet, as Anru Lee has argued, slowly through the 1990s, the system took on a level of discipline and performance that propelled it to the forefront of a new social awareness and citizen pride. It is now considered by many the jewel of everyday life in Taipei.

In the MRT we have a new transit system that was both a practical response to troublesome traffic patterns, such as massive gridlock on the congested downtown streets in the 1980s, and a symbolic embodiment of a new citizenry, this time the globalized, cosmopolitan "New Taiwanese." Of the latter, Anru Lee has written:

> Globally and economically, the willingness to cooperate observed among MRT riders reflects a shift in reference of Taipei residents' self-identification to an increasingly globalized world. The completion of the MRT coincided with Taiwan's recent economic restructuring on the one hand and the emergence of global cities as the main site of global competition on the other. Behaving in an orderly way and keeping a positive image of the MRT, therefore, resonates with the Taipei residents' efforts and desire to keep their city economically competitive.[68]

The MRT space for the performance of this new citizenry has created an "MRT tribe" (*jieyunzu*) of everyday riders who embody well-disciplined and prideful behavior—they are smart, efficient, and considerate participants in the running of the city (fig. 3.6). As Lee has argued, this performance is both commanded by state authorities and welcomed by the riders. She argues that the MRT created a space of "cultural intimacy wherein people of Taipei reiterate or reconstruct their ambiguous and contradictory relationship with the state as well as their collective identity."[69] In this acceptance of state discipline, one sees an echo of earlier behavior in "the same space" of the Qing wall and Japanese boulevard: the cooperation, albeit somewhat coerced, of the leaders of Mengjia and Dadaocheng in the construction of the wall, and the modern circulation of colonial subjects in

3.6 Passengers at MRT Station, 2010

traffic along the boulevard and around the gate. In the diachronic transformation of wall to boulevard, and boulevard to subway, we also find an ideological transformation: the imperial into the colonial and the colonial into the global.

In 2004 the official poster for Taipei's 120th anniversary (*Taibei jiancheng yibaiershi zhounian*) featured a large rectangular stone standing on end, tied with a red sash and dramatically lit against a dark background of similar but barely visible stones. Though unexplained there, these stones have become a feature in the politics of the city: they are from the foundation of the old wall that was excavated in 1993 during the construction of the MRT. In addition to the elaborate archaeological report that was produced for this very modest find, the excavation is featured in large, three-dimensional murals incorporated into the underground MRT mall near the main train station, alongside retail boutiques and various eateries.

In 2000 a display of these stones was included in the international exhibition Qiang (The Wall) at the National History Museum. It featured representations of various walls and wall-related installations from China and around the world, in whose setting the Taipei materials seem to fall somewhere between archaeology and installation art.[70] One reason the wall became so celebrated is that it is connected ideologically both with the localization movement and with the larger Chinese identity that lay behind Nationalist Party policy—the wall could be seen both as local and as national (Chinese). Moreover, in the context of the exhibition, it was embedded into an international rationale as well, associated with walls of Europe and the Middle East, as well as China. The disinterred stone-as-art-object on the 2004 poster was accompanied by the slogan "Our thoughts rest on the old wall; Our dreams sail toward the world" (*Xin anju gucheng; meng hangxiang shijie*). The celebrated subway system that is, in fact, an elaborate vertical displacement of their old wall is one way in which the people of Taipei are sailing toward a new world.

FOUR

A Park in the City

The conventional metaphor for a public park lodged in the heart of the modern city is that of a jewel—a gemstone glistening in the gray bedrock of urban planning, a small piece of nature inside the mechanical clicking of the city. That metaphor does not work very well for the small park that lies in the heart of downtown Taipei.[1] The six-block trapezoid of public space framed by two Japanese towers (the former Sōtokufu and the chic Shin Kong Mitsukoshi office building and department store) seems too purposeful to elicit metaphors of a natural object.

All parks are by definition unnatural and purposeful, yet Taipei Park seems to wear that purpose more plainly than most, and this is related to its Japanese colonial origins. The term *gongyuan* has a long history in Chinese literature, but not until the twentieth century is it used to designate a public park.[2] The designation was translated back from Japanese, for the term *kōen* (the Japanese pronunciation of the same two-character expression) was used as early as 1873 to designate Tokyo's first park, Ueno Park.[3] While Japanese parks were obviously derived from a European model (Seidensticker calls Ueno Park "another Meiji novelty introduced under the influence of the West"), in their new context they take on a style and function distinct from those of their European models.[4] Broadly speaking, early European parks were associated with the "healthful life" in open nature, separated

4.1 Taipei Park in 2003, viewed from the north; museum in foreground, lily pond and pavilions, middle left; February 28th Museum, far left; band shell, middle right; administration building, far right; February 28th Monument in center

symbolically and actually from the city: "They offered an antidote to the urban world, a space where Nature could be experienced, allowing recuperation and revitalization."⁵ The *kōen/gongyuan*, on the other hand, became more closely associated with the activities of civic life in a modern society. In Japan, this was particularly true of Hibiya Park, the small central park and civic center of modern Tokyo, with which Taipei Park shares affinities. We also see versions of the park as a civic construction in the colonial parks of Korea, which date from 1910; these institutions were, according to Todd Henry, "used to draw newly colonized Koreans into the expanding imperial community dominated by colonizing Japanese."⁶

Currently, Taipei Park is a labyrinth of buildings, monuments, and other constructions that overlap and intersect with different civic moments and motivations (fig. 4.1). Even the foliage has been brought into these civic designs: in the middle of the park stands a huge topiary spelling out (in Latin letters): TAIPEI. A wide walkway, formerly a street, slices the park into north-south sections. The north entrance is dominated by the neoclassical National Taiwan Museum, a colonial building dating from 1915.

At the south entrance (just off Ketagalan Boulevard) now stands a recent gift to the city from the Taipei Taiwan Lions Club: a large, ancient-style Chinese bell. The east side of the park is held down by the new MRT station and an elaborate set of Chinese pavilions and a central pool. The west side is lined with various office buildings associated with the park administration office, in the middle of which is the band shell and amphitheater, where various public performances, both official and otherwise, are held. In the very center is the park's latest civic monument, the February 28th Monument (Ererba Jinianbei), which boldly announces a new civic consciousness. Among these dominating structures, a series of walkways winds through a plethora of smaller sites that contribute just as significantly to the configuration of the park. As it is, Taipei Park resembles neither a space of serenity nor a space of thoughtful design, but rather a jumble of incongruous and competing spatial statements. Yet it is within those complications that one finds the telling signs of the political and cultural displacements of the park and, indeed, of the city.

Like the colonial parks in Korea that were inserted into the spaces of the royal Taehan Palaces of Seoul, Taipei Park also displaced an earlier political order, although somewhat more benignly. The park was built on the original site of the city's major intramural temple, Tianhougong for Mazu, dating from 1888.[7] As with the city itself, this temple delineated a neutral, or "imperial," space within the Qing wall that negotiated local identities. Most temples of the late Qing period in Taiwan were closely associated with ethnic and subethnic groups, and they often functioned as headquarters for their organizational activities, including the planning and execution of ethnic feuds; for example, the Sanyi group was closely associated with the Longshan Temple (1738) in Mengjia, which served as a base of operations during its feud with the Tong'an group, which subsequently established the Xiahai Temple (1859) of Dadaocheng.[8] Despite being dedicated to the popular local goddess Mazu, the intramural Tianhougong was more aligned with the provincial *yamen* built in the northwestern part of the city in 1887.[9] The temple, in fact, occupied the geographic center of the city, at the intersection of the two main streets, Back Prefecture Street (Fuhoujie, today's Guanqianlu) and West Gate Street (Ximenjie, today's Hengyanglu). In this position, the temple also served as an entryway to the nearby academy and provincial examination hall, another monument of imperial status.[10] Thus, the Tianhougong and its grounds were physically and socially removed from, or at least neutrally positioned between, the tensions of local ethnic politics.

A Story of Recovery

Today the temple has long since disappeared from the park. The only remnants of that early architecture are a dozen or so pillar-stones that have been turned into small stools where citizens of Taipei can rest their weary legs. There has been, however, a recent, unexpected recovery of one of the Tianhougong idols; the story of that recovery is told as a narrative of Chinese nationalism and Taiwanese local identity.

While historical records have noted that the original idols of the Tianhougong were saved and placed elsewhere by the Japanese when the temple was confiscated for secular purposes, the idols had long been lost (at least to official sources). Then, in 2004, one of the original Mazu figures was found in a temple in the town of Sanzhi on the north coast of the island, placed there for safekeeping.[11] In 2005 this idol was transported back to the park for ten days in celebration of the goddess's birthday, the twenty-third day of the third lunar month (April 23, 2005). This was a high-profile municipal event, full of pomp and ceremony, organized by Taipei's Cultural Affairs Bureau. Mayor Ma Yingjeou (Ma Yingjiu) and Commissioner Liao Xianhao were both on hand to welcome the goddess back to the city, and when she was returned to Sanzhi, the mayor was one of her palanquin bearers. Reports of this event were couched in praises for the mayor as well as for Mazu. The official news release reads:

> On May 2nd, the Cultural Bureau brought the "Taipei Mazu Festival" to a conclusion, escorting the Mazu palanquin back to Sanzhi. Mayor Ma Yingjeou made a special point of helping to carry the palanquin. As they made a 1.5-kilometer circumambulation of the village of Sanzhi, they drew a large crowd of people along the way who responded with enthusiastic applause. Ma Ying-jeou pointed out that this year was the 110th anniversary of the Sino-Japanese War that resulted in the ceding of Taiwan to Japan, and it was the 100th anniversary of the Japanese tearing down the Tianhougong. But the intended attempt of the Japanese Colonial Government to destroy Chinese culture was never realized. Faith in Mazu is deep and long-lasting. Every year the Taipei City Government will welcome Mazu back to the old intramural city to thank Her for protecting all sentient beings and to assure that this historical lineage is unbroken.[12]

The story of cultural loss and recovery told here by the mayor invokes the rhetoric of Chinese nationalism and anticolonialism. When he elicits "Chinese culture" (Zhonghua wenhua), into which he wants to draw all Han Taiwanese, Mayor Ma Ying-jeou is promoting the role of the original Tian-hougong as a neutral, "imperial" space set aside from factional politics and local power. In other news releases, the story of the construction of the Tianhougong is linked to the public works of Liu Mingchuan, the famous and widely revered Qing appointed provincial governor.[13] In this we hear the faint echoes of the "one China" policy to which the Nationalists, the United States, and the People's Republic of China espouse. Yet, the close identifica-tion of Mazu worship with the Fukienese/Taiwanese population also makes this appeal much more regional and local, separated from a broader Han nationalism. That tension between the official, sanctioned voice of power and the subaltern, resistant voice of the local is one that defines the history of Taipei Park as well.

A Park in the City

When the Japanese claimed Taipei City as their new colonial capital of Tai-hoku, they inherited the Tianhougong and its surrounding grounds as part of its intramural spatiality. While the Taiwanese temples outside the city walls were allowed to function relatively undisturbed for most of the colo-nial period, the Japanese authorities moved quickly to change the nature of the intramural Tianhougong.[14] Apparently, the ruling powers regarded this religious space as part of the colonial core, which needed to be neutralized by its quick secularization—by 1901 it was already designated as the Taihoku Business Office (Benmusho/Banwushu) (see fig. 1.3).[15]

Taipei Park was included in the earliest plans for the transformation of the city, with an announcement in the public record of 1899, which found graphic form in the planning map of 1900.[16] Technically, this was the colo-ny's second park, with Murayama/Yuanshan Park being built north of the city in 1897, but as Li Lixue points out, at the time of its construction, the Murayama space was not really a public park.[17] Nonetheless, these are our earliest designations of *kōen/gongyuan* in Taiwan and may be the first time the term was used outside of Japan.[18] Although it is not clear on the 1900 map, the park would come to encompass the entire trapezoidal space formed by the old Chinese streets and a newly designed street planned for east of the temple. Like the building of the colonial city as a whole, the park would first take shape in the relatively empty space south of the temple grounds, leaving the north section relatively unchanged. The commonly quoted official documents state that the park was built between 1905 and 1907 and completed by the end of Kodama's and Gotō's rule in the colony.[19] Indeed, in 1906 departure ceremonies for the two administrators (posthumous for Kodama) were held in the park area and contributed an early signifier of its overtly civic nature, the statue of Kodama at the south entrance of the park (see chapter 6). Yet, as we shall see, the park as a fully colonial space was really a product of its 1915 reconfigurations.

Many modernization efforts in Taiwan, from railroad construction to popular entertainment, were modeled on European practices, but there was always space for local interjections into these colonial projects. These came from both the Japanese colonizers and their Taiwanese subjects. For example, Edward Seidensticker has remarked on the hybrid quality of Hibiya Park; it is often referred to as Tokyo's "first genuinely Western park," but, in actuality, he says, "a good deal of the park is fairly Japanese."[20] That European-Japanese hybridity was also found throughout Taipei Park in what C. J. Hsia calls the "double transplantation of cultural dependency."[21] In fact, Hibiya Park, which was under construction just as Taipei Park was being conceived, was its apparent model: as such, Taipei Park was an obvious site of this doubled (perhaps even tripled) cultural transplantation.[22]

Despite the early designations and deliberate insertions of public monuments, the Taipei Park project was always transforming in shape and definition. This was certainly true during the Japanese period, but it was also true afterward, even up to the present day. Standing at the beginning of the twenty-first century, our retroactive gaze tends to draw the pieces of these efforts into an ideological whole of current value. Yet, a closer parsing of the historical contingencies and incremental changes to the park, with attentiveness to transplantation and displacements of colonial, neocolonial, and postcolonial efforts, allows for a subtler rendering of that ideological whole.

The Club in the Park

The first building to appear in the empty space designated as the park in the 1900 map is very much an edifice of this "double transplantation" of colonialism. This is the somewhat enigmatic Taipei Club (Taihoku Kurabu), which first appears in maps from 1904 and 1905.[23] According to archival sources, construction of the club was approved in 1902, which would make it not only the earliest colonial building in the park area but also one of the earliest in the city, shortly following the residences of the governor-general and civil administrator (1901).[24] Although the club building is not featured as much in the photographic record as are those official residences, we do have a few incidental photographs that show a large, two-story, hybrid construction—Japanese materials (wood and tile) with semi-European design (see fig. 6.1). [25]

The Taipei Club was certainly a privileged site for the colonialists, as were other such "colonial clubs" in Asia; yet, rather than being secluded in a walled or hedge-fringed compound, this privileged space was placed within the parameters of the most self-consciously public space, the new park. At this early stage of development (1902), however, we might better view the club building as not so much part of the park as part of the other exclusive facilities of colonial rule in the area. The site lay not only between the two official colonial residences of Kodama Gentarō and Gotō Shimpei but also near the new sports facilities just to the west and south.[26] In 1904 Takekoshi Yosaburō wrote:

> There is a [horse] racecourse in Taihoku; and also in front of Baron Gotō's official residence a fine recreational ground surrounded by a fence. Outside of the fence is a regular bicycle track, much better than anything to be found in Tokyo. The Government bore the first cost of laying these out, but all now belong to the Athletic Society and can be used by members of that society.[27]

A 1906 photo album commemorating Governor-General Kodama's official tours of the island provides a partial record of the facilities and the activities of which Takekoshi writes. For a reception held in Kodama's honor by the Athletic Club (Tai'iku Kurabu), the record features equestrian events, bicycle races, and footraces.[28] The club would have clearly functioned as a meeting ground for members of this Athletic Club as well as for the political players of the city, among whom there was no doubt extensive overlap. In the later stages of the colony, these groups might have included individuals of the Taiwanese elite, but in the days of Kodama and Gotō, membership would have been composed exclusively of Japanese colonial officials and bureaucrats.[29]

There is explicit testimony to the composition of that membership. A 1901 photo album, "Photographs of the Club," contains portraits of approximately ninety-six individuals, accompanied by short introductions and biographies.[30] As we would expect, the portraits are presented in order and in categories that represent the colonial hierarchy, from the top-ranking

4.2 Portraits of
newspaper men, 1901.
Source: *Shashin kurabu*;
courtesy of National
Taiwan Library

military and civilian officials, Kodama Gentarō and Gotō Shimpei, down to
the photographer himself. Interim pages trace the various levels of the elite
colonial society, including bureaucrats and business leaders. Both photographic and sartorial style offer overwhelming evidence of another "double
transplantation" of colonial discipline: the men are depicted largely in poses
that mimic those of formal European portraiture, if not in military or civilian uniform, then in the uniform of modernization, the Western suit and
tie (with some exceptions). For example, three-quarters of the way through
this gallery, we find portraits of four men associated with the most important newspaper of the day, *Taiwan nichinichi shimpō*: its president, the editor in chief, a reporter, and an editor (fig. 4.2). The editor in chief and the
young reporter appear in suits and ties in standard three-quarter profiles;
the president is presented in tails with top hat in hand against a vague studio

background, with a small array of medals displayed on his chest—we will return to the distinctive portrait of the editor below.

In addition to these formal portraits, the album opens with six full-page photographs related to club activities. Three are group portraits that document public moments of club members and associates. The most formal of these is not particularly related to the club—a carefully staged outdoor portrait of a large send-off party for the consul from Holland, 1900. The other two group photographs present select subsets of club members. The first is of the club's most elite members on a tour of southern China in 1899 as part of a delegation led by Gotō Shimpei. Standing on the steps of the Nanputuo Temple in Xiamen (Amoy), the group appears with a delegation of islanders (*hontōjin*) who have hosted them—presumably these were Taiwanese living in Xiamen at the time. The colonial order is fully arrayed, with top hats and uniforms dominating the front, suits and derbies in the middle, and finally the Chinese robes of the local hosts toward the back. The third group photograph is a much more relaxed affair, but the affected seriousness is almost as uniform: a group of reporters attending a social gathering at a Japanese-style restaurant, The East (Azuma), in downtown Taipei on December 3, 1899. Thirty-eight individuals from ten different publications and organizations sit and stand in an informal portrait commemorating the event: here many are in traditional Japanese clothing, although there are also Western suits and perhaps a uniform or two represented. In the relatively impromptu quality of the scene, the photograph approaches the style of a snapshot (a commodity that was becoming available at this time).

The three full-frame photographs of individuals that open the album offer another glimpse into the club's activities. In the last one, Soeda Rōichi, doctor of law and head of the Taiwan Bank, appears in a most "clubby" pose, with his springer spaniel, double-barreled shotgun, and bag of birds. The photograph is captioned "Dr. Soeda on Hunting Trip" (Yūryōjū Soeda hakushi).[31] James Ryan has noted that the photograph of a hunter "posed with a gun beside his recently killed prey" is a common representation of an "archetypal colonial figure."[32] That certainly fits the depiction of Mr. Soeda, even though his is a studio photograph with rather puny prey. The first two photographs in the album are, as we might expect, of Kodama Gentarō and Gotō Shimpei, but they diverge widely from the formal portraits in the opening gallery. Here, they are documented as participants of the "club culture." Gotō Shimpei's photograph is not entirely unexpected. Taken at the time of his delegation's visit to the temple in Xiamen, it shows him as his

4.3 Informal portrait of Governor General Kodama Gentarō, 1901. Source: *Shashin kurabu*; courtesy of National Taiwan Library

typical dapper self: top hat, double-breasted coat, and walking cane. But the photograph of Kodama is remarkable in many ways, particularly in its deviation from the norm set by his numerous formal portraits, in which he is always dead serious in his medal-laden military uniform. Here he is pictured on the back lawn of his residence, posing casually during a round of croquet (fig. 4.3). The playfulness of this representation is not just in the activity, with its obvious references to British colonial culture, but also in his jaunty "sports clothes" and Mona Lisa–like smile.

Physical education and public sports were part of a larger Japanese effort during the Meiji period to form a new civil society, both in the Japanese homeland and in the new colony. One of the functions of the Taipei Club was the promotion of sports on the island, so that even in their more playful poses, Dr. Soeda and Governor-General Kodama are playing their colonial role. This cultural work of the club would continue throughout the colonial period, and perhaps even after.[33]

Winding Paths

As a formal colonial monument, Taipei Park took definite shape around 1915, with the completion of the memorial museum to Kodama and Gotō at its north entrance, which I discuss in detail in chapter 5. This reconstruction yielded the configuration of space that we recognize as the present-day park. Just before this dramatic change, the park grounds were depicted in the 1911 "bird's eye" map, where "viewers without special cartographic training, such as women and children, [could] comprehend easily the layout of the whole city."[34] Captured in those details are a mélange of park structures that plot the winding path that the space took toward becoming the park we now know. According to the map, the northern part of the park still had one foot in its earlier Chinese space: not only was the Tianhougong building still standing, now housing the Taiwan Association of Chinese Studies (Taiwan Chūgakukai), but there was also an accompanying building represented in a traditional Chinese, four-sided compound style, with a cartouche that claims it as the site of the planned memorial museum.[35]

Other buildings in this space came closer to fitting the agenda of the colony, if not the park. They included dormitories for the hospital and monopoly bureau staff, both important enterprises in the colonization agenda, with offices in the area. There were also living quarters for a unit of the army, barracks for military police, and, at the northern edge of the park area, a small police box (*hashutsujo*). At this time, the civil police force was emerging under the leadership of Gotō Shimpei as the most important organ of social control on the island, moving it away from a military-dominated state toward one of more mature colonial civil administration.[36] The ubiquitous police boxes were the neighborhood manifestation of that policy.

Even more declarative of Qing heritage in the park are two memorial arches (*paifang*), one located between the erstwhile temple and the compound building and another nearer to the club. Although these arches are imperial in their construction, they are very much colonial in their (dis)placement: both were moved to the park area to make way for construction projects of the new colonial government, and both are still within the park grounds. The first arch, celebrating the good works of the Widow Huang, was moved to the northwestern corner of the park in 1901 to allow for the building of the governor-general's residence near East Gate.[37] This arch was built in 1882 by order of the Tongzhi emperor when the widow was sixty-two years old.[38] The second arch was erected in 1888 to commemorate the city's imperial examination halls; this one originally stood on the main thoroughfare (currently Hengyanglu) that led from West Gate to the Tianhougong and on to the examination grounds. When the colonial government came to broaden and renovate this street as part of its 1905 urban development plan, it dismantled the arch and moved it to the park area.[39] This and the preservation of the city gates are two of the most important preservation projects carried out under the Kodama-Gotō administration.

Let me digress here to examine the implications of these acts of conservation. While European colonialists may have held aspects of indigenous cultures in some regard (typically as signs of the exotic other or monuments of transformable high art), the Japanese elite had a more complicated relationship with traditional Chinese culture. Certain aspects of this culture, especially that of the elite literati class, had been esteemed and integrated into Japanese society over the centuries. When the colonialists encountered elements from that culture in association with their new colonial subjects, they faced a certain dilemma: How should they treat these representations of the colonized local culture? Speaking first of the problems of racism in Japan's treatment of its colonial subjects, Mark Peattie also remarks:

> Yet . . . it was possible for the Japanese to view their colonial charges in quite a different light. If one stressed affinities of race and culture between Japan and the people of its two most populous colonies, one could believe that the latter were, in Tsurumi's words, "not quite Japanese, but capable of becoming Japanese."[40]

Is it possible, however, that this contemplation of "shared culture" might produce a tension that was in fact more unsettling? Could not these monuments of Chinese culture actually challenge the assumed superiority of the colonialists over their subjects, in the sense that the Chinese cultural objects were "more authentic" than the Japanese versions? This was especially so in the area of literary culture, since the Meiji Japanese continued to hold classical Chinese and its written language in high regard, even while disparaging the local spoken languages of Taiwan. For example, the photo album commemorating Gotō Shimpei's departure from the island contains, along with portraits and photographs of the celebration, a document written in formal classical Chinese, apparently in his calligraphy.[41] If the colonialists were to promote the so-called *dōbun* (shared script) policy, everyone would know where the *bun/wen* had originated. Takeoshi Yosaburō reports on a very clear example of this conflicted mentality:

> Here [at Governor-General Kodama's country house, Nansaien] the Viscount [Kodama] loved to assemble the learned men of the island and compose Chinese poems, the result of which appeared in the form of a collection of verse under the name of *Nansaien Shishu* (Collection of Poems from Nansaisen). I believe acts like this enabled him to touch the hearts of the natives.[42]

If so, those natives were clearly the educated elite of the Han population who also had command, and no doubt often better command, of classical poetics. Even as they moved closer to "becoming Japanese" but never actually getting there, members of the Taiwanese elite clung to practices of their "Chineseness," especially as represented by these literary arts. From their perspective, there must have been a good deal of irony in the Japanese regard for classical Chinese language and literature.

The colonialists could promote the use of Japanese as the official language of colonial life at the same time that they promoted and participated in celebrations of classical Chinese language, including calligraphy exhibitions and Chinese poetry clubs. In practical terms, the Japanese colonialists in Taiwan might have viewed most of the local Han cultures, whether Hoklo or Haka, as not authentically "Chinese," but elements of the elite Mandarin culture could not have been so easily dismissed. This paradox brings us back to the portrait of the fourth Japanese newspaperman in the club album, the editor in his very un-European pose, legs spread and hands of his knees ala the formal Chinese portrait, and in his "Mandarin outfit" of Chinese tunic, robe, and silk shoes. Although we see similar cross-cultural dressing in other colonial photography (such as in Jean Geiser's 1870 "Couple européen en costume algérien"), in contrast to the European colonialists sporting "native dress" or adopting local attire for practical purposes, here I understand this to be a sign of sartorial respect, not parody, play, or practicality.[43] A high regard for Mandarin culture would have extended to emblematic material culture as well, including these robes. The Qing dynasty memorial arches stood in the way of the construction projects of colonization and modernization, so they needed to be removed, yet since they were an emblem of the imperial and literary cultures, the monuments could not be simply razed. A better solution was to preserve them inside the new public space of the park, where they would be relatively safe—safe from modernization efforts, but also safely displaced, away from a position of power in local culture.

Civic Life

This transitional architecture, from converted temple to police box, would succumb to the full assertion of the park as a new type of public space that was soon to follow. Even the 1911 map begins to plot that change with significant park-like monuments, especially the music pavilion (*ongakudō*) that stood just east of the former temple.[44] Built in 1908, nothing is more emblematic of the authorities' vision of the future park than this small pavilion, in both its style and its function. With column and cornice copied from pavilions in European parks, it was constructed for the performance of Western, particularly classical and military, music, which the colonialists had also brought with them as part of their cultural "transplantation" program.[45] At the program's inception, it was perhaps intended only for the colonialists and not for the colonized population, but that would quickly change.

The period from 1915 to 1930 might be viewed as the glory years of colonialism on Taiwan; this is the time when material and social conditions on the island advanced rapidly, and under the influence of international geopolitics, such as Wilsonian self-determination, a new sense of civic life emerged. During the 1920s, the colonial government seemed to contemplate seriously a policy of assimilation (*dōka*), with Taiwanese elites arguing vigorously for some form of self-rule.[46] This new sense of civic involvement was entangled with a concerted effort to promote modernity on the island. Along with the typical trade exhibitions of agricultural and commercial products, the colonial government held numerous other types of public events aimed at creating a modern civil society in the city.[47] Most of these activities took place in the public spaces that various colonial agencies were producing throughout the city. The music pavilions (there would be several) in Taipei Park became an early site for the performance of this modern civic life that Japanese rulers and the Taiwanese elite were meant to share, however unequally.

Over the decades, the 1908 music pavilion slowly transformed the park and was transformed by it; five different music pavilions were erected in three park locations. The first three pavilions were very much in the design of Victorian garden pavilions (similar to the one in Hibiya Park, which was built in 1905); the second pavilion's location was moved south of the bisecting street with the completion of the museum in 1915.[48] A fourth pavilion, of modernist design, was built in this location in 1925—a well-known photograph depicts it with a mixed audience of men, women, and schoolchildren. The fifth and final construction was the art-deco band shell and amphitheater built in preparation for the 1935 exposition; significantly, this structure also mimicked one built in Hibiya Park (1923).[49]

That final colonial structure for musical performances, the band shell and amphitheater, was inherited by the postwar Chinese government, which also used it for early performances of military music. Then, during the 1960s, the facade of the original art deco building underwent an ugly "modernization" of concrete and tile, although the basic structure of the building remained. Today the area of the band shell, stage, and small amphitheatre (now called *yinyuetai*) is one of the most vibrant spaces in both official and public life-use of the park. The stage is often the site of government sanctioned social events and performances, from Sunday afternoon children's festivals to evening rock concerts hosted by local TV celebrities. Just as important, on most days the stage functions as a casual, impromptu performance space, available on a first-come, first-served basis.[50] During the early part of the day, one often sees young children playing at performing, attended by mothers seated in the front rows, or an old man doing his martial arts routine applauded by other old men sitting in the shade. Later in the afternoon, it is time for teenagers to work on their dramatic performances or dance routines—often these will be the Bei'yi'nü (Number One Girls High) students in their telltale green blouses and black pleated skirts, whose school is next door to the park.

The wooden seats that fill the small amphitheatre function as a casual gathering place for a variety of citizens—from the chatty elderly men of the neighborhood to well-heeled office workers on their lunch break—with the nature and function of the gatherings changing throughout the day. The seating area is also used in less sanctioned ways: the homeless nap on the long red benches during the day, while at night, gay men use the space as a place to meet.[51] The earlier music pavilions must have functioned in a similar way: space not only for public colonial displays but also for those now lost life uses that would make the space more part of everyday activities.

A Small Kingdom

Often when I mentioned to people who were familiar with Taiwan that I was doing research on New Park (Xin Gongyuan), as it is still commonly called, it was assumed that I was investigating the park in terms of its in/famous gay activities. In fact, the most interesting studies of the park are exactly of this phenomenon, including those by the students of C. J. Hsia (Xia Zhujiu) that feature innovative investigations of urban space and planning.[52] The studies of the park by Lai Zhengzhe and Xie Peijuan are much in that vein. In the English abstract to his master's thesis, Lai, now a celebrated gay rights advocate known by the nickname A'zhe, wrote:

> The park, which carries a heavy burden of state ideology, has had the ironic co-existence of forty years of gay culture. In such a rich culture, love and lust take on a spatial performance, transgressing and appropriating the intended meaning of this public space, giving multiple definitions to symbolism and utility of the park.[53]

The status of Taipei Park as a site for gay cruising had been widely known, if seldom mentioned, during those forty years, and Lai believes this may have also been so during the Japanese period. The explicit association of New Park and gay activities was made public by Bai Xianyong in his 1983 novel *Crystal Boys* (Niezi), which describes the subculture of gay life in the "company" (*gongsi*) during the previous decades. He opens his novel:

> In our small kingdom there was no daytime, only night. As the sky lightened each day, our kingdom disappeared, for we existed as a highly illegal nation. We had no government, no constitution; we were not recognized, not respected; all we had was a motley crew of citizens. . . . As for the borders of our kingdom, they were pitifully small: no more than two or three hundred meters long, and just over a hundred meters wide. We were confined to that small rectangle of land surrounding the lily pond inside New Park near Guanqian Street in Taipei.[54]

The official rhetoric during the 1960s and 1970s, which effectively permeated all public discourse, was that homosexuality did not exist in Taiwan or China (and if it did, it was the effect of social corruption from the West).[55] This meant, of course, that there could be no public campaign against these activities as there were against other "deviant" behaviors (like the wearing of long hair); thus, the authorities effectively looked the other way, allowing this "little kingdom" to flourish at night. Jens Damm describes how a new discourse of same-sex desire began to emerge in Taiwan as early as the 1970s and 1980s, albeit then always framed in authoritarian terms. Even the 1986 film adaptation of Bai Xianyong's novel has been accused of failing to deal directly with homosexuality and of marginalizing the park.[56] That situation changed rapidly after 1987, when gay rights became a broadly debated issue and public gay culture emerged from the shadows. Currently, gay culture is found throughout the city, from bars and restaurants to Lai's bookstore, Gin Gin (Jingjing), which offers a wide range of gay publications and materials.[57] Yet, even with the substantial expansion of public gay space and activities in the city, Taipei Park continues to be a place for the "company" to gather.

Through a series of interviews with men in the park, Lai Zhengzhe's study of gay life describes the complex codes and circulations in that space. From these interviews, Lai plots the park into zones of different expectations and desires—there are spaces for older men, young boys, blind dates, and so on. Although the spaces Lai describes are contemporaneous with his study (1998), there is ample evidence that throughout the decades similar spaces existed, most of which were located in the northern half of the park near the museum. These were especially the pond-pavilion complex (i.e., the lily pond), the area near the TAIPEI topiary, and the men's room near the northwestern corner of the park; after the 1960s, the restroom in the southern part of the park was added to these spaces. Interviewees describe their habitual movement through the park and their behaviors in different spaces, such as "fishing" on the benches. A Mr. Chen says of his habits in the 1970s and 1980s:

> I would go to New Park by motorcycle, and because of the parking problems, would enter the park from the direction of National Taiwan University Hospital. At that time there was no MRT station, so I could walk along the row of seats near Gongyuan Road. Then I would go around the TAIPEI topiary and pool where a lot of people gathered. The way it worked in New Park was that I would usually pick out a spot and stand there and wait for a while. Later I would walk all around checking things out. I could wander round and round inside the park, going to the wooded areas, to the children's playground, and around the lily pond. I would stop in each of these for a while, walking back and forth between them.[58]

A narrative from the 1990s is a little more explicit, but parts of the itinerary described are identical to Mr. Chen's. Mr. Ye says:

> Most often when I go to New Park, I first go straight to the restroom; the restroom is a great place to satisfy your sexual desires. I know there will be some people in there performing sex for others; I myself have done this in the past. So you can imagine how the renovated bathroom [in the southern part of the park], with its large, low windows, eliminated the possibility of any exciting action in there for anyone. The place where most gay guys go to meet someone is the area near the TAIPEI topiary; the trees around the topiary are the prime location for most of my activity.[59]

Changes in the structure of the park, such as the addition of an MRT station and additional lighting, have affected the specific dynamics of the venues, but cruising and other activities seem to continue apace. From these narratives, one gets the sense of how and where the park comes to life after dark. The diurnal use of the museum and band shell gives way to the nocturnal use of the restrooms and lily pond. At dusk one often sees those types of activities meet and merge, as two populations slide by each other in very different occupations of the park.

Another Temple

Tucked into a corner of the park, against the perimeter fence of the administration building, stands a quite elaborate Tudigongmiao (Earth God Shrine). The Tudigongmiao is one of the most ubiquitous types of shrines in the mélange of the island's local folk religion. Earth Gods are minor deities whose domain is restricted to a village, a rural area, or a city neighborhood. Often compared to a local police officer, the Earth God offers protection for that area's residents.[60] The story of the temple's presence in the park is complicated, but all agree that it has not been an easy arrangement.

According to an elderly neighbor who was maintaining the shrine in 1999, the temple was originally located nearby but had to be moved into the park to make way for a government construction project in the 1960s—a narrative that places responsibility for the temple's location on the authorities.[61] This explanation is complicated by an official narrative of 2003, which contends that the area near the shrine had been recognized as an auspicious site for nearly two hundred years, with a small temple dating back to that time.[62]

According to this account, the present shrine was constructed in the 1980s with support from the staff of the park administration building, but since there was no organization established to maintain the site, it fell into disrepair.[63] Although we have no information on its status before the Nationalist period, in recent years, the shrine has been a site clearly contested by authorities and neighbors. Not only does the temple never appear in official descriptions or maps of the park, in the past, park officials have also denied any responsibility for the temple and spoken disparagingly of it. This sense of antagonism went both ways: the caretakers I spoke with in 1999 were very clear about their dislike for park authorities, speaking with pride about the temple's connection to the local neighborhood. Tensions reached a crisis around 2002, when the city government threatened to tear down the temple, whereupon local residents organized support and petitioned for official status for the temple. They were successful. On October 24, 2003, the city government recognized the temple as the February 28th Peace Park Fude Temple.[64] Since that time, the temple has been thoroughly renovated and now claims rather garish new facilities. The elevation of this temple to official visibility is testimony to the sense of local political action that has pervaded civic culture in Taipei since the lifting of martial law.

Despite the Tudigongmiao's contested history, it is currently one of the most frequented sites in the park, albeit usually for only moments at a time. In large part, this is because the temple lies on a direct, if informal, path from the new MRT subway station to the office buildings in the central government area. On any given weekday morning, a stream of workers, well dressed and striding hard on the way to their appointed tasks, makes its way past the small temple. By my estimate, about a third of those passing by, mostly younger people and many women, stop briefly in front of the temple and do the standard three bows to the god, just in case (fig. 4.4). This happens again at the end of the work day, although to a lesser extent. In addition to these passersby and the regular caretakers, a group of elderly men use this temple as a neighborhood gathering point during the day and a group of medium-level users come to do their daily obeisance in a more measured and complete fashion. These include businessmen and bureaucrats who visit during their lunch hour. Thus, this small temple is currently one of the park's strongest life-use areas, although it still does not appear on any map (except mine).[65]

In its new official status, there may be a sense of return to the original function of the space defined in the Qing by the Tianhougong, yet the dif-

4.4 Earth God Temple, Taipei Park, 2010

ferences are striking. If the Tianhougong was imperially sanctioned and ethnically neutral, the Tudigongmiao has been unauthorized and is strongly aligned with local affairs. It still is not a likely candidate for official literature on the park.

When Japanese city officials developed the 1932 plan wherein the eastern suburbs were mapped into a series of parkways connecting a system of sixteen parks, the old Murayama/Yuanshan Park was designated as No. 1, but Taipei Park was left unnumbered. Its lack of a number was a sign not of its insignificance but rather of its exclusive nature in the minds of the city planners—when Li Lixue annotated the Japanese map in 1989, she labeled Taipei Park as "0."[66] Although Taipei Park developed as a site of civic life, parks introduced in the ensuing decades were more oriented toward sports and the natural world—we might say that they became more closely aligned with Western conceptualizations of what a park should be.[67] Between the 1905 and 1932 plans, a series of new parks, sports facilities, and entertainment areas were added incrementally to the Taihoku cityscape: these included two swimming pools, a sports stadium, a zoo, a botanical garden, a horse track, and a children's entertainment park.[68] The parks planned for east of the city were intended to extend those types of facilities out into the suburbs and into the future. In the 1930s, under the increasing demands of military expansion, work on the park system stalled, and then came to an abrupt halt with the outbreak of war.

This Japanese plan for a park system is what the Nationalist government adopted as its own when it, too, projected in its 1956 urban plan a utopia of parks, schools, and boulevards for the eastern suburbs.[69] Over time, many of those public spaces were eventually developed, although not necessarily in the fashion envisioned in these maps: for example, designated Park No. 6 became the Father of the Nation (Sun Yat-sen) Memorial Hall (Guofu Jinianguan). One mark of the irony in the Nationalists' plan is how the area that had become the city's biggest sprawling shantytown of poor immigrants, similar to the one featured in *The Taste of Apples*, was still labeled "No. 7 Park" in their 1956 map. Even a 1971 planning map has the area tinted a nice leafy green, with the legend telling us that it is designated "Park and Greenbelt."[70] This was delusional urban planning on the same scale of proclaimed plans in the 1970s to "retake the mainland." But this park and greenbelt would finally come to be; for here is where the Da'an District Forest Park now stands, what Hsiao-hung Chang and Chih-hung Wang called a "Paradise Regained."[71] In part this was possible because during these seventy years the area continued to be called "No. 7 Park," even though it was never a park at all.[72] Thus, the Japanese-imagined park was displaced but not erased by the shantytown, allowing for its reconfigured return.

FIVE

Display in the City

In the world of cultural displacements, there are few on the scale of the National Palace Museum (Guoli Gugong Bowuyuan) in Taiwan: the term "National" in its title is a telling sign. The museum, nestled in the hills of the Taipei suburb of Shilin, is currently the home of 655,713 objects related to Chinese art and culture, primarily from dynastic China, including 386,729 Qing imperial documents and 1,651 fans.[1] This constitutes the second-largest collection of Chinese artifacts in the world, and even though only a small percentage can be exhibited at any one time, the museum galleries daily offer the largest single display of such objects to the general public. There is much irony in such dynastic riches being on display in Taiwan, with its very tenuous connection to imperial China.

The common narrative is that "Chiang Kai-shek's forces moved the 600,000 items from the Forbidden City in Beijing and took them to the island in the waning stages of the Chinese civil war,"[2] but the complete story of how this collection ended up in the suburbs of Taipei is much more complicated and of nearly mind-boggling logic and logistics. In several ways, the museum now stands as an emblem of Taiwan's local and international condition.

This monument to traditional Chinese art and culture was originally the "inheritance" of the Republic of China when the imperial treasury came to the victors of the 1911 revolution that ended Qing dynastic rule. In the early years, the ownership and status of the treasure were disputed and in constant flux, but over time materials from various imperial sites were all collected in Beijing and held by the erstwhile imperial family, although secured for the public, at least in name. Then in October 1925, after the expulsion of the Last Emperor from the old imperial palace (or Forbidden City) and the inventorying of the remaining collection (for much had slipped out of the palace by various means), the (Beijing) Palace Museum (Gugong Bowuyuan) was established. The treasure was immense, including nine thousand paintings and calligraphies, ten thousand porcelains, five thousand bronze mirrors, and sixteen hundred seals.[3] Among these many wonderful objects, the palace itself was the museum's most important possession, where the identities of architecture and artifact combine. This is obvious to any tourist who has visited China in recent years: for the general public, the visit to the Palace Museum is defined as a passage through a select set of its seventy halls and nine thousand rooms on the palace grounds; except for a few dusty displays, the important objects of the old treasury that remain in Beijing are held in highly restricted areas, far from tourists' cameras.[4]

The building and its treasury became dissociated in 1933 when the majority of the collection was packed up and shipped south to Shanghai and Nanjing to keep it out of the hands of Japanese invaders who were pressing on Beijing at the time. The removal of the objects from Beijing was a desperate act of nationalism that was widely supported by all Chinese political parties in the country, Nationalist, Communist, and the unaligned; no one wanted the "Japanese bandits" to get their hands on the great Chinese treasure. The young curators who packed up those hundreds of thousands of objects, using techniques learned directly from the imperial stores, were themselves cultural heroes in a larger war of Chinese identity formation.[5]

Over the next ten years, the 19,557 large wooden crates were trundled back and forth across war-torn China by train, truck, and boat, following a complex set of itineraries that kept the treasure just out of reach of the Japanese and their machines of war. With the fall of Nanjing in 1937, the treasure was hastily evacuated from its newly established quarters there, with the crates traveling in three different groups, along complicated itineraries and attended by their curators. En route, the objects were temporarily stored in museums, temples, and caves and on ships anchored in harbors. Then, miracle of miracles, at the end of the war, the entire hoard was collected together in Chongqing and in 1947 returned to the war-time capital city of

Nanjing. Most remarkably, not one crate was missing, not one object broken. It was then time to return these "war refugees" to their rightful home in the palace, but another war intervened: the Chinese civil war. The Nationalists held onto their part of the collection, and just before retreating to Taiwan, they sent 2,972 crates, deemed to contain the best pieces, along with rare books and other antiquities from the Central Library, to the island for "safekeeping"—this was only about 20 percent of the Nanjing collection.[6] The plan was to hold everything there until the Nationalists could carry the crates back in a triumphant return to Beijing. The crème de la crème of objects came in three shipments to Jilong Harbor (from December 1948 to February 1949) and were soon transported by train to Taizhong, where they were put into storage in an empty Japanese sugar factory near the train station. In 1949 the treasure was moved to new storage facilities built in the countryside outside of Taizhong, in the neighborhood of Beigou.

During these trying twenty years of war and dislocation, the curators continued to work, as best they could, on the materials in their possession; in fact, in 1935 and 1940 they sent materials abroad for international exhibitions in London and Moscow. After settling into the relatively spacious and secure facilities in Beigou, the researchers increased their inventorying, cataloguing, and international outreach efforts. The American scholar James Cahill writes of his first visit to the collection:

> I first visited the National Palace Museum collection in 1955, when I was a graduate student doing doctoral dissertation work on the "Four Great Masters" of Yuan dynasty landscape painting, and needed access to this greatest single concentration of their major works. The collection was then kept in storehouses near the village of Pei-k'ou [Beigou] some miles outside Taichung [Taizhong], reachable by bus but also, as I chose more often to do, by bicycle. The Palace Museum staff were generous in bringing out the paintings I needed to study, and helpful with advice; I remember especially the wise, sharp-eyed, and highly informed counsel of Mr. Chuang Yen [Zhuang Yan], . . . Director of the Museum.[7]

As indicated in Cahill's account, during this time, almost all materials remained in the original crates that had been packed in 1933, piled high in neat rows throughout the storage facility, which was augmented with an underground bunker in 1953.[8] A small exhibition hall with twenty-four display cases was finally opened to the public in 1957.[9]

These conditions changed dramatically in 1965, when the National Palace Museum moved into the Sun Yat-sen Museum (Zhongshan Bowuyuan) building in Shilin, whose construction was supported by substantial donations from the U.S. government. As discussed in chapters 1 and 2, the mid-1960s was a time when the Nationalists' rationale for being on Taiwan began to shift: their temporary exile began to look more permanent, the early years of their "economic miracle" gave the island more visibility in the international market, and the deep freeze of the cold war gave the Nationalists, with promotion by the United States, a strong presence in the United Nations and other international organizations. The new museum in Shilin embodied much of that changing rationale, built in a style that blended traditional and international architectural styles—basically, a modern box with a Chinese pavilion on the roof, what Yi-wen Wang and Tim Heath call a type of "regional modernism."[10] The intended audience for this new building was also decidedly elite and international. The museum was presented to the world as a monument of "free China" and the bastion of "traditional Chinese values" in the modern world. The objects on public display were presumed to be the embodiment of those values, and their very possession was evidence of those claims: Allen Chun has aligned this possession with other forms of cultural conservatism as "rallying points for shared national sentiment."[11] The logic was that the "palace" of the National Palace Museum may have been lost, but its treasury was still largely in the "nation," the Republic of China.

Over the decades, that initial logic gave the National Palace Museum its position in the geopolitics of the region and the world, and the institution has furthered that rationale in several ways. During the 1960s and 1970s, while the People's Republic of China was dragging itself from one political and cultural nightmare to the next (from the Anti-rightist Movement to the Great Leap Forward, and onward to the Cultural Revolution), the National Palace Museum in Taiwan could easily be praised for its responsible and progressive policies of object treatment and preservation.[12] They could argue that being in "exile" was the best thing for these treasures.[13] Over the ensuing forty years, the museum went through a series of renovations and expansions, beginning with the "crates to cabinets" (*gaixiang weigui*) work of replacing the storage crates with modern cabinets, to the most recent upgrading of public spaces to contemporary international standards.[14] Until at least the 1990s, the museum was by default and design the international center for the display and study of Chinese classical art—with the museums in China largely shuttered, only the Metropolitan Museum of Art in New York and the British Museum in London had similar stature. Beginning with such scholars as James Cahill, several generations of Chinese art historians received their training in Taiwan, in a palace collection without its palace.

All museums, especially museums of fine arts, are largely removed from the daily lives of their public: they are removed both by their function (the preservation and presentation of art objects in restricted settings) and in their contents (objects representing an elite form of culture that largely does not intersect with the mundane lives of the viewers). This is perhaps a necessary condition of the art museum. In Taiwan, the public is estranged from the National Palace Museum in especially extreme ways: it is a matter not just of the distance of the elite from the mundane but also of the isolating "palace" and "nation" that remain intact from the Nationalist rationale—Edward Vickers says that a visit to the museum was meant to be a pilgrimage to an ancient national heritage.[15] Although any local or international visitor to the museum may take delight in the pieces in the collection as art objects of the finest kind, it is difficult for those with a sense of Taiwanese consciousness not also to see the museum as another institution of Chinese nationalist imposition, on the order of the 1960s architecture of Sinicization. In the early raucous years of Taiwan's democratization movement, I heard this sentiment expressed several times by pro-independence citizens: "Okay, give the mainland back its Palace Museum stuff, and let us keep the island." If this "return to the Palace" were actually to happen (and why not?), it certainly would be in accord with the physics of cultural displacement: six hundred thousand displaced objects moving back into the original location but forever altered by their interim condition.

Even members of the institutional elite in Taiwan cannot overcome the irony of this condition. In the spring of 2009, the director of the National Palace Museum in Taiwan, Chou Kung-shin (Zhou Gongxin), made an unprecedented visit to the Palace Museum in Beijing to begin discussions on the exchange of objects. Yet, while she was there, she needed to reduce her "national" position: "She [Zhou] said the contacts with Beijing were on a museum-to-museum basis, thus avoiding the use of the word 'National' in her museum's name."[16] There was a certain incongruity in the results of these discussions: Beijing agreed to lend Taiwan artifacts for a fall 2009 exhibition on Emperor Yongzheng of the Qing dynasty (sending twenty-nine *more* objects to Taiwan), but "Taiwan remains reluctant to send any of the treasures it holds to China for fear that they may be impounded, although it has lent them to other countries."[17] Given the current politics of returning museum objects of dubious acquisition to their rightful owners, it seems that the curators in Taiwan are right to be worried.

The Colonial Museum

Steven Lavine and Ivan Karp open their study *Exhibiting Cultures* with the statement that "every museum exhibition, whatever its overt subject, inevitably draws on the cultural assumptions and resources of the people who make it."[18] They further speculate that the modern museum, which encourages our participation in narratives of national identity, shared traditions, and civilization, is a "uniquely Western institution" associated with imperialism and colonial appropriation.[19] Thus, we are not surprised to see that the first efforts in museum building in Taiwan are linked directly to the leadership of Governor-General Kodama Gentarō and Civil Administrator Gotō Shimpei, the architects of so many other early colonial institutions that relied on European models.

Although the museum in Taipei Park was generally called the Museum of the Colonial Administration (Sōtokufu Hakubutsukan), it was officially designated as the Memorial Hall for Kodama and Gotō (Kodama Gotō Kinenkan).[20] Its association with these two architects of colonial policy remained strong until the end of the Japanese period: statues of the two men stood in alcoves on either side of the central rotunda and the museum periodically held exhibitions celebrating the anniversaries of their rule.[21] Their early efforts provided a legacy of modern cultural display that continued throughout the colonial, neocolonial, and postcolonial period.

In both form and content, the museum building represented an example of what C. J. Hsia has called the "double translation" of colonial architecture to the island—from Europe to Japan, and then from Japan to Taiwan. In this case, the translation may have been tripled, given that the building is largely European neoclassical in style. The elegant stone building is wide and narrow, with its main north-facing entrance modeled on a Greek temple, with a wide stairway leading through a rank of classical columns (see fig. 4.1). Entrance into the building brings the visitor into an elaborate three-story rotunda capped by a Romanesque dome; an elaborate staircase leads toward the second floor with the galleries off to each side (fig. 5.1). A recent publication by the museum describes the entrance (in English):

5.1 Cross section elevation of Colonial Administration Museum plan, entrance, rotunda, statue, 1915. Source: *Kinen hakubutsukan shashinchō*; courtesy of National Taiwan Library

> The lobby is the essence of the entire building. It is surrounded by 32 Corinthian embellishments, decorated lavishly with carvings of acanthus leaves. Standing at the center of the lobby looking up, you see a vaulted roof ceiling and a stained glass window. In addition to decorati, the window allows natural sunlight to flow through. On sunny days, the glittering colors shine through the room, creating an elegant and splendid atmosphere.[22]

The English "you" in this description implies a contemporary sense of the public nature of the museum, yet for most of the Japanese period, this museum was also distant from the interests of the Taiwanese public, in both its science and its displays. Not only were the Taiwanese *not* its expected patrons, they were often the subject of its ethnographic studies; this was especially true for the aboriginal peoples: objects, not observers, in the museum.

The implementation of museums and exhibitions as tools in colonizing and nationalizing projects is well attested, especially by Timothy Mitchell in *Colonizing Egypt*. Of the late nineteenth century, he writes:

Exhibitions, museums and other spectacles were not just reflections of this certainty [of colonial order], however, but the means of its production, by their technique of rendering history, progress, culture and empire in "objective" form. They were occasions for making sure of such objective truths, in a world where truth had become a question of what Heidegger calls, "the certainty of representation."[23]

The Japanese colonial museum, like British museums, was very much concerned with projecting the world in a "colonial order," and it focused its attention primarily on the natural world of Taiwan. There were ten departments in the museum, ranging from Soil and Minerals to History; perhaps most important was Anthropology, which was devoted to the study of aboriginal groups—a focus on indigenous cultures remains a specialty of the museum. In essence, this museum became the natural history museum for the island and then for other parts of the empire, as the Japanese expanded their control into Southeast Asia and the Pacific. As such, the museum was the principal organ and site for a series of expeditions, exhibitions, and conferences for the scientific exploration of the flora and fauna of the new empire. This scientific interest in the island's natural environment was embedded in the "scientific colonialism" that the Japanese, especially Gotō Shimpei, promoted, generally modeled on German colonial policy.[24]

Renamed the Taiwan Provincial Museum (Taiwan Shengli Bowuguan) in 1945, for most of the postwar period, the museum attracted little official interest or investment from the Nationalist central government, being overshadowed by the museums of "real" Chinese culture: the National Palace Museum and the National History Museum (Guoli Lishi Bowuguan).[25] Faced with these two well-funded and ideologically engaged national museums, the Taiwan Provincial Museum languished as a remnant of Japanese colonialism. During these years, there was no strong political culture that promoted an understanding of Taiwan, scientifically or otherwise; in fact, the museum was used primarily as a site for second-order exhibits of Chinese historical materials and as a gallery for the arts, including traditional painting, calligraphy, and contemporary works. Occasionally the museum was used to promote the blatantly ideological messages of the central government, as, for example, with the 1959 Exhibition of Criminal Materials from the Communist Bandits People's Communes (Gongfei Renminshe Zuixing Ziliaozhan).[26] By and large, the provincial museum plodded through a series of relatively low-profile activities and exhibits. One index of the general neglect was its old, beat-up cabinetry dating from the colonial period that was used for displays until quite recently. Yet, as we might expect, changes are afoot.

In 2003 the museum was renamed once more, this time the National Taiwan Museum (Guoli Taiwan Bowuguan), erasing its "provincial" designation. It went through extensive renovations in 2005, which included opening up the third floor as display space, and there are now ambitious plans to develop the museum as the center of a Capital Culture Park (Shoudu Wenhua Yuanqu) in the downtown area. These plans include converting a nearby ten-story office and a colonial bank building into new wings for the museum, as well as installing an underground mall, all to be joined by a greenway for pedestrians that would extend out from the park along major streets to the north. This plan, if fully implemented, will be the first major reconfiguration of the park parameters and structure since the museum was built in 1915. The planned renovations have already attained a street presence that dramatically changes the approach (both physical and psychological) to the museum. The old fence in front that restricted entrance into the park has been removed, leaving a series of walkways leading to the museum.

The current investment in and planning for the museum are in line with the attention paid to other locally oriented institutions in recent years. There is some irony, however, in that this attention comes only after the museum has become, like the History Museum and the Palace Museum, a "national" institution. That "nation" is still nominally the Republic of China in exile, but there is a sense that this is being overshadowed by a stronger Taiwanese element. In 2007 the museum director, Hsiao Tsung-huang (Xiao Zonghuang), declared, "The National Taiwan Museum, the first museum in Taiwan, provides the public with a new understanding about Taiwan's history and culture, which should not only be a part of knowledge exploration, but also a reunion of Taiwan pluralistic cultural values and an important link to represent Taiwan's lively vitality."[27] The minister of the Council of Cultural Affairs of the Central Government, Wong Chin-chu (Weng Jinzhu), was even clearer in his introduction to the new museum: "We have been aggressively transforming Taiwan to become a major cultural nation [*wenhua daguo*]."[28] In this vein, one cannot help but notice that the flag that is on display in the lobby of the museum is now that of the short-lived 1895 "Republic of Taiwan," a designation that is sometimes tendered, not always tongue-in-cheek, as a possible alternative to the "Republic of China." We assume Taipei is the capital referred to in Capital Culture Park, but capital of what?

The Exposition

During the thirty-five years when the museum in Taipei Park operated as part of the larger Japanese colonial project (1915–45), only once was it promoted as a place for the ordinary citizen of Taiwan. This was during the Taiwan Exposition: In Commemoration of the First Forty Years of Colonial Rule (Shisei Yonjisshunen Kinen Taiwan Hakurankai) held in the fall of 1935. The Taiwan Exposition was an extravagant display of cultural and political power that Japan wanted to show everyone, even the villager from Taidong.[29] In 1935 Japan was at the pinnacle of its colonial rule, poised to overwhelm East and Southeast Asia with its imperial schemes. From that high point, the exhibition was not only a celebration of forty years of colonial rule, it was, as were all international exhibitions, a projection of things to come, a signpost pointing the way to the future of the colony.

The exposition's principal sites were in Taipei, but the whole colony participated in this display of power, with most cities and townships throughout the island holding branch expositions of their own. The celebration was widely promoted via a variety of new technologies, including radio broadcasts, lighted billboards, and flyers dropped from airplanes. Not only was the citizenry of the island encouraged (nearly harassed) to come to Taipei (with special trains and travel arrangements available along both coasts) but advertising and special promotions were also directed overseas, especially to the Japanese homeland: "Come to Treasure Island and see the Taiwan Expo," "Autumn Travel: To the Taiwan Exposition," read the slogans.[30] In a span of fifty days (October 10–November 28), the exposition attracted 2,758,895 visitors; the vast majority of them must have been Taiwanese and Japanese from the island, but this figure also includes Japanese from the homeland, Koreans, Chinese, and others.[31]

We get a sense of the social complexities of the exposition at the local level through a 1937 short story by Zhu Dianren, "Autumn Letter" (Qiu xin). In the story, the village police officer, a Japanese bureaucrat who speaks Taiwanese, is the principal conduit for official promotion of the event, while an elderly scholar, Chen Douwen, represents stubborn resistance to Zhu's invitations and suggestions. In the end, encouraged by a letter from his son, old Chen reluctantly makes the prescribed pilgrimage to the exposition, but when he arrives, he is confused and angered by the exhibits and the recent changes to the city:

On the street before the Taipei [train] station, the crowd swarmed toward the museum like a wave. Master Douwen was like a rudderless boat without a sense of direction: the geography of Taipei was no longer what he had remembered [from fifteen years before]. Somehow, while he was at a loss, he was pushed right to the entrance of Exhibit Hall No. 2. . . . [After taking in the exhibits on education, in a confrontation with Japanese students, he says,] "Runts! Bandits! Japanese barbarians!" He could not help but let it go, regardless of whether they could understand or not. "Even though the rise and fall of a nation is fated, and the Qing dynasty has already ended, yet it doesn't necessarily mean that the Chinese people . . . all this fuss about the Exhibit—it's just meant to brag about. . . . Forget it . . . 'The Great Leap Forward of Taiwan's Productivity' [the exhibit's slogan], indeed! Only you Japanese devils are able to have a 'great leap forward.' I am afraid Taiwan's youth don't even have a chance to inch forward. All this talk about education, indeed!"[32]

Chen Fangming has cited this story as an example of an attack on the modernization efforts celebrated by the exposition: for the Taiwanese, these represented "destruction and loss" of the local way of life.[33] Yet, the age and extreme conservative views of Master Chen Douwen (he is portrayed as an ossified remnant of the Qing dynasty) conspire to undermine his biting criticism of the exposition; in the end, the story seems to project the inevitability, if not the acceptability, of modernization and colonial rule.

Another villager seems to represent the more commonly held position on the exposition when he speaks to the old man:

It's really a shame not to go [to the exposition]. I don't know about other villages, but in our village every family has someone going to see it. I heard that there are many tourists' groups today. Maybe the train is going to be all jammed again. Xiucai [Scholar] Chen, life is short, and you're quite old. If you don't see it now, when are you going to see it? Come on, let's go. Isn't it nice to see something different?[34]

The "something different" that is projected in this appeal was found throughout the exposition in its celebration of the material culture of the modern world, contrasted with traditional and precolonial conditions.

The pavilions and performance sites for the exposition, most of which were built in the international modernist/art deco style, hosted an array of the latest technology—robotic humanoids, dioramas, automated displays, three-dimensional maps, amusement-park rides, recorded music, and films. Columbia Music was a principal retailer at the site. Taking its cue from the international exhibitions of the early twentieth century, in which Japan participated and learned a new form of display, the colonial government sought to hold its own "world's fair" to display its colonial possessions and imperial aspirations.[35] Japan's inclusion in international expositions in Europe and the Americas had always been mediated through the country's ambivalent position in geopolitics. As the most progressive of the emerging "oriental" nations, Japan was seen as neither modern nor traditional, its people neither white nor colored, neither "us" nor "them," but rather some exotic hybrid; they were called, for example, the "Yankees of the East" and "Anglo Saxons of the Orient."[36] A similarly ambivalent positioning was also seen at the Taiwan Exposition; there, however, the Japanese were the "us" and the Taiwanese the "them" who had the potential to become the "Japanese of China," as it were.

When planning for the exposition began, Japanese authorities hoped to find a single large site in the city's suburbs, but they were not able to identify an appropriate location with adequate facilities. They thereupon decided to mount the exhibition in three separate sites, two in the downtown area and one (a hotel and spa) in the suburban mountains. Subsequently, a fourth site was established on the initiative of local business leaders; it was located in the Dadaocheng neighborhood.[37] Here I would like to concentrate on the second exhibition site, which occupied Taipei Park.

In contrast to the emphasis on commodity display and administrative activities at Exhibition Site No. 1 (located near West Gate), the park site offered a wider variety of display types and themes.[38] This was, for example, the primary site for exhibits dedicated to the presentation of modern colonial culture in Taiwan, implying that Taiwan (under Japan's tutelage) was an emerging member of the modern world. These exhibits included Electrification Hall, Monopoly Hall, Maritime Hall, and two large halls for cultural displays. As might be expected, the colonial museum was the center of attention at this site; it held the Number One Cultural Exhibit Hall (Dai'ichi Bunga Shisetsukan), featuring models, displays, and dioramas of modern life on the island, including scenes celebrating the educational system and the Shinto shrines on the island. The museum's neoclassical architecture also allowed it to serve as the exposition's miniature "white city" (the grand, neoclassical halls associated with the international exhibitions of the late nineteenth and early twentieth centuries).[39]

The open area east of the museum (the sports and parade grounds) was most fully and systemically developed: this was one of the few areas in the park that allowed for a formal, geometric array of display halls and space, forming a small quadrangle and mall. Of special note here was the National Defense Hall, one of the largest on the site (only the museum was larger). This part of the exhibition clearly announced the growing Japanese militarism of the time. Displays included full-scale equipment, models, and dioramas. In one of these displays, a full-size parachute with an oddly feminine mannequin descended from the sky; there were also model amphibious planes, bombs falling from planes, mortar launchers, technical communication equipment, and the like. These exhibits, like the other displays of technology, both promoted contemporaneous accomplishments and designated future directions: two dioramas featured military uniforms for tropical climates—not much would be lost on the Taiwanese audience about Japanese intentions there—and another diorama exhibited "food rations of future wars" against a painted landscape that looked suspiciously like north China. In fact, according to Shih-wei Lo, the exposition served as a cover for high-level meetings to discuss Japan's secret plans for military expansion in the region.[40] Even the Children's Country (Kodomo no Kuni) amusement area participated in this militarization: among the rides was one in airplanes sporting the distinctive Japanese sun on their wings.

Along with the themed exhibits surrounding the mall was a group of buildings representing the most important urban centers of the metropole: Tokyo, Kyoto, and Osaka. These pavilions were very much in the style of the international exhibitions of the time: celebrations of local traditions and modern successes, with product displays, distinctive scenery, and urban models. A comparison of the Tokyo and Kyoto halls suggests the range: the array of exhibits in the Tokyo Hall celebrated the modernity of that city, featuring electric appliances and other modern commodities; while the Kyoto Hall featured more traditional cultural displays, such as panoramas of Kyoto's temple grounds, bamboo pavilions, and teahouse mannequins in kimonos. In many ways, these two halls represent the Janus-faced nature of the Japanese position in geopolitics at that time. The Tokyo Hall was the face the metropole turned toward its colonies, while it was with the face of the Kyoto Hall (oriental, charming, and feminized) that Japan typically looked toward the non-Asian world. The latter look was the one, for example, that Japan presented at international exhibitions in Europe and the Americas. In 1935 this was quickly changing, and the new face that Japan abruptly offered the non-Asian world in December 1941 was a shock to many in the United States simply because they were much more used to the "Kyoto look," despite Japan's colonial empire, the Russo-Japanese War (1904–5), and the country's aggression in China during the 1930s.

It is instructive to compare this display of the Japanese homeland with those of Japan's colonial holdings and aspirations, such as Korea, Manchuria, and the various representations of the "South" (southern China, Southeast Asia, and the Pacific islands). The "South" was done in "authentic" architectural styles, suggesting the still purportedly traditional, nonprogressive state of these areas. Perhaps most interesting of these was the Fujian Hall of southern China, which was configured in a local architectural style: since this was the ancestral homeland of most of the Taiwanese on the island, it stood in contrast to the progressive nature of the colony. Nor is it insignificant that these southern halls were all located in the Dadaocheng exhibition area, which was organized and run by local Taiwanese businessmen, not by colonial authorities.

This sort of ethnographic construction was even more clearly articulated in the displays dedicated to the aboriginal people of Taiwan. Throughout the exposition, the aborigines were seen almost entirely as "anthropological subjects" rather than as potential members of the Japanese nation. Although there were many types of performances by Taiwanese, Japanese, and aboriginal groups, the last of these (usually "folk" dancing) were most often held outside on the open grounds, not in the performance hall or onstage. And the central exhibit of aboriginal groups was also outside, presented as a type of "living museum," popular in international exhibitions; the Philippine Reservation in a 1904 Saint Louis exposition is the most famous example of this type of display.[41] Small groups of aboriginal people were placed in replicas of village and tribal dwellings, often working on handicrafts (fig. 5.2). Use of live subjects as opposed to dioramas or plastic models presents the aboriginal peoples as actually (and permanently) "primitive."[42] In contrast, the gaze trained on the Han Taiwanese (who were generally not live models) is more modulated, with an allowance for their potential modernity/civilization.[43] These two types of displays are graphic examples of the exhibiting strategies that Ivan Karp terms "exoticising" and "assimilating."[44]

Building on a series of trade shows and expositions held on the island, especially on the decadal anniversaries of the establishment of colonial rule (1915, 1925), the Taiwan Exposition of 1935 was an unprecedented success. Quite unimaginable at the time was that this exposition would be the colony's last.

5.2 Outdoor display of aborigine dwelling and couple, 1935 Colonial Exposition. Source: *Shisei yonjisshūnen kinen Taiwan hakurankai shi,* 1939

There would be some heady intervening years, including the rapid occupation of eastern China in 1937, celebrations of the imperial family's lineage in 1940 and early naval battles against the United States in the Pacific, but by the time the fiftieth anniversary rolled around in October 1945, things had changed dramatically. Japan had surrendered to the Allies, the island's infrastructure was suffering from war damage, the local economy was in shambles, and new authorities were occupying the government buildings downtown.

The Nationalist Displays

During the heyday of the Chinese Nationalist rule, there were several important sites of exhibition, performance, and display. I have already mentioned the National Palace Museum and National History Museum. There were also display sites with more overt political intents, such as buildings built or refashioned in honor of Sun Yat-sen, Father of the Nation. In Taipei Park, he is represented in the relatively abstract terms of the pavilion and pond complex constructed as part of the neoclassical architecture of the 1960s (the lily pond mentioned in chapter 4 and discussed in more detail in chapter 6; see fig 4.1).[45] At the other extreme, in both intention and locality, is the gigantic

5.3 Chiang Kai-shek Memorial viewed from National Library, Concert Hall on left, Memorial Hall at center rear, 1999

Father of the Nation Memorial Hall (Guofu Jinianguan), which was built in the eastern suburbs on the site designated by Japanese planners as Park No. 6. The hall, another example of a blend of modern and traditional Chinese temple structure (but heavier on the modern), is surrounded by a large park and open plaza. Finished in 1972, it quickly became a premier site for elite social and artistic functions; in 1975 it also served as the site for Chiang Kai-shek's elaborate lying-in-state and funeral.

With Chiang Kai-shek's death, such overtly ideological architecture reached its zenith, some would say its logical absurdity, with the building of his Memorial Hall (Zhongzheng Jiniantang, 1976–80). The massive grounds just beyond East Gate were a decommissioned military area (inherited from the Japanese), and the various buildings were fashioned as gargantuan versions of palace and temple architecture, very loud echoes of the neoclassical architecture of the 1960s (fig. 5.3). The two main auxiliary buildings, the theater and concert halls, contain most of the formal public activity on the site and have become the premier performance spaces of the city. The wide main plaza between the halls provides space for ceremonial and outdoor performances along with occasional public demonstrations. Informal uses of the grounds tend to occur in the elaborate garden areas and smaller open spaces between them. The Chiang Kai-shek Memorial Hall, which rises high in the center on its stone platform (alluding to the imperial architecture of Beijing), challenges human scale and is largely neglected, except for brave joggers who use the steep steps for extreme conditioning. The hall contains a gigantic Lincoln Memorial–like seated bronze figure of Chiang dressed in a traditional Chinese robe. Beneath the memorial building huddle display halls that still seem to participate in the idol worship of a former time: there we can read that the Generalissimo was the direct descendant of the Duke of Zhou or gaze on Chiang's beat-up briefcase; in another room, the polished surfaces of his Cadillac limousine reflect old portraits and calligraphy samples. Under current circumstances, this display would seem to be in the realm of high camp, yet Jeremy Taylor's close observation of these displays, comparing them to their former condition, suggests a more nuanced understanding.

Taylor argues that during the eight years in which the Nationalists were the minority party (2000–2008), sites depicting their presence on Taiwan became historicized by the new powers (this was done not to commemorate such sites but to "wrest control" of them from Nationalist ideology), including renaming the Memorial Hall and giving it national "historic site" (*guji*) status. With the 2008 election of President Ma Ying-jeou, the Nationalist party began to embrace its history (and these sites) in Taiwan as an important part of its new legitimizing narrative, saying, in effect, that the Nationalists, too, share a Taiwanese heritage. With this in mind, Taylor revisits the displays:

> Yet it must be clear to those who have visited the hall both before and after its short-lived transformation under the DDP [majority party] that things are not quite the same as they once were. To be sure, much of the hagiographic material has returned. But there is also a far stronger emphasis on Chiang's life in Taiwan now. And most crucially of all, unlike in the heyday of the Chiang personality cult, the statues, paintings, and photography that decorate the exhibition halls are all now authored. It is not simply Chiang who is on display anymore, but also the products (and producers) of the Chiang cult itself.[46]

Here I would argue that Taylor is describing a recent and clearly formed dynamic of displacement in which the display materials, decommissioned during the period of DDP governance, have returned to their original site but reconditioned by that hiatus. In this case, that condition is strongly marked by the new signs of their provenance and authorship, a return of agency, as it were.[47]

Returning to Sun Yat-sen Hall

In the old intramural area where the recovery of such agency is relatively more layered and complex, we have the recent restoration of the Sun Yat-sen Hall (Zhongshantang) that was carried out during Ma Ying-jeou's mayorship of the city. That restoration is celebrated in a volume of essays and photographs, *Returning to Sun Yat-sen Hall* (Huidao Zhongshantang), edited by Long Yingtai, writer, public intellectual, and then Taipei City commissioner of Cultural Affairs. The photographs in the volume range from early historic scenes of the Japanese period through a series of contemporary shots of the hall and its environs. As the title suggests, the essays are primarily reflections by well-known writers on their experiences with the hall and the surrounding downtown area: at restaurants, coffee shops, bookstores, movie houses, and other sites of popular culture. We can consider the volume, as well as the restoration itself, as a type of "display."

As noted above, this hall was originally the Japanese Civic Hall (Kōkaidō) and very much part of the legacy of the 1935 Taiwan Exposition. The initial motivation for the construction of the hall was the commemoration of the enthroning of the Shōwa Emperor; its obvious model, in both style and function, was the Civic Hall in Tokyo, located in Hibiya Park and built in 1925.[48] After the removal of the old *yamen* buildings, construction of the hall in Taipei began in 1932 and was finished in time for the opening of the Taiwan Exposition, where it functioned as the exposition's most formal ceremonial site. Events there included the opening ceremonies, welcoming speeches for important guests, and various performances. The visit of one dignitary to this hall, Fujian provincial governor Chen Yi (the Chinese representative to the exposition), has drawn the critical analysis of the contemporary scholar Chen Fangming. In his essay, Chen notes the deep irony that surrounds Chen Yi and this building. During his visit to the 1935 exposition, Chen Yi praised the modernization and progress of the colony, noting the benefits it brought to the people of Taiwan; in a 1937 planning document, he even suggested that Taiwan act as a model for development in Fujian province.[49] Ten years later, Chen Yi stood in the same hall as the newly appointed administrator of the Taiwan Provincial Administrative Executive

Office (Taiwansheng Xingzheng Zhangguan Gongshu) and commander of the Taiwan Garrison (a dual position that darkly resembled that of the Japanese governor-general).[50] Professor Chen writes:

> Chen Yi's political power in Taiwan emanated from the Sun Yat-sen Hall. After accepting the documents of surrender from the last Japanese governor-general, Chen Yi promptly declared that the Taiwanese people who had been baptized (*xili*) by Japanese modernization had received a "slave education" (*nuhua jiaoyu*). And with this began the tensions between Taiwanese citizens and new Chinese officials.[51]

The immediate renaming of the hall for the 1945 ceremonies was the first step in the symbolic refashioning of the building for the Nationalist civic cause.[52] The Japanese imperial crests were removed from the entryway, and the new name was announced in large characters across the front of the building.[53] The major interior spaces were also named in the spirit of the Nationalist agenda: the 2,056-seat auditorium was the Chiang Kai-shek Chamber (Zhongzheng ting), and the large banquet room was the Retrocession Chamber (Guangfu ting).[54]

Despite the renaming of the space and the addition of exterior signage (there had been none on the Japanese building), the spatiality of the building remained largely unchanged during the postwar period. Nor were there major changes to the building's overt functions, principally large-scale performances and formal gatherings. Until the completion of the Father of the Nation Memorial Hall in the eastern suburbs, the auditorium was the site of all major musical and theatrical performances in the city, both Chinese and international. Several of the essays in *Returning* recall these performances fondly, such as artist Jiang Xun's description of his mother's nights at the Peking opera and her elaborate preparations.[55] Architect Li Qingzhi's essay, on the other hand, describes his grandmother's devotion to Western classical music, which brought her hurrying up from Taizhong by train for the big performances, including one that was sold out and left her crying on the front steps of the hall. When a member of the staff discovered her, he "kindly led grandmother into the hall through the backstage door and let her watch the performance from the front of the stage. With this, my weeping grandmother broke into a smile."[56]

A number of these essays recall, in similar nostalgic terms, other types of performances during these years: movies, folk song concerts, poetry readings, college graduation ceremonies, and the like. Given the age of most of these essayists, their recollections are filled with thoughts of youthful friendship, romantic courtship, and urban adventure. In these recollections, the hall often functioned merely as a convenient, high-profile place to meet, whence dalliances and adventures would move onward. In their liaisons, few of the young people actually entered the hall at all. Rather, they met in its courtyard or under its covered portico and then went off to the various eateries nearby, such as the Chaofeng Café or the many entertainment venues of West Gate District (Ximending). [57] In these cases, the open space in front of the hall was the building's important "architecture." Sun Yat-sen Hall was not always about youthful innocence, however.

Long Yingtai opens *Returning to Sun Yat-sen Hall* with a short, elegant preface that begins:

> During the years of martial law, the Sun Yat-sen Hall continued to project a solemn atmosphere; even though they showed movies there, even though they held ceremonies celebrating the holidays there, and even though the courtyard was often used for gatherings and activities, still the sense of the place was not altered. [58]

Long Yingtai then goes on to note some of the formal activities that cast the solemn (*yansu*) shadow over these entertainments and celebrations: the hall's colonial origins, the Retrocession Ceremonies held there, and its association with early Nationalist government propaganda. Yet the "even though" (*suiran*) construction of this passage leaves other, even more somber, things unmentioned. As Chen Fangming's essay reminds us, during the postwar years, one of the primary official functions of the Sun Yat-sen Hall was to host gatherings of the National Assembly (Guomin Dahui), the principal electoral body of the Republic of China, which selected the president (in most cases, Chiang Kai-shek) and voted on constitutional amendments. In Taiwan, the assembly embodied political displacement at the highest level. Elected in 1947 and convened in Nanjing in 1948, the assembly was composed of 2,691 representatives from a variety of geographic and demographic groups in China. In 1949 this body was transferred to Taiwan, where it remained largely intact, although growing increasingly decrepit and absurd, throughout the martial law period. [59] To me, this is the looming "even though" presence to which Long Yingtai's preface alludes and which also underlies C. J. Hsia's deep suspicion of the "public" (*gonggong*) nature of the space. [60]

When the renovated Sun Yat-sen Hall reopened in 2001 as the new home of the Taipei Metropolitan Symphony, its interior spaces had been restored but not much altered. The principal addition was a chic new restaurant on the second floor, the Fortress (Baolei Candian), specializing in Spanish-style tapas cuisine; yet that too may be a form of restoration since the hall originally had a Western-style restaurant.[61] The most dramatic changes came to the exterior plaza. During the postwar period, the plaza had slowly been encroached upon by the parking lot of the central police station next door. As motor vehicle ownership grew, things worsened, until the space "was transformed into a city public parking lot, ruining the most valuable open public space in the downtown area."[62] To me, the restoration of the plaza area is one of the most successful recoveries of public space in the city, especially as it has been appropriated in some unintended ways.

There is plenty of intentionality in the design of the new plaza—dramatic plantings, a large stone stage, and even the Retrocession Monument to Those Who Brought Victory to Taiwan in the War against Japan (Kangri Zhanzheng Shengliji Taiwan Guangfu Jinianbei), with a time line beginning in 1895.[63] Such official designs, activities, and intentions certainly contribute to the success of the newly reclaimed plaza, but what is more exciting is how the space is appropriated by its neighbors once the sun goes down. Under the harsh sunlight of day, the plaza is not particularly attractive or useful space, but in the tropical evenings, when there are no official activities planned, it is physically and socially transformed. It must be remembered that the hall and its plaza are located in one of the most densely packed areas of the city, where open space is at a premium, especially space that allows for a variety of activities in a safe and welcoming area. Dramatic lights on the hall's facade are complemented by landscape lighting that subtly illuminates the various features of the plaza, creating an ambience of usable space and intimacy.

In his early essay on the semiotics of the city, Roland Barthes introduces the potential "eroticism/sociality" of the city, calling on us to be attentive to the "play of signs" in these special places, which he associates with young people. He says:

> When they [adolescents] express their image of the city, they always have
> a tendency to limit, to concentrate, to condense the center; the city center
> is felt as the place of exchange of social activities and I would almost say
> erotic activities in the broad sense of the word. Better still, the city center

is always felt as the space where subversive forces, forces of rupture, ludic forces act and meet.[64]

In Taipei, this first brings to mind the role that Taipei Park has played as an erotic, ludic, and subversive center of the city, and if we want to see adolescents "at play" then the entertainment area of West Gate District is a riot of such behavior. But I think we can also include the plaza outside of Sun Yat-sen Hall as a similarly "erotic" space. First, as one might expect, the plaza has recaptured its romantic function as a place for young couples not only to meet but to spend time; often they sit together late into the night along the darkened edges of the plaza. Heavy petting in the bamboos seems to be the norm. At the same time, in the early evening, young children, with their parents, gravitate to the central open area, where they are pushed in strollers, play with their dogs, or practice riding their bikes and roller-skating.

The most dynamic area of the plaza is on and around the stage and stone structures, which are taken over by teenage skateboarders and trick bikers performing their stunts on, around, and over the monuments and mundane built space (fig. 5.4). Although these teenage activities were certainly not intended in the design of these spaces, and a recently installed sign prohibits skateboarding, still they proceed without much real interference (no metal bumpers to deter slides and grinds). For example, one Sunday in the summer of 2010, a group of approximately fifty skateboarders, from rank amateurs to high-flying fanatics, careened across the space, all watched by a dour

5.4 Trick biker in plaza in front of Sun Yat-sen Hall, 2010

but silent security guard. The *Returning* volume even includes photos of the skateboarders as part of its celebration of the building's restoration.[65] There is something both familiar and exciting about the lively yet relaxed ebb and flow across the plaza in the evening, when this social cross section of downtown Taipei gathers. It is certainly a site of both eroticism and sociality.

Numerous display sites in Taiwan have emerged in recent years that are related to the post–martial law politics of localization (*bentuhua*) and multiculturalism (*duoyuanhua*). Usually these involve the exploration of Chinese (Fukinese or Haka) experiences—the exhibitions considered in chapter 1 being examples. Another display type that is noteworthy, especially as a challenge to Chinese Han chauvinism, are new museums dedicated to the explanation and celebration of aboriginal culture.[66] Michael Rudolph has discussed such sites as an instrument of elite aboriginal leaders (teachers, ministers, and social scientists) to promote an "authentic difference" within the discourse of multiculturalism.[67] That discourse of difference is central to an institution such as the Ketagalan Culture Center of Taipei City (Taibeishi Zhengfu Yuanzhumin Shiwu Weiyuanhui Gaidagelan Wenhuaguan), established in 2002 in the suburb of Beitou on the site of an old military police station. The center's mission combines exhibition, performance, and education (especially language education) related to aboriginal cultures—clearly all signs of authentic difference. Although these new museums are much more than the "aboriginal folk villages" of former years, they still concentrate their displays on "traditional" cultural materials, which, in effect, continue to define the identity of native people primarily by the past—past conditions are "authentic" but present ones are not. In this way, as Rudolph has said, the aboriginal difference remains cultural not political.

The Ketagalan Culture Center does give evidence of beginning a new, more political mission: to "build up the living network of [the] city's indigenous peoples" and to "boost aboriginal group competitiveness."[68] This reflects the more assertive "we are still here" stance taken in the conceptualization of other international museums of native peoples, such as the National Museum of the American Indian in Washington, D.C. This is especially important to the aboriginal plains peoples of Taiwan, such as the Ketagalan, who have been completely displaced by the Han population, becoming nearly invisible in the present.

These new museums are welcome attempts to restore some of that visibility, even if it must be done belatedly through questionable authorities, such as Executive Yuan's establishment in 1996 of the Council on Indigenous Peoples, parallel to other Chinese "minorities," such as Tibetan, Mongolian, and Hakka. [69] Perhaps the most ironic aspect of this recently discovered visibility is that the Alliance of Taiwan Aboriginals, established in the 1980s, found representation in the United Nation's Working Group on Indigenous Populations long before it found that visibility in the Republic of China.[70] Now the Republic of China is no longer in the United Nations, except as represented, however problematically, by these indigenous people of Taiwan.

SIX

Statues in the City

One afternoon in the fall of 1999, I was returning from a bicycle trip through Yangming Mountain National Park, which lies north of Taipei, and stopped to rest in a rather sprawling park just inside the city limits. This section of New Life Park (Xinsheng Gongyuan) stands directly under the flyway of the Matsuyama/Songshan Airport; every few minutes, an aircraft would roar by just a few hundred feet overhead.[1] When I looked up, I noticed that I was seated at the base of a statue of General Claire Lee Chennault, famed commander of the contingent of American"Flying Tigers" who worked with the Nationalists in the air war against the Japanese during the early 1940s.[2] I had inadvertently found the "missing" statue.[3]

This bronze bust of General Chennault atop a tall stone pedestal was originally installed at the south entrance of Taipei Park on April 14, 1960. It was designed and crafted by Yang Yingfeng; the pedestal was Japanese in origin.[4] In an elaborate ceremony presided over by Madame Chiang Kai-shek (Song Meiling) and attended by Chinese and American officials, as well as the general's widow, Anna Chan Chennault (Chen Xiangmei), and their two daughters, the statue was unveiled at this site of prestige and high visibility. The front-page news estimated that more than three hundred people were in attendance:

The ceremony began at 10:30 in the morning. Following a spirited playing of the American national anthem, Taipei City mayor Huang Qiduan delivered his words of praise on behalf of the 800,000 citizens of Taipei City. After which the First Lady, Madame Chiang Kai-shek, accompanied by Mrs. Chennault, unveiled the bronze image.[5]

In Madame Chiang's statement praising the general and his contributions to the Chinese nation, she said:

> This commemorative bronze statue of the late General Chennault erected
> in New Park of Taipei City is the apt expression of the reverence that the
> people of our nation [*woguo renmin*] have for this great American general.
> Although his physical body has left this world, his true self without bodily
> form—his spirit that devoted itself to the service of our nation when
> China was experiencing the most difficult time in its history—is still with
> us here. That spirit continues to urge us to struggle on with the goal of
> liberating our people from the shackles of Communism. Such a great spirit
> will never die. . . .
>   Moved with emotion, the people of our nation will long remember
> General Chennault and the spirit of dedication he brought to his sacrifice
> and contributions to our people [*minzu*]. As thousands upon thousands
> of visitors make their way each day to New Park to look upon the bronze
> statue that commemorates this great American general, they will find a rare
> example in him, one who never allowed any obstacle to stand in the way of
> finishing the work of his life's mission.[6]

The "nation" and "people" of whom Madame Chiang spoke were, of course, those in exile on the island with the Chiang regime; it is highly unlikely that "thousands upon thousands" (*chengqian chengwan*) of Taiwanese would come to the park to visit this statue. But there the statue stood for thirty-five years, an emblem of the Cold War alliance between the Nationalist and U.S. governments, looking out onto the expansive Long Live Kai Boulevard.

Then suddenly in 1995, General Chennault's statue was dismantled and moved to the much less elegant New Life Park, a victim of the political realignment of the city and the park—this was when the park was renamed and memorials to the February 28th Incident were being built.[7] For the statue's 1995 reinstallment, there were no words of praise from the First Lady, no national anthem, and no invitation to the Chennault family: indeed, Mrs.

Chennault learned of the event from a sister living in Taipei, who sent her the brief announcement of the relocation that was carried in a local newspaper. Then, in another unlikely event ten years later, another bronze image of General Chennault, similar in style but this time standing full-length, was installed in the Chinese People's Anti-Japanese War Memorial Hall (Zhongguo Renmin Kangri Zhanzheng Jinianguan) located in southwest Beijing.[8] For this event, there was plenty of pomp and ritual, and family members and friends did attend.

Renewed interest in General Chennault and the Flying Tigers on the Chinese mainland is part of a reconsideration of the early years of the Republic of China in which the position of Sun Yat-sen (and even Chiang Kai-shek) is being elevated to higher levels of national prominence. Although Sun Yat-sen has always been nominally the "Father of the Nation," since the 1990s there has been a renewed effort to bring him closer to a broader Chinese nationalism. Nothing marks Sun's visibility in China more than the large portrait of him that is installed on special occasions in Tian'anmen Square, directly facing the famous portrait of Mao Zedong on the wall of the gate: as if the father has come back to gaze upon the son. In fact, Mao's portrait hangs where the portrait of Sun Yat-sen was first hung in 1929, so the elevation of the father of the nation is perhaps not yet complete.[9] The glow from Sun Yat-sen and the early Republican years is being cast much wider, however. At another war museum in Shenyang (far northeastern China), which memorializes the Japanese invasion of Manchuria in 1931, the exhibits were recently revamped to include more representation of the Nationalist war efforts. The director of the museum noted (in English) that "there were only photos concerned with the Communist Party in China–led war against the Japanese in the museum previously. This time, we'll add photos about the KMT-led fight against the Japanese army in the main battlefield."[10] Thus, the wheels of nationalism turn.

Although this rehabilitation of Sun, Chennault, and even Chiang makes sense in terms of a more complete "national" narrative, the ramifications for Taiwan are somewhat ominous. For those committed to the sovereignty of Taiwan, the recalibration of the story of China's "liberation," whereby the Japanese invaders are placed in the foreground instead of Chiang and the Nationalist forces, can be read as part of a "one-China" rationale meant to draw the two sides together around the "Father of the Nation." Although Sun Yat-sen and the Republic of China had little to do with Taiwan in the first half of the twentieth century, his dominating presence in the ideology of the exiled Nationalist government, which we have seen manifested in numerous ways, gives that argument substantial weight. Just how much Sun Yat-sen's symbolic presence matters in the future resolution of Taiwan's national sovereignty depends in part on the cast of its "national" government. The positions that Chiang Kai-shek and, by association, General Chennault hold in the Chinese national narrative will also be determined largely by political resolutions found in Taiwan.

The complications of the Chennault legacy were not quite over, however. In July 2006, General Chennault's bust was moved from its second Taipei location in New Life Park and installed (refurbished but without the pedestal) in a new museum honoring him and the Flying Tigers. The new museum is located in the east coast city of Hualian, on the airbase of the 401st Tactical Combined Wing of the Taiwan Air Force under the command of Major General Tian Zaimai (Mike Tien). It was General Tian's initiative that got the museum built.[11] This time, Mrs. Chennault, along with U.S. government representatives and several former members of the Flying Tigers, were invited to the ceremonies, during which Mrs. Chennault called Taiwan her "home away from home." In some ways, this new location situates General Chennault even farther from the center of power in Taiwan (he certainly had no association with the Hualian area), yet the dignity of the museum and its strong military connections compensate. General Tian's comments that "General Chennault's statue is home now" and the Air Force "will take care of him now" reflect the sense of estrangement and neglect that the Taipei relocation had implied. The irony is that General Chennault is again allied with the Air Force of the Republic of China, whose primary function is to protect the island from aggression by the Chinese mainland, where he has also found a new "home."

Civic Statuary

Statuary in East Asia was traditionally dominated by the religious icon, particularly in its associations with Buddhism, which entered China through Central Asia in the first few centuries CE and moved on to Japan, where it became the principal religion of the court and society. In China, plastic forms of the human figure, both monumental and miniature, were found primarily in funerary art. This monumental art is most dramatically manifested by the terra-cotta army found in the tomb area of the first emperor of the Qin, Qin Shihuang (259–210 BCE), but also in large stone figures such as those that line the approaches to the Ming tombs outside Beijing, the statuary Victor Segalen called "funerary but profane."[12] The Chinese bronze industry was extremely long lived and well developed, especially in its production of vessels; during the middle and late imperial periods, numerous bronze figures, from figurines to monuments, were created, with religious icons again predominant in the medium. Thus, despite China's wide-ranging achievement in plastic arts, its humanistic philosophies, and strong bureaucratic forms of government, there was almost no tradition of secular statuary in China: no emperors, princes, generals, or even mythical figures.[13]

In Japan, there is a stronger tradition of portrait statuary in realistic form, especially of priests and members of the court. Yet, neither in China nor in Japan was there a dissociation of these figures into stand-alone art, such as is seen in the Western Renaissance treatment of Greek and Roman statuary.[14] Sergiusz Michalski traces the beginnings of public statuary in the West to the late sixteenth century, which commenced "an almost three-century-long process of evolution in the course of which the fledgling public monument lost most of its monarchical or aristocratic strictures and became—in the late nineteenth century—the preserve of bourgeois political culture and representation."[15] This led to the "statumania" of Paris in the late nineteenth century, where historical and allegorical figures meet in large bronze public monuments, with narrative themes celebrating the meritocracy of the Third Republic. In turn-of-the-century Germany, this development took a more conservative and nationalistic form in large stone statuary, especially the many figures of Bismarck. And in Victorian England, there was a strong association of the portrait statue with the public park.[16]

These European practices came to East Asia in new forms of art associated with modernization, nationalism, and colonization. As part of its Meiji Restoration, Japan was certainly at the forefront in introducing this new iconography, including the public monument, to the region. Japan's "statumania" was nearly contemporaneous with that of Paris, reaching full force at the end of the century, when it was declared that "bronze statues became so fashionable that even cats and ladles (*neko demo shakushi demo*) had bronze statues erected for them."[17] Most of the Japanese statuary was of public figures, especially military heroes: among the earliest were those of Ōmura Masujirō at the Yasukuni Shrine (1893) and Saigo Takamori installed in Ueno Park (1898). Tracing these figures to forms of European neoclassicism that came to Asia on the back of imperialism is an obvious way to account for them—as early as 1881 they were identified in Japan as "a form of commemoration that was learned from the West."[18] At the same time, we need to be attentive to the intersection of the new art with indigenous forms. Note, for example, that in the world of Japanese bronze ware, the Meiji promotion of Shintoism as the official state religion diminished the production of Buddhist icons, which meant that these craftsmen "had to start looking for new markets."[19] One of those markets certainly was civic statuary.

Along with other modern representational media, these plastic forms came to Taiwan in the early years of colonization. For example, they paralleled the introduction of Western landscape painting and the development of photographic portraiture, all of which contributed to a new colonial art form on the island.[20]

Colonial Monuments

Not coincidentally, the first important example of colonial civic statuary in Taiwan was placed exactly where General Chennault's statue would later be installed in 1960. On October 1, 1906, a full-length stone statue of the late Governor-General Kodama Gentarō was unveiled at the southern entrance to Taipei Park (fig. 6.1).[21] Although the statue, on a wide base and pedestal,

臺 北 新 公 園

6.1 Stone statue of the Governor-General Kodama Gentarō, south entrance of Taipei Park; background left, civil adminstrator's residence; background right, Taipei Club, 1906.
Source: *Taiwan miyage*; courtesy of National Taiwan Library

reveals none of the dynamism and innovation of the Paris bronzes, it still is an overtly European-style military figure standing (literally) over the colonization of the island; appropriately, the style is similar to the portrait statuary of the Victorian park.

This emplacement of the Kodama statue established the early southward orientation of the park, linking it to the most emblematic colonial buildings of the downtown area. Although Terry Wyke warns against overstating the significance of public statues in the design and rationale of the Victorian public park, in colonial Taiwan, I believe such statues *were* definitional in the highly articulated civic motivation for its parks.[22] Thus, I would argue that the installation of Kodama's statue was the first conspicuous marker of the civic nature of Taipei Park.[23]

The self-consciousness of that design is found in a graphic representation that prefaced the installation of the Kodama statue: a detailed blueprint that shows the statue surrounded by elaborate curvilinear paths, plantings, and geometric beds filling the entire park area.[24] This idealization of the space of Kodama's memorial is striking. Except for the club, there is no sign of other buildings or constructions in these drawings, although we know that there were still a number of other transitional buildings, including the erstwhile Tianhougong, in the park at this time. Clearly, this statue was not a "serendipitous object," as Wyke termed statuary in the Victorian garden. In this design it was intended to *be* the park. Although the park never reached the height of idealization that this plan suggests, its principal restructuring in 1915 did incorporate a number of features from the 1906 blueprint, especially its winding pathways. With the addition, ten years later, of the north-facing Kodama-Gotō Memorial Museum, Governor-General Kodama came to hold a commanding presence at both entrances. The statue at the south entrance stood until destroyed by Nationalist authorities in 1945. After a hiatus of fifteen years, the installation of the Chennault statue on this site placed the general close to those same buildings but under a different political power.[25]

In the decades following the installation of the Kodama statue, Taiwan, especially Taihoku, became populated with civic monuments of a similar sort, but most of them cast in bronze.[26] Taipei Park itself contained bronze statues of two other Japanese officials. First was the 1911 installation of Gotō Shimpei's full-length bronze image and stone pedestal, which occupied the center of the park, looking north toward the soon-to-be-built museum. Gotō was perhaps the most commemorated of all colonial figures, including an identical bronze figure installed in the central park of Taichū/Taizhong.[27] After the war, Gotō's statue was also destroyed, but the pedestal remained in its original location for decades, converted into a stand for a clock and an air-raid siren. Additionally, a 1918 bronze statue of Yagyū Kazuyoshi, first president of the Bank of Taiwan, stood in a stone alcove at the north end of the park near the museum. As with the Gotō statue, the bronze was destroyed but the pedestal lived on, this time to become the base for General Chennault's bust.

Finally, the bronze statue that held the most prominent location in colonial Taihoku was a monumental figure of the fifth civil administrator, Ōshima Kumaji, erected in 1913, which stood on a tall pedestal surrounded by a pool and fountain at the central intersection of the city, facing the Taihoku District office building. This location was the postwar intersection of Sun Yat-sen and Chiang Kai-shek roads, where the statue of Chiang, similarly posed but in military garb, was installed on the original Japanese base.[28] The provenance of such early Nationalist statuary is not clear. Were they cast on the island? If so, was the bronze from the Japanese statues melted down and used to recast the new ones? There certainly would not have been an abundance of bronze on the island in the early postwar years. Or was there a hiatus between the destruction and the new installations that would have precluded this?[29] Either way, these exchanges suggest a highly symbolic "recasting" of power from the colonial form to the Nationalist, perhaps neo-colonial, one.

Loyal Taiwan

Not all present-day statuary in Taipei Park derives from Japanese inspiration, site, or materials, however. When the park came under the Nationalist government's purview (largely undamaged by the Allied bombings), the sports and parade grounds that stood just east of the museum continued to function as such until the 1960s: baseball and tennis were civic activities that fit well into the new "international" (read American) conditions of Nationalist policy.[30] A frequent visitor to the park, Mr. Zhang (sixty-eight years old in 2004), remembered fondly the baseball games played there during the 1950s and 1960s, especially by the famous Kainan Shanggong Vocational High School teams.[31] Yet, in the early 1960s, this space was dramatically reformed with the construction of a large, formal pond-pavilion complex, which turned the relatively open space associated with the colony and sports into a square, formal, Chinese architectural frame (visible in fig. 4.1).[32] The pavilions that form the complex are all in the "northern palace" style that was part of the neoclassical projects of the time. The complex did allow some acknowledgment of local historic conditions. As mentioned above, the central pavilion represents Sun Yat-sen, but each of the four flanking pavilions is dedicated to an important personage in Taiwan's history. These four figures are, however, all officially sanctioned by the ideology of Chinese nationalism: the Ming loyalist Zheng Chenggong (Koxinga), who has been celebrated across the island as fighting for authentic China in the face of non-Chinese (Manchu) rule; the Qing official and first governor of the province, Liu Mingchuan, famed for his modernizing reforms, especially in Taipei City; the local military official Qiu Fengjia, who is known for his strong mid-island resistance against the Japanese in 1895; and the conservative Taiwan historian Lian Yatang, who wrote the anti-Japanese *Complete History of Taiwan* (Taiwan tongshi) and had family ties with the Nationalist government. The message here is anything but subtle: Sun Yat-sen and the Nationalist government, as the displaced Chinese nation, are supported on all sides by such loyal local patriots.

When the complex was built, this ideological construction may not have been particularly overt: the calligraphic panels on each of the pavilions named them with versions of the dedicatee's professional name (*hao*), not his common name. Thus, the Liu Mingchuan pavilion is named Daqian Pavilion (in Xu Shiying's calligraphy), based on the abbreviation of Liu's professional name (Daqian Shanren). To fully appreciate the loyalties expressed here, the visitor to the park would have to have known the relatively obscure reference to the governor (or perhaps the pedigree of the ninety-two-year-old Nationalist official and calligrapher Xu).[33] In the late 1970s, these tests of cultural knowledge were reduced when the pavilions were outfitted with life-size stone busts and plaques engraved with hagiographic accounts of the four figures. These materials were mounted on small pedestals that stand, somewhat awkwardly, in the center of each pavilion, placed there by the Taipei City Archives (Taibeishi Wenxianhui).[34] The engraved texts are old-fashioned in style and written in unpunctuated, semi-classical Chinese, thus maintaining the formal dignity of the site, yet they do clarify the pavilion's referent and provide an assessment of his historic relationship with the island in terms of Chinese nationalism. We are told, for example:

When the Japanese armies invaded Taiwan, they perpetrated cruel treatment on the Taiwanese people and levied limitless taxes. In response, [Lian Yatang] wrote poems that criticized this and urged them to desist. When this came to naught, he went to Xiamen [in Fujian province] and started the *Fujian Daily News*, petitioning the Manchu government to dispatch an official delegation to put a stop to these practices.

Thus, the ideological work that began rather subtly with the construction of the Sun Yat-sen complex was recast in a more thorough and transparent fashion by these additions.

The February 28th Monument

With the installation of the busts of the four heroes of Taiwan in their pavilions, new portrait statuary in Taipei Park came to an end. Despite that, several subsequent civic monuments stand in the stead of such statuary.[35] The most important of these is the February 28th Monument (Ererba Jinianbei) that now dominates the center of the park, having been built on the site of the former Gotō Shimpei statue. This stone and bronze monument, dedicated to the memory of those who suffered and died in the incident, does not contain any overt human figures (although the bronze lamps circling the monument are elegantly anthropomorphic in shape), yet it carries the full cultural weight of earlier statues (fig. 6.2). Its representation is in more abstract allegorical terms. An official brochure introducing the monument states: "The cubes [which form the main structure of the monument] stand on end, symbolizing an independent and autonomous individual; the three cubes together form a stable structure symbolizing that only when we are united can we work peacefully together."[36] As we might expect, this monument is *the* ideological vehicle of the early post–martial law period: an architectural and ideological answer to the colonial museum, the Chennault statue, and the Sun Yat-sen pavilion complex. Wu Jinyong describes this cultural condition through the critical language of Michel Foucault and Raymond Williams:

The February 28th Monument was constructed during a time in which structures of feeling [Williams's term] were being reorganized. Following the reorganization of the hegemonic entities and the recalibration of power relationships [after the lifting of martial law], Taiwanese society underwent a reorganization of the structures of feeling. These changes bore no resemblance to the various formal and systematic features that formerly supported Chinese nationalist ideology; rather, they united in the sudden rise of the

6.2 February 28th Monument, Taipei Park, with center anthropomorphic lamp and plaque, 2010

Taiwanese ethnic community and, in the context of a new historical direction, reconstructed the formerly repressed February 28th Incident. In the process of building the February 28th Monument, various forms passed through various relationships, situations, and occasions.[37]

Like the prose of this paragraph (and I hope my translation has been faithful to its texture as well as its meaning), the process of the monument's coming into being was long and torturous, yet in that process are also profound social and cultural meanings.

Since the complicated process of building the February 28th Monument in Taipei Park was conducted during a time of relative transparency and open discussion, it allows us to see this civic monument as both a product and an instrument of overt and covert ideologies. Nearly every step of the process is documented, and the many contending voices in those records make the story intriguing and revealing. Although the monument in Taipei Park was not completed until 1997, as soon as the shroud of martial law was lifted in 1987, public discussion of the theretofore tabooed incident erupted in a wide variety of media. During this time, memorials of various kinds—holidays, museums, and monuments—were suggested, debated, and often established.

In the early years, public monuments to the February 28th Incident were concentrated in the southern part of the island, where the government opposition forces were strongest.[38] When the process began in Taipei, it was especially complicated because two contending authorities were involved: one political, one civic. In the early 1990s, the Taipei City administration was still aligned with the Nationalist Party through the appointment of Mayor Huang Dazhou, directly under the jurisdiction of the central government as a special metropolitan district. This created a political climate in the city that was generally reluctant, even opposed, to the establishment of the memorial. The other force was the moral authority generated by the critical exposure of the 1947 incident itself, which had played out most dramatically in Taipei City. This second authority was represented by the families of the victims of the incident, who were concentrated in the city and generally aligned with the opposition party. The earliest action committee in the city was organized in 1991 around these families by the Presbyterian Church; it was known as the United Concerned for February 28th (Ererba Guanhuai Lianhehui) and was headed by Lin Zongyi.[39]

The first meeting between Lin Zongyi and Mayor Huang, on August 5, 1991, did not go well: the mayor indicated that he was not interested in having a memorial in Taipei at all. Nonetheless, the central government, under the presidency of Lee Teng-hui, established its own organization to deal with these issues, the February 28th Incident Memorial Committee (Ererba Shijian Jianbei Weiyuanhui). This committee was headed by Qiu Chuanghuan, an official from the president's office, and included members of the United Concerned as well as government representatives, most importantly, Mayor Huang Dazhou and Wu Boxiong, a high-level Nationalist Party official. This committee met, and often wrangled, throughout 1992 and 1993. Stephen Phillips has described the political party alignments of the time:

> The outline of the future struggles over February 28 became clear. The DPP [opposition party] would raise the issue to satisfy its supporters and to attack the Nationalists. The Nationalists, particularly mainlanders, would grudgingly acquiesce to some DPP demands in order to prevent the issue from energizing the Taiwanese majority at the ballot box. Lee [Teng-hui] would take substantive steps to claim the middle ground between the two parties.[40]

These electoral politics took even more concrete shape in the process of establishing the Taipei memorial.

Once the decision was made to establish a memorial in Taipei, the first issue to decide was its location. This is where the contending forces, represented by Mayor Huang and Lin Zongyi, had their first and most dramatic dispute. In the beginning, the mayor and his forces suggested one of two small parks in the Dadaocheng area, arguing, "In building the memorial, we should consider the historical circumstances. If we can build it at the location where the incident first flared up, that would be best; otherwise, it should be nearby."[41] This certainly made historic sense, but it was soon noted that these parks (really only neighborhood "pocket parks") were not big enough for a substantial memorial. Less articulated, but also significant for historic reasons, is that these two parks are in a relatively marginalized old Taiwanese neighborhood, distant (both physically and culturally) from the arenas of public life and political power.

In the second meeting of the committee, on February 1, 1992, the list of possible sites was expanded, and by March it included four more parks, an outdoor entertainment area, and the plaza in front of the central train station. During this time, the mayor and other government representatives advocated for the adoption of a site in New Life Park at the northern edge of the city, which they said "was large in area, convenient to transportation [the freeway], and at the same time ready for construction to begin immediately."[42] After inspection of the seven proposed sites in March, the Memorial Committee eliminated five from consideration, leaving only New Life Park and Youth Park (Qingnian Gongyuan), which is in the far southern part of the city.[43] At that point, Lin Zongyi brought up the elephant in the room: he suggested that Taipei Park be considered as a site. Other representatives from the United Concerned agreed, noting the importance of a historical context for the memorial. In this sense, Taipei Park was logical because in 1947 it had served as a rallying stage and headquarters (via the commandeered radio station located on its grounds) for the island-wide movement—the old radio station would soon become the February 28th Museum (Ererba Jinianguan). Quickly, United Concerned issued a public statement that supported Taipei Park as the best location for the memorial and argued that New Life Park was "the most inappropriate location."[44] At the same time, they asked the government to replace Qiu Chuanghuan as head of the memorial committee. The battle lines were drawn.

Over the next few months, the two sides bickered, and did so very publicly. After the community expressed support for the Taipei Park location, the Memorial Committee met to make a final decision. Those supporting New Life Park expressed their concerns that Taipei Park was too small and was also a "gathering place for homosexuals," thus not appropriate for the memorial. Lin Zongyi and his supporters complained that New Life Park was too noisy, yet when Qiu Chuanghuan declared (there was no formal vote) that the New Life Park location had the most support, Lin and the others went along. Not for long, however. Within a fortnight, Lin Zongyi, the mayor, and others made an inspection tour of New Life Park, at which time Lin suddenly declared that he refused to accept it as a location because of the noise: "The families of the victims who will come here to pray and recollect need peace and quiet. How can they stand to have an airplane flying overhead every five minutes?"[45] In the coming days, Lin hardened his stand, wrote letters to the authorities, and threatened to boycott meetings of the Memorial Committee. He also visited Taipei Park (with Qiu Chuanghuan's approval) and identified a specific site: the area of the central clock (on the base that had held Gotō Shimpei's statue).

In the meantime, the city government commissioned a sound assessment of New Life Park, which declared that over a twenty-four-hour period the *average* noise level was acceptable, between sixty and seventy decibels. Lin pointed out the illogic of that sort of reading, explaining that the question was the noise level at the moment of the plane's approach, not some technical average. But this was becoming a debate about much more than noise pollution and gay cruising; it was about political sensitivities. The government wanted to marginalize the memorial by (dis)placing it as far from the center of political and cultural power as possible; the families wanted the memorial to be placed at a site that brought public attention to the incident and their plight.

Under the leadership of Wu Boxiong, who reasoned that without the support of the victims' families, any memorial would be a failure, the Memorial Committee met and agreed that the memorial would be built in Taipei Park. The wrangling was hardly over, however. As Wu Jingyong has chronicled, the coming months were consumed with disputes about the actual site, the selection of the monument, the text of the inscription, and other parts of the process. And Stephen Phillips has described how the political maneuvering and debates continued into the next century. Nonetheless, on February 28, 1997, the fiftieth anniversary of the incident, Taipei's (and in many ways Taiwan's) February 28th Monument was officially opened at a site so strategically located that it was a sign of a new era: the city government was under the mayorship of Chen Shuibian, leader of the opposition party, and the park's name had already been changed.[46]

The irony is that while the February 28th Monument was rescued from the marginalization intended by the Nationalist powers and placed prominently in the February 28th Peace Park, General Chennault's monument was almost simultaneously removed from the park by Chen Shuibian's government and sent to the distant and noisy environs of the New Life Park to stand alone, night and day, under those approaching airplanes.

The Displacement of Chiang Kai-shek

The rapid changes following the lifting of martial law in 1987, including the ascension of oppositional leader Chen Shuibian to a position of power, first in the city and then in the nation, elicited a number of cultural recoveries, including an open review, verging on nostalgia, of the Japanese period. Those cultural recoveries were also accompanied by the diminishment and dismissal of events and personages that had held center stage during the interim martial law period. The Chiang presidencies, father and son, were very much part of that reassessment. These effects were seen even in loyal Nationalist camps. Witness, for example, the restructuring of the exhibitions in the Chiang Kai-shek Memorial Hall that positioned Taiwan more in the Chiang Kai-shek narrative, as described by Jeremy Taylor (see chapter 5). Another example of the Nationalist realignment of the Chiang legacy was the promotion of Chiang Ching-kuo's presidency in the story of the late martial law period, especially his role in the Taiwanization of the party and his critical decision, for whatever reason, to lift martial law just before he died. In this narrative, his father is diminished, and Chiang Ching-kuo's role in the early years of martial law, when he was the director of the secret police (1950–65), is elided. In a recent tourist brochure for the Taoyuan area, *The Culture Park of the Two Chiangs*, the story told is as much about the younger as the older Chiang:

> Even at the last moment of his life, Jiang Jing-guo (Chiang Ching-kuo) still served his country. Six months after saying [when he lifted martial law], "I am also a Taiwanese," he passed away and became an honorable and solemn part of our history. As a political figure, the path Jiang Jing-guo took in Taiwan for half of his life was both harsh and magnificent.[47]

As an index of the intended audience for this new narrative, the brochure is written in traditional and simplified Chinese, Japanese, and English. The realignment of the Chiang narrative also extends to the commemorative statuary dating from the time of the family's rule.

According to one estimate, at the end of martial law, there were approximately forty-five hundred statues of Chiang Kai-shek, large and small, installed in various locations across the island.[48] Given the size of the island and the distribution of its population, this is a remarkable density of images: approximately three per square mile, and many times that in populated areas, especially in the Nationalist stronghold of Taipei. As a comparison, Sergiusz Michalski notes that at the height of German statumania (1914), throughout the German Reich there were about five hundred images of Bismarck, "the leitmotif of German national imagery";[49] perhaps only the statuary of Lenin in the Soviet Union compares to such a concentration. With the changing political winds in Taiwan in the 1990s, the ubiquitous image of Chiang Kai-shek became an ironic reminder of the past and the focus of cynical thoughts and some embarrassment. In 2007 a young student in Taipei remarked, "Most of those statues were built by the KMT [Nationalists] when they were trying to control the thinking of the people. It's ridiculous to have them on every campus."[50] Over the years, there has been a relatively quiet campaign to remove these statues from public spaces: not to destroy them, just to hide them away, in basements, backyards, and other out-of-the-way places. This was carried out most rigorously in the south, especially in the Gaoxiong area, where opposition forces are the strongest. The practice climaxed in 2007, when Chiang's statue was removed from all military bases.[51] This did not rest well with many supporters of the Nationalist Party, to say the least; yet, there was a relatively benign quality to this wave of displacement, especially when compared to the fate of communist statuary all over Eastern Europe after the fall of the Soviet Union, or Japanese statuary in Taiwan at the end of the colonial period.[52]

In a highly unusual way, the town fathers of Daxi, a historic town in the countryside south of Taipei City, decided to do something about this demotion of the Chiang statuary. Seeking to capitalize on the associations of the region with the Chiang family, they developed a plan to promote tourism in the area; they already had an "old town" center filled with baroque architecture from the Qing and Japanese periods that had generated a lively tourist trade. Quite unrelated to this old town area was a series of sites associated with the Chiang family, whose members often vacationed in the scenic area. This association had left a legacy of strong Nationalist support in Daxi: the park in the center of town is still called Chiang Kai-shek Park (Zhongzheng Gongyuan) and contains a bronze statue of Chiang in military regalia atop his horse. Of the sites associated with the Chiang family, the most important is Chiang Kai-shek's temporary mausoleum in the Cihu Lake area (temporary until his body can be returned to his home in Zhejiang province). During the heyday of Chiang rule, this site functioned as both a vacation home and a military command center. In 1975 the small villa-cum-mausoleum was opened to the public and became a relatively popular site for tourists, especially given Cihu's lovely rural setting.

In 1997, under the leadership of Daxi mayor Zeng Rongjian, the town established the Cihu Memorial Sculpture Park (Cihu Diaosu Jinian Gongyuan) next to the mausoleum parking lot. This site is dedicated to collecting the various abandoned statues associated with the early Nationalist period, primarily those of Chiang Kai-shek. Mayor Zeng announced to the island that the city would accept any statue donated to the park, and pay for shipping.[53] After the park was constructed (in 2000), the collection began with a donation from Gaoxiong County; as of 2010 there were 152 statues on-site, with space to hold approximately 200. The park is designed around walkways that meander past the statues, which are gathered together in two basic configurations: busts standing about ten feet apart on waist-high pedestals that line the curving walkways; and full-length standing or seated figures in the center of a low circular brick wall, with other figures surrounding the wall facing in.

The purpose of the park is clearly to commemorate the Chiang legacy: a plaque for a statue that came from the Chiang Kai-shek Grammar School (Zhongzheng Guoxiao) in Xindian says (in English): "Most people who exercise and walk in the school every morning would spontaneously bow to the CKS statue, and students follow this action. It had always been the spiritual emblem of the people there." Nonetheless, the actual effect of the site seems somewhat at odds with this intent. First, there is the recasting of the former commemorative materials into objects of more historical interest, similar to the process seen at the exhibition rooms of the Chiang Memorial. The contingent and historical nature of the images in the park is reinforced by the small plaques that accompany each piece, giving the original location and the date of reinstallation; there is also a finding map where the numbered sites are identified by the statue's original location. Occasionally, the artistic agency of a sculpture that was invisible in its original installation is also recovered. For a large equestrian figure of Chiang Kai-shek removed from the Taiping Market in Taizhong County, for example, the plaque also names the artist, Xie Dongliang. In addition, a display board standing next to the statue recounts the details of Xie's life and work, making clear his Taiwanese heritage and training; here the hagiography (in English and Chinese) has moved from the subject of the sculpture to its creator:

> Hsieh Tongliang [Xie Dongliang] was born in Wufong of Taichung County, 1949, whose family register is Yulin. Being graduated from Taichung Second Senior High School, Hsieh passed the exam for the admission of entering National Taiwan Junior College of Arts and thus started his life in exploring arts. In the beginning, he was assigned to the traditional Chinese Painting division of the Department of Arts; later he found himself not interested in that field. Not successfully transferring to the western painting division, he grieved for having only one grade less than the standard admission score of entering the Department of Arts in National Taiwan Normal University and then entered the Department of Sculpture against his will. This decision has been a turning point in his life, and later proved to lead him to achievements. . . . Hsieh has been clinging to humane concern and discovery, and this is what Hsieh has been trying to present, the true emotion that his artwork implicates.

The turn of attention away from the subject of the art to its creator is especially pronounced here, in that within the review of Xie's career and in the accompanying details of his résumé, there is not one mention of the statue that stands so prominently alongside: clearly this piece of sculpture does not represent "the true emotion that his artwork implicates."

This type of displacement and historicization may well be within the intentions of the creators of the sculpture park, but there is another level of realignment of these materials that is more profound and not likely something that the Daxi town fathers sought. The array and repetition of images, many from the same mold, combine to reduce its referent (Chiang Kai-shek) to a product of some mere mechanical process. This reduction to and reproduction of materiality in effect extinguishes the work's original aura, either ideological or aesthetic. Julia Ross has suggested that this gives the site the feeling of a "Chiang Kai-shek Memorial Dump." Given the public display of that process/form, I believe the site more approaches the configuration of installation art, with a decidedly postmodern feel. The postmodern quotation of the mundane object merges the everyday and the iconic in ways that confuse those two apparent extremes. This confusion involves a sense of play and even humor, often irreverent humor.

With the first configuration of statues (busts standing in a line), we walk past bust after (exact or nearly exact) bust until the effect approaches the bizarre, in this case unintentionally reinforced by Chiang's Cheshire cat grin. In the case of the second configuration in which the Chiang Kai-shek figures stand around "looking at themselves," the effect is quizzical, if not comic. One has to wonder whether these effects are not, in fact, intentional, at least at some subversive level of design. The configurations seem to contain a playful reference to the necessary narcissistic condition of the original statuary. At one level, the site as a whole alludes to the narcissism of such self-image-making: as the brochure says, it is the "only sculpture park in Taiwan (and in the world) dedicated to a single individual." And in the sense that the site is a "dump," it witnesses the public rejection of that narcissism, although nothing like the "Temporary Museum of Totalitarian Art" in Moscow that included displays of overturned and mutilated figures.[54] Although it would not be known which statues would come to stand on which bases when the arrangements were first plotted, it does not actually matter because they are "all the same." The postmodern effect is in the very structure of the design.[55]

This postmodern effect may have been coincidental to the original design of the sculpture park, but later it becomes openly operational, at least at one installation. In 2007 a monumental seated bronze of Chiang Kai-shek held in Gaoxiong's (Chiang Kai-shek) Cultural Center was dismantled with a cutting torch (ostensibly so it could be removed from its site). After shipment to Daxi, it was impossible to reconstruct the statue because the careless dismantling had left it in a bewildering number of unidentified and missing pieces—the Humpty Dumpty of the Daxi sculpture park. Not to be deterred, the authorities turned the commemorative piece into pure installation art. What could be salvaged was attached to a steel substructure so that the gaps and fissures of the dismantled statue came to be part of its display: "Due to extreme incompleteness of the original piece, it was restored through resemblance [rather] than reconstruction," says the plaque (in English). The statue now stands by itself on the hillside with a commanding view of the entire park; the fragmented Chiang looks down on an array of his complete forms (fig. 6.3). The explanation on the plaque contains elements of historicization, naming the original artist, Lin Muchuan, and its original installation; it also says that "the primary principle is to respect originality

6.3 Cihu Memorial Sculpture Park, Chiang Kai-shek statues, with large "postmodern" restoration in background, 2010

and historic documentation." Yet most interesting is the claim that this type of display is meant to "preserve true features of arts for postmodern representation" (or in Chinese, *yi baoliu zhenxiang he weihu yishu qianti, zuo houxiandai zhuyi fenge de biaoxian*). In keeping with that spirit of artistic make-over, the statue is renamed "Hacks · Revivals" (Shanghen · Zaisheng). The statement of postmodernity may be somewhat facile here (the plaque also claims "academic and artistic representation without ideology"), but, in fact, to my mind, the entire site is a *houxiandai zhuyi fenge de biaoxian*.

How far removed we are from the seriousness of the Chiang Kai-shek commemorative statues in their original condition and locations becomes clear with a visit to the sculpture park's information center and gift shop. On the patio of the building are two more bronze statues of the Chiangs, father and son, standing side by side. These contemporary pieces are half-life-size parodies of the two, rendered in the cartoonish style of bobble-head figures, with a toothy grin for dad and exaggerated square eyeglasses for the son, who raises his hand in a peace sign, which is *the* pose of East Asian snapshots. Thirty years ago, such irreverence could have landed a person in the Green Island gulag.

The statues of Kodama Gentarō and Gotō Shimpei that stood in the Colonial Museum dedicated to them (see chapter 5) were clearly the most thoughtfully coordinated commemoration of their rule of the island (fig. 6.4). Their position in the specially designed alcoves facing each other across the elaborate central marble rotunda was designated in the earliest drawings of the museum plans (see fig. 5.1).[56] Bronze, life-size, full-length figures of particularly good quality presented a pair of distinguished colonial leaders in full regalia. There they stood, overseeing their museum until 1945, when they were not destroyed but spirited away into storage. The preservation of these

6.4 Bronze statue of Governor General Kodama Gentarō in original alcove of the Colonial Administration Museum, 1915. Source: *Kinen hakubutsukan shashinchō*; courtesy of National Taiwan Library

two statues was probably the fortunate combination of the museum's relatively low profile and the cautious work of the early transition team, which retained four Japanese and two Taiwanese members from the colonial staff.[57] It would behoove any museum professional to see such objects not merely as political paraphernalia but also as historic treasures.

Over subsequent decades, the two statues remained in storage, safe but unseen except by curatorial staff. Then in January of 1999, I happened to stop by the museum and found Gotō Shimpei's statue in one of the museum's rear galleries, unlabeled and unexplained. Even as late as 1999, I was surprised. A few weeks later, it disappeared again: the slightly deceptive entrepreneurial work of a curator having apparently upset certain authorities, the statue went back into storage.[58] It did not stay there for long, however. In 2008 the museum put both statues on display, with full labeling and explanation (in Chinese, Japanese, and English). The English reads:

BRONZE STATUES OF KODAMA GENTARO AND GOTO SHIMPEI
AND THE VICEROY KODAMA AND GOVERNOR GOTO MEMORIAL HALL

During the Japanese Administration, the building that houses today's National Taiwan Museum was called the Viceroy Kodama and Governor Goto Memorial Museum. As the name implies, it was built to honor Kodama Gentaro, Japan's fourth Viceroy and Governor Goto Shimpei. Construction began in April 1913 on a site located in Taipei New Park and the building was completed in March 1915. An example of classical architecture, the stately structure is a symmetrical rectangle featuring a raised dome flanked by Doric columns. A month following its completion, bronze statues of Kodama Gentaro and Goto Shimpei created by the Japanese sculptor Shinkai Taketaro were placed in the alcoves at both sides of the main hall. Kodama's statue sat in the eastern alcove, while Goto's statue was situated in the western alcove. Following the Second World War, the Nationalist government took control of the building, renaming it the Taiwan Provincial Museum and moved the statues from their original position into storage. In 2008, to commemorate the museum's approaching 100th anniversary, the museum has brought the Memorial Hall's original signboard and statues out of storage for the public to enjoy.

What a difference eight (to say nothing of sixty-three) years make. The full detailed disclosure of the provenance of the statues and the origins of the museum is emblematic of the times. Clearly the effort here is to historicize the statues and thereby diminish their commemorative nature, but there is nonetheless something close to a full rehabilitation of Kodama and Gotō. Note also that the 100th anniversary being celebrated is of the original (1908) colonial museum, which was *not* a memorial to Kodama and Gotō. Using the 2008 date to return the statues to public view seems slightly opportunistic; logically, they should have waited until 2015.

Here there seems to be a complete reversal of the displacement of the colonial figures, as they are returned to their original home. Yet the return is not quite complete. Not only has there been the intervening historicization of the statues, but they also have not been returned to their original rotunda alcoves, in which massive Ming-style vases still stand on the original stone bases. Rather, the bronzes have been placed in the relatively marginal display area on the third floor, occupying plywood alcoves that offer a diminished mimicry of the colonial elegance of the first floor. This type of cultural recovery can only go so far, at least for the time being.

SEVEN

A Horse in a Park in a City on an Island in the Sea

O n Thanksgiving Day, 2006, I set out on an expedition around the island of Taiwan, traveling by train, taxi, and bicycle to a number of cities and towns. I was in search of lost horses. With some sketchy information gleaned from old photographs, colonial records, and ruminations on several Web sites, I plotted a circuit around the island. For weeks I had been looking over materials in various archives around Taipei and had made short trips to areas near the city, especially to Taoyuan, Zhongli, and Yilan. This new trip was intended to cover the rest of the island. The materials suggested the sites, but the trip was open-ended—no time lines, no specific itinerary, and no reservations. The weather was excellent, and after weeks in libraries and archives I looked forward to the adventure: a hunting trip of sorts.

At the various stops along the way—Taizhong, Tainan, Xinying, Gaoxiong, Taidong, and Hualian—people were, as they invariably are in Taiwan, warm and helpful. I remember two people in particular. Mr. Zhuang Weicheng of the Xinying City Cultural Office not only plied me with materials from his library for my research but also patiently explained the special conditions of that small city. The other person who comes to mind was a young schoolboy in Gaoxiong. During my travels, my modus operandi was to arrive at the train station and begin searching for a nearby "business hotel"—clean, practical, and economical lodging. Yet, as I wandered down the streets away from the Gaoxiong train station, I found only hotels that suggested another sort of profession and service. I walked on toward the city center and Love River (Aihe). After many luckless blocks, I stopped in front of the Metropolitan Middle School (Shili Zhongxue) to peruse my map and collect my thoughts. As I stood there, a boy, around twelve years old, stopped and asked what I was doing. When I told him I was visiting for a few days and looking for a business hotel, he casually and confidently suggested a place a few more blocks down the street on the left. How he knew about this place I have no idea—perhaps it was operated by a relative or friend of the family. I asked his name (Zhou Danlong), thanked him, and went off to find it—and thus began my enjoyable stay in Gaoxiong. That trip and this account start (and end) in Taipei Park, but really this is a story of the whole island, in both its historical and contemporary conditions.

My Horse

In the southwest corner of Taipei Park, not far from the site of the Kodama, Chennault, and Peace Bell monuments, stands a majestic, three-quarter-size bronze horse, head back, front hoof raised, tail streaming. Unlike other monuments in the park, the horse stands unlabeled, except for a small sign on the low base that reads "Do Not Climb." Despite the sign, most days a small but steady flow of children and their parents come by, and the children climb or are placed on the horse, for a small diversion, for a photograph, for the fun of being there (fig. 7.1).[1] The back of the horse is cracked and polished to a golden shine, an index of all those happy sittings. No one seems to know why the horse is there or where it came from, yet all agree it is a handsome horse and a fine addition to the park, especially being right next to the playground. Even administrators of the park appear not to know the provenance of the horse, or if they know, they are not talking.

Signs of the horse's origins are not that far to seek, however. Close inspection of its torso reveals an effaced engraving that is still just readable below the erasure. We have what appears to be a *shimmon* (crest) of a Japanese Shinto shrine: in this case, a *sakura* (cherry) surrounding the stylized, simplified character *tai* (as in Taiwan)—the stylized *tai* was the insignia of the Taiwan Colonial Administration.[2] Although not widely known, during the Japanese colonial period, bronze horses of this type were donated to various shrines in Taiwan, which displayed them at their entrances and on their grounds (fig. 7.2).[3] Along with historic photographs of this practice, we

7.1 Bronze horse, Taipei Park, 2000

7.2 Entrance to the Shinchiku/Xinzhu Shinto shrine, with flanking horses displaying family crest; donated by Shida Yosaburō, 1921. Courtesy of Tsai Chin-tang.

have horses and other material evidence that remain, also largely unlabeled, at several sites around the island.[4] In addition, there is a pair of fiberglass horses that are full imitations of the bronze ones, dating from the postwar period and held by the Zhongxun temple in Muzha. Several other horses from the Japanese period are known to have been lost to the vicissitudes of time and politics, and others may be waiting to be discovered.[5] These sites offer horses in different configurations and conditions, but they all represent blatant forms of cultural displacement.

These bronze horses were a type of the *shimme* (votive horses) that in Shinto belief serve as mounts for the *kami* (tutelary spirits); as we shall see, even the new plastic ones imitate that worship function to some extent. *Shimme* were originally live horses (and sometimes still are), but material substitutes are now the rule and range from paper images (*ema*) to these bronze ones. The horses in Taiwan were often displayed in pairs, each horse a mirror image of its mate (always both stallions) and with matching crests on both sides of each torso. This specific form of statuary seems particular to the Japanese colonial areas and is most strongly represented in Taiwan; there is evidence of similar horses in the colonial city of Dairen, Manchukuo, and in colonial Korea, but none I know of in Japan.[6] The horses in Taiwan are all very similar in style and size (as were, judging from photographs, the Manchurian and Korean examples). With one exception, they all have one foreleg raised, head held back, and tail streaming; in size, the horse in Taipei Park is typical, standing approximately six feet tall from hoof to ear, and eight feet from tail to nose.[7] Because of their near uniformity, I assume that the horses were produced in some reference to each other, perhaps even in the same factory, and I assume that they were all produced in Japan (except for the replicas, discussed below). Thus, it appears that the present-day hobby horse in Taipei Park originally stood, like the others for which we have more evidence, in a Shinto shrine. But in that knowledge is the problem: which shrine?

Some of these horses, such as those in Taizhong, retain a tangible connection to their original location or, like the Tainan ones, to their ceremonial role, while others have had both their location and their condition partially recovered, as in Taoyuan and Yilan. Their various conditions of displacement represent transformations of cultural power in Taiwan over the last hundred years, informed by the interplay of history, politics, and locale. The Taipei Park horse is the most extreme example of displacement; it has been stripped of both location and function, reduced to a piece of playground equipment.[8] Before discussing the conditions of displacement, let's first consider the earliest manifestations of this complex story of cultural production: the horses themselves.

Shinto and the Military

The influence of European equestrian statuary, including the semiotics of posture, is obvious here, but the horses also need to be calibrated against the long tradition of horse statuary in East Asia, including samurai iconography.[9] Although none of the bronze horses in Taiwan carries a rider or overt military paraphernalia, they all display a martial bearing that suggests the relationship between the Shinto shrine and colonial governmentality. For example, the Taiwan *shimme* are nearly identical with the horse carrying the famous fourteenth-century samurai Kusunoki Masashige, as seen in the large statue located outside the Tokyo Imperial Palace (there was a similar, smaller statue in Taiwan during the colonial period).[10] Kusunoki Masashige was closely associated with Japanese militarism and state Shintoism; he even became the patron saint of the kamikaze pilots during World War II. In general, the definition and promotion of the Shinto religion were an important part of nation-building by the Meiji government; in fact, it has been argued that Shintoism was largely an "invented tradition" of the modern Japanese state.[11] Helen Hardacre writes:

> In this era [1905–30], popular religious life became profoundly influenced by the state's relation with Shintō. The Russo-Japanese War [1904–5] produced many apotheosized "glorious war dead," and the death of so many in war, followed by their public worship, both at the Yasukuni Shrine and in its prefectural branches, the Nation Protecting Shrines, brought state-sponsored shrine rites into popular consciousness in a new and deeper way.[12]

This is the same era during which most of the shrines in Taiwan were built and their horses installed, and the following period (1930–45) was characterized by an even more intense form of military nationalism. As Hardacre says, the Shinto shrines in the colonies "were used to promote patriotism, and they became symbolic emblems of the subjection of the colonized territories."[13]

In the case of Taiwan, the imperial/military nature of its Shinto shrines is overdetermined by their specific origins. The island's two major imperial shrines (*kanpeisha*) were both dedicated to the imperial prince Kitashirakawa Yoshihisa, who died in Tainan, October 1895, leading the initial military occupation of the island. And like Kusunoki Masashige, Kitashirakawa's military career was commemorated in Tokyo with a statue depicting him riding a mount posed exactly like the Taiwan *shimme*.[14] Writing in 1935, Richard Ponsonby Fane begins his biography of the prince:

> Many men have started as soldiers and ended as priests, and in the middle ages, it was by no means uncommon, both in the East and in the West, to combine the two roles, but it is given to few to start as a priest, and finish as a distinguished General, as did the late Prince Kitashirakawa.[15]

The prince-general became the earliest and most important of the war dead worshiped at the Taiwan shrines. The first shrine on the island, just north of Taipei, the large Taiwan Shinto Shrine (Taiwan Jinja), was constructed in 1901 specifically to enshrine Kitashirakawa's spirit. Although the other *kanpeisha* in Tainan did not attain official status until the mid-1920s, this one began as a memorial for Kitashirakawa, established in 1902 at the site of his death, and functioned as an important early homage to him.[16] Many other shrines in Taiwan extended this worship of Kitashirakawa and/or the Japanese military in general, including the well-known Kenkō Shrine in Taipei, to which I will return in a moment. From these associations, the mounted military officer became an iconic symbol of the colonial occupation of Taiwan, as seen in various illustrations and depictions of the island, such as the 1905 postcard commemorating the Taiwan Shrine.[17] The prominence of Prince Kitashirakawa in Taiwan Shinto worship helps explain the use of this type of bronze military horse as *shimme* on the island and, by extension, in other parts of the colonial empire. As mounts designated for spirits, the *shimme* are presented to the *kami* without military tack, girded only by a ceremonial cloth.[18]

Crests

Along with their general military bearing, the bronze horses in Taiwan also all displayed Japanese crests on the girdle wrapping their torsos. These crests, in their different present-day conditions, offer us a site where we can explore the cultural production and transformations of the horses. The specific sources and representations of the crests are complicated, although they generally fall into two possible configurations: as a form of shrine crest or the more commonly known family crest (*kamon*), which can become associated with the shrine through donorship or some other agency. We apparently have both types of crests on the island, although the former is certainly more widely used.

Two of the most important temples in the Taipei area had very specific and distinctive shrine crests. Because of its direct association with the imperial family through Prince Kitashirakawa, the Taiwan Shrine used variations of the imperial, sixteen-petal chrysanthemum crest: the shrine's most common crest was the fourteen-petal chrysanthemum with a stylized *tai* character incorporated at its center, although one source displays the full imperial chrysanthemum crest of sixteen petals, also with the stylized *tai* character.[19] The graphic configuration of these crests (chrysanthemum petals surrounding the *tai*) represents the imperial-colonial condition of the shrine, a location where the imperial homeland incorporates the colony but keeps it separate.

The second shrine crest for which we have clear evidence is that of the Kenkō Shrine located in Taipei's Botanical Garden, which was established to enshrine military and civilian officials who died in service to the state. Shrine records from 1928, the year of its completion, list 15,354 enshrined individuals with information about their origins, positions, and the circumstances of their deaths.[20] In 1936 Richard Posonby Fane reported that of the 16,805 people enshrined at that time, 13,185 were Japanese, 3,339 Taiwanese, and 281 aborigines.[21] Clearly the nature of this shrine was far more civilian and local than the Taiwan Shrine, although the imperial is still present. Ponsonby Fane also described the peculiar representational form of the shrine:

> No one passing in front of Kenkō Jinja would suppose it to be a shrine, though the presence of many *tōrō* and a gateway, reminiscent of a *torii*, would give the impression that it was some place of worship. But for the absence of minarets it resembles somewhat a mosque. . . . It was argued that it was not an ordinary shrine [in] that the worshippers would not all of them be Japanese, and that they would not necessarily be believers in Shinto doctrines, and that, therefore, a combination of different styles would be fitting. The interior of the *Go-Honden*, alone, is in accordance with Shinto Canons. I cannot say that I personally admire the result, but there is undoubtedly something to be said for introducing a Chinese, or perhaps I should say a Taiwanese, element.[22]

7.3 Postcard of Kenkō Shrine with crest seal, 1928. Source: *Jianzheng Taiwan zongdufu*, vol. 2, 104.

The crest chosen for this unusually designed shrine was also an intentional mixture of references to both colonial rulers and their subjects. The official shrine record explains the origins of this crest:

> The decision to give this shrine for the war dead the name Kenkō Shrine [Established Merit Shrine] was derived from the nature of works performed by the enshrined spirits, as was announced in a public notice by the Sōtokufu on January 12, 1928. The crest of the shrine is a Sacred Mirror [Yata no Kagami] within which is inscribed a pair of facing phoenixes [*hōō*], with the character *tai* centered above them. The Sacred Mirror expresses the spirit of our great nation, while for people of this island the phoenix is considered their most auspicious bird. Moreover, the *tai* character clearly refers to Taiwan.[23]

A vivid depiction of this unusual shrine building and crest is found on postcards commemorating the building's construction, dated July 14, 1928 (fig. 7.3).[24] The origins and representations of these two important shrine crests, although very different from each other, are parallel in their motivations: both self-consciously seek to represent the merged imperial and colonial conditions of their respective shrines.

The second form of shrine crests, those that use an adopted family crest, is a more ambiguous representational medium. In Taiwan, this ambiguity is compounded by the lack of detailed records. In Japan, the patron family crest (*patoron no kamon*) becomes the shrine's by association with the good services and donations provided through the patronage of a family or clan. For example, the Oda family crest, *goka ni toka* (Chinese blossom within five melon slices), is used along with the imperial crest for the famous Yasaka shrine in the Gion district of Kyoto. This is presumably the same process by which family crests would have become associated with the shrines, and their horses, in Taiwan.

Contemporaneous materials in Taiwan that record the gift of the *shimme* to temples give us some insight into the sources that may have led to this type of family-cum-shrine crests. In addition to the gifts given to the shrines by the imperial family and government officials (largely ceremonial materials such as swords, official garments from imperial members, planted trees, and the like), donations from individuals and organizations were also a common form of devotional and civic practice: these typically were stone lanterns, stone dogs or lions, and other statuary. In most shrine records, there is a separate list of gifts made of metal, and that is where we find information on the *shimme*. For example, the Taizhong horses were a 1928 donation from the Taizhong Architectural Contractors Union (Taichū Mokkuto Ukeo Kumiai).[25] We have a similar donation recorded for the Taiwan Shrine, this time in 1922 from the Taipei Contractors' Union (Taihoku Ukeo Kumiai).[26] For these gifts, one supposes professional organizations would have used the shrine crest, since there is no evidence that they had their own crests. As we have seen, shrine donations from individuals and families could very well have come with family crests. For example, in 1926, three individuals—Sasaki Noritsuna, Ochi Toraichi, and Sumiyoshi Hidematsu—donated a horse to the Tainan shrine; at the same time there was a similar donation to the Taiwan Shrine from two other individuals—Iwahashi Tei and Furuya Seisaburō.[27] In both of these cases, the family crest of the donors might have been used.

Returning to the residual physical evidence, I believe that there are perhaps two crests that have these patronage origins. The first is on the horse in Taipei Park; the defaced version of the *sakura*, a known, albeit relatively rare, family crest. However, the embedded stylized *tai* character suggests that the *sakura* here perhaps is being used as a nationalist symbol of Japan;

7.4 Bronze Horse at restored Taoyuan Shinto Shrine with detail of partially effaced crest, 2003

if true, this would be another representation of the dual condition of shrines on the island. The other example, also somewhat defaced, is found on a single horse in the restored Taoyuan (Tōgen) shrine (fig. 7.4). Although the effacement makes identification problematic, it appears to be the common crest of a *kikuyu* (bellflower) in some sort of surround. The Taoyuan crest is the only example found thus far that does not include the stylized Sōtokufu *tai*, and it appears to be a pure family crest. However, from the photographic record, we know that the Shinchiku/Xinzhu horses, which were donated to the shrine by Shida Yosaburō (1921), also carried a crest with no stylized *tai*; this appears to be a family crest of gingko leaves in a surround. Note that the lanterns next to the horses display the common bellflower family crest (see fig. 7.2).[28]

As an aside, it is interesting that the fiberglass horses at the Zhongxun temple in Muzha, which seem to have been molded directly from Japanese-era bronze horses, reproduce this patronage context. The brightly colored saddles and other tack that have been added to the Zhongxun temple horses align them with the martial origins of the temple's principal deity, Baoyi Daifu,[29] but on these saddles, which replace the girdle and crest of the Japanese *shimme*, are the names of two temple patrons and donors: Ke Jintie and Wu Jiawu. Given that these horses are said to be from the 1950s, it is likely that the patrons would have been familiar with the Shinto donational practices of a slightly earlier time, reproducing them here in a different religious context.[30]

The Shrine and the Taiwanese Community

The blatant role that state-sponsored Shinto played in the imposition of colonial rule in Taiwan is seen in many manifestations. This is especially evident when Shinto became wedded to the *kōminka* policy of the final war years, during which Taiwanese native religious practices were suppressed in favor of the promotion of Shinto in Chinese communities, as they desperately sought to "make Japan and Taiwan as one."[31] Yet, even in the earlier periods of colonial rule, the integration of Shinto into Taiwanese society, particularly elite society, was substantial. For example, there are records of shrine visitors, analyzed by ethnicity, for both the Taiwan Shrine and the Kenkō Shrine: for the former, in 1910 there were 52,917 Japanese (Naichijin) visitors and 13,745 Taiwanese (Hontōjin) visitors, and in 1920 the ratio at this shrine was 85,770 Japanese to 42,047 Taiwanese; for the Kenkō Shrine, the 1930 ratio was 118,907 Japanese to 63,886 Taiwanese.[32] As Chen Jinchuan's study of the function of the Yilan shrine in the lives of Taiwanese shows, the nature of these visits could differ greatly, ranging from religious practice, civic/school visits, and secular ceremonies (such as weddings) to very casual tourism. Clearly, the shrines were not just spaces for the native Japanese; that is to say, not only were the Taiwanese familiar with these shrines in general but a significant body of the local population was also familiar with the details of specific sites.

In the end, the shrines were still spaces of exclusion. Although the Taiwanese were allowed (sometimes forced) to visit and participate, they were never able to "be Japanese" in these or other colonial spaces; the Taiwanese were always partitioned off from the Japanese core. They were like the stylized *tai* surrounded by the Japanese crest: contained within the Japanese sphere, but not of it.

When the Chinese Nationalist government arrived on the island after years of devastating and humiliating warfare with the Japanese on the mainland, they abhorred these icons of Japanese nationalism. Throughout the late 1940s and early 1950s, the new government dismantled or converted the Shinto shrines on the island. The authorities deemed the shrines, along with military and civil statuary, as too Japanese to be enfolded into their new plans for the island. The brochure for the recently restored Taoyuan/Tōgen Shinto shrine explains:

> When the Nationalist government came to Taiwan, because of its opposition to the Japanese, it instituted a policy in the 1950s to eliminate completely the architecture and symbols left behind by Japan. From the capital on down to the villages, it consciously expunged all the Shinto shrines and related materials. . . . The only thing it left to be used were the *wudedian* [*butokuden*, the Japanese martial arts halls] that were used by the police and military or for shrines for Chinese martyrs. Because it was not easy to convert the Shinto shrines to secular [*siren*, or private] use, they were dismantled or left to collapse in the wind and rain.[33]

The Nationalist agenda of cultural purification, meant to rid the island of the most Japanese of all cultural icons, the Shinto shrine, largely succeeded. But, given the opportunity, a *shimme* was very well suited to resist the "wind and rain" of that policy. It could remain available, albeit always in some condition of displacement, as a sign of the former shrine, waiting another reading.

Effacements

But who decided to give these various horses an opportunity to resist those Nationalist forces? Who saved them from being destroyed along with the shrines and other bronze statuary from the Japanese period? The decision to do so must have been a conscious act with its own complicated, perhaps even dangerous, implications. Was this act of preservation a statement of some subversive cultural agenda, or was it a more benign act of historic conservation, akin to the Japanese colonial government's relocation of the Qing memorial arches to the park? The pervasive effacement of the crests on the horses suggests something in between.

Although there are different forms of effacement, clearly the very *need* for erasure immediately marks this act of preservation as significantly different from an act of historical conservation.[34] In the case of the Qing arches, the Japanese colonial powers held, at the least, a nonantagonistic view of the materials. Their decision seems to have been motivated by relatively positive, albeit self-serving, policy: preservation of important symbolic materials of Chinese elite culture on the island in the service of trying to recruit

7.5 Bronze horse at Hualian Martyrs Shrine with crest covered with Nationalist insignia, 2006

that elite class to the colonialist cause. There was a certain amount of displacement in the preservation of the arches, but their provenance and role in the old society was also acknowledged (similar to the discarded Chiang Kai-shek statues placed in the sculpture park). In contrast, the Nationalist policy toward Japanese materials was defined by aggression and contempt, and those who were responsible for the erasure of the horse crests were motivated by that policy, whether they approved of it or not.

Note that it was the crest not the horse per se that attracted this attention. The horse could quite easily be assimilated into the ranks of other European-style colonial objects, but the crest was the "label" that established its Japaneseness: it placed the object in the context of its original symbolic value. Two horses display vivid examples of this postwar sensitivity toward the Japanese crest. In these cases, the crest is not only removed but replaced by a new symbol of political authority: the Nationalist Party insignia (the white sunburst on a blue background). In the example from Taizhong, the crest is cut away and the insignia painted inside the resulting lacuna; in the example from Hualian, the crest is covered with a metal plate that bears a three-dimensional, painted party insignia (fig. 7.5). Although other forms of effacement were not as blatantly political as this, they all expressed a similar ideology: the necessary erasure of the Japanese value of the horse.

Yet, in the case of several horses, including the one in Taipei Park, the crest was only partially effaced, leaving enough of the design to be read by anyone familiar with the symbols of Japanese culture and colonization; this would certainly have included a large segment of the Taiwanese elite citizenry in the early postwar period. Could this have been intentional, or was it merely the result of carelessness or inattention? Or could it be merely a sign of contempt? Given the extreme measures taken in other effacements and the highly visible location (and probably re-location) of this horse in downtown Taipei, should we not assume intent and agency here? In any event, it is clear that the ideological work of effacement was subverted, intentionally or not, when readable traces were allowed to remain. With the Taipei horse, the subversion worked. Standing in the shadows of major institutions of Nationalist authority, the horse continued to announce its cultural origins to those who could read the still-visible crest. Over time, the subversive strength of the partial erasure must have slowly dissipated as the general population became unfamiliar with Japanese heraldry. With that, the displacement of the horse increased in intensity, as it evolved into a handsome object associated with a day at the park, and little more.[35] In fact, I had one young woman tell me that as a child she played on the horse, thinking that the design was a plum blossom: the national flower of the Republic of China!

Under the current political-cultural climate, we might anticipate the original symbolic value of the horse (its association with colonial Shinto), to be reinstated by a figurative rewriting of the effaced design. Such an affirmation of Taiwan's colonial experience would correspond well with other acts of cultural nostalgia that have occurred throughout the city in recent years, including the rehabilitation of colonial and Japanese architecture whereby intervening coverings, interpretations, and reuse of those structures are stripped away. Indeed, recoveries of this sort have already occurred.

Recoveries

The first recovery was the rehabilitation of the Shinto shrine in Taoyuan, which includes the bronze horse with a defaced family crest. In 1946 the original shrine was converted into a shrine for Chinese martyrs (*zhonglieci*), although its architecture apparently remained largely unchanged. Plans in 1985 to demolish the shrine buildings met with opposition from people in the architectural community who "recognized that this exquisite cultural property should be preserved."[36] In the following two years, the shrine was restored to its original condition and is now a celebrated architectural monument. How this Japanese shrine remained relatively intact for such a long time through the political "wind and rain" is an intriguing question; the shrine brochure calls its preservation a "miracle" (*qiji*). One assumes that its relative distance from the gaze of the central government was partly responsible. And we should note that Fu Chaoqing's remark above intends to transform the site into a relatively neutral "cultural property," quite divorced from the Shinto ideology that constructed it. At the site itself, almost no explanatory materials were incorporated into the restoration: commentary is provided by a caretaker and a small handmade brochure. In that sense, this is a recovery of a very partial kind.

At two other sites, in Xinying and Yilan, the level of recovery is more complete and more complicated. Along with the original Japanese horses, each site features recent reproductions, combining acknowledgment of the horse's provenance with its aestheticization. In each case, the original horse is marked by another form of displacement, moving it into a position or location that transforms it into a form of secular art or historic object. In Xinying the original horse has also been placed in a park without signage or explanation, again associated within a playground area (and used as an incidental hobby horse). In Yilan, the original horse stands in the courtyard of the Wenchang temple, paired with a Chinese unicorn (*qilin*) and labeled with the aphorism *ma dao chenggong* ("instant success," or, literally, "a horse reaches achievement").

To some extent, this recontexualization of the original horses extends to the reproductions as well. In Xinying, the two replicas are labeled in classical Chinese as Steeds of Xinying (Xinying zhi Ji): *ji* (steed) is a classical Chinese term closely associated with a passage from the Confucian *Analects*. Taking this aestheticization a step further, the Xinying reproductions inspired a new public monument of "eight stallions" (*bajun*) in a small park facing the large Carrefour Department Store on the edge of town.[37] This large monument is composed of eight bronze horses of approximately the same size and style as those found in the Shinto shrine, but here they cavort wildly in a fountain, to a somewhat bizarre effect. The Yilan replica has a complicated overlay of public disclosure that I will discuss below, but it has also been discussed in purely artistic terms, by both the artist Lin Zhengren and the scholar Chen Yijun. They celebrate the horse as an example of European-style realist art quite foreign to Taiwanese artistic practices, and they place the replica in the context of public art in Yilan.[38] In Yilan, this treatment takes an extreme form at the site where the new horse stands: using pieces of broken and discarded materials from the original shrine, along with sections of the recently cast horse, the artist constructed an "installation" (*zhuangzhi yishu*) embedded in the ground around the horse.[39] These forms of aestheticization are, of course, also ideological acts: the object is stripped of its original political content, removing it from both its Japanese associations and the discourse of colonization and militarization that produced it.

Strategies to transform the horses into cultural objects or works of "conceptual sculpture" (*gainian diaosu*) are complicated by a countervailing drive to restore them to their historic context, that is, to reverse their cultural displacement, now that this is allowed. Although the original horse in Xinying stands alone and unlabeled, there are full explanatory plaques accompanying its two replicas. Both explain the provenance of the horse; one of the plaques reads:

> On this site in 1921, where originally stood the Japanese Shinto shrine, two bronze horses were installed, one of which was unfortunately later lost. Because of the striking and elegant bearing of this horse, people took special care of it. Shortly after Retrocession [1945] the shrine was converted into the Sun Yatsen Park, and a Chinese Martyrs' Shrine was established within it. Still, the bronze horse stood in its original location, accompanying the spirits of the fallen martyrs. The site became a popular tourist attraction. When later the Martyr's Shrine was moved to Hutoupi and in its place was built the Provincial Xinying Hospital, the horse disappeared in the confusion. Thus, the people of Xinying lost what they so loved. Hoping to recover the glory of these antiquities and thereby bring back fond memories of our youth, we took up the challenge and exerted ourselves to search for them. As we had hoped, the missing horse was fortunately found and replicas were made of it. The original horse was placed in the square facing First [Market?—character obscured], while the replica was placed here at its original location, offered to our citizens so they might reminisce as they enjoy their visit here.
>
> Respectfully,
> Yan Jibin, Mayor, June 1990

Although the inscription does indeed recall the origins of the horse, those thoughts are quickly obscured by nostalgic reflections on the horse as a cultural, if not artistic, object. In the official history of Xinying, this type of recollection is cast in even more innocent tones, recalling how the older generation remembers the horse so fondly: "taking its picture or climbing onto its back is a memory almost everyone shares. Because of this, the horse is practically a spiritual symbol of Xinying."[40] Such refractive nostalgia reduces the Japanese colonial and military provenance of the horse, masking its signs of religious persuasion and colonial oppression. This tension between the aestheticization and contextualization of the horse is even stronger at the Yilan site.

What is most remarkable about the original Yilan horse at the Wenchang temple is that its crest and manufacturer's name remain completely intact: a twelve-petal chrysanthemum with the stylized *tai* at the center, along with a cast inscription naming the Kubota Company of Hiroshima as its manufacturer (the side with the manufacturer's name is turned toward the wall, away from view). These are certainly glaring signs of its Japanese origins that we would expect to have been expunged in the early postwar period. But this horse was protected by its placement inside a cultural institution, shielded from the interference of postwar politics. It was both out of sight and restructured as part of the temple architecture. In fact, when government authorities recently wanted to reclaim the horse and move it to the park, temple elders refused to give it up, resulting in the need for a replica.[41] The replica faithfully reproduces the original, including its crest and manufacture's name, and these are now openly visible (fig. 7.6).

The process of recovery in Yilan was also publicly announced in a plaque on the base of the replica:

In 1918 the Japanese built a Shinto shrine at this location for the worship of the Sun Goddess, creator of the world. Three or four years after the establishment of the shrine, a bronze horse was installed to serve as a mount for the gods. Along with bronze lions and stone lanterns, the horse stood at the foot of the staircase, projecting an extremely stern and solemn air. After the war in late 1945, the national central government had come to Taiwan, but things were still in turmoil throughout the island; cultural objects [*wenwu*] that were left behind by the Japanese were all destroyed. However, some thoughtful person [*youxin renshi*] could not stand to have this horse meet such a fate, so it was moved and placed in the Wenchang

7.6 Replica of Yilan horse with details of crest and manufacturer information, 2005

temple, where it remains to this day. According to a local legend, because
the horse was no longer cared for after Retrocession [1945], it escaped and
damaged field crops and village farms. These stories were so realistic that
it made it [the horse] even more mysterious. In 1958, the Shinto Shrine
was converted into the Shrine for Chinese Martyrs of Yilan. The structure
of the site remained as before, but the horse was missing; only the inscription plaque remained. Now with the completion of the construction of
Yuanshan Park, a reproduction of the bronze horse has been placed upon
its original site; here we can nearly espy the scene of former times, but the
vicissitudes of life are hard to describe.[42]

    August 1997

The writing of this text and the act that it so publicly documents could have
occurred only in a mature phase of the post–martial law period, which
allowed for this straightforward act of cultural recovery and its implicit
praise for the subversive preservation of the original horse by some "thoughtful person." The explicit nature of this narrative of restoration stands in contrast to that of the earlier restorations in Taoyuan and Xinying. We should
note, however, the slight hesitancy in that enigmatic closing phrase, "but the
vicissitudes of life are hard to describe" (*er shishi cangsang ze nanyan yi*),

which avoids specific mention of either the colonial or the neocolonial politics of oppression, so that the aesthetic condition of the horse (as a "cultural object") is foregrounded and its political conditions slightly masked.

Extreme Displacement

Although the horse in Taipei Park has gone unnoticed in the general literature and official publications,[43] it has recently caught the attention of a young man who writes a travel blog about Taiwan. In his introduction to the history of the park and its materials, he argues for the Shinto origins of the horse, although he remains perplexed over its provenance:

> At first I supposed it came from the Taiwan Shrine, but the crest for the Taiwan Shrine is that of the chrysanthemum, and the crest on this horse is the cherry blossom. If the cherry blossom crest might also be used for that shrine, then my speculation could hold true. But I am unclear if the Taiwan Shrine could have other crests. Perhaps the horse is from another shrine. The Jiangong (Kenkō) Shrine? Or the Huguo (Gokoku) Shrine? But I don't know the crests for these shrines, and there is no way to establish what they were.[44]

Later in the entry, he wonders whether the horse could have been originally situated in the park and whether it perhaps once had a rider. (In the end, he doubts both of those speculations.) He closes by asking, "Who can solve the mystery of this bronze horse?"

Here I would like to investigate that mystery: specifically when, how, and why the horse might have come to this location in Taipei Park. Although these questions can be answered only speculatively, at best, I hope that by addressing them, we can explore the ideology and agency of the horse's extreme displacement. Judging from the above evidence, the horse clearly must have come from a Shinto shrine or similar site, and one would assume its original location to have been in the park's vicinity, there being no such shrine in the park itself (as there was in Taizhong Park, for example). As the blogger suggested, the two shrines most likely to be sources for this horse are the Taiwan Shrine north of the city and the Kenkō Shrine in the Botanical Garden south of the park. In fact, there was a *third* Shinto shrine just a few blocks west of the park, in the West Gate district: the Taihoku Inari (Harvest) Shrine, established in 1911. All three of these shrines deserve consideration as possible sites for the original emplacement of this horse.

As for the Inari Shrine, there is little documentary or photographic evidence with which to work. We know that the shrine was set up inside the first municipal public market, which was constructed in the West Gate area in 1908. It was not an important temple, however: Ponsonby Fane tells us that in 1936 it was still a *mukakusha* (unranked shrine) of only 179 *tsubo* (approximately six thousand square feet); it became a *gōsha* (district shrine) in 1937.[45] A photograph depicts it as very modest, with limited statuary.[46] It seems unlikely that such a minor shrine would be the site for a large bronze horse.[47] As for the belatedly constructed Gokufu (1942), I know of no physical, documentary, or photographic evidence of its holdings (but see note 60).

We do know that the two major shrines in the Taipei area did have bronze horses. Although there is no photographic record of the horse or horses at the Kenkō Shrine, there is a newspaper notice of the installation of a single horse on June 22, 1937.[48] Moreover, a horse of remarkable condition still exists that must have come from the site and *is* associated with the park; this horse is held by the park's National Taiwan Museum, stored in its Xindian warehouse.[49] Although severely damaged, the horse in storage sports a Phoenix crest that is completely intact and is identical to the one for the Kenkō Shrine discussed above. Clearly, this is not the mate to the horse standing in the park—but could there have been two horses at the Kenkō Shrine, one with the shrine crest and one with a *sakura* crest? And could the two horses then have come into the museum's possession together, with the damaged one put into storage while the other one was placed in the park? This could very well be, but, unfortunately, the official record for the Kenkō Shrine does not contain a materials list, such as are in the records for the Taiwan, Taizhong, and Tainan shrines, and I have found no further evidence in the media of a second horse.

What about the Taiwan Shrine? This appears the most likely source for two reasons. First, there is an argument by analogy: the two bronze oxen that currently flank the north entrance of Taipei Park (in front of the museum) were moved from the Taiwan Shrine after the war, and the inscriptions on their torsos were effaced in a fashion very similar to the method used to remove the crest of the horse in the park.[50] Second, as mentioned above, there were two horses donated to the shrine: one by the Taipei Contractors' Union in 1922 and another by Iwahashi Tei and Furuya Seisaburō in 1926.[51] Given the provenance of these horses, it appears that either one could have sported the *sakura* crest. I was very excited to locate two newspaper accounts of these events, with photographs, as well as another incidental photograph of these two horses flanking the main entrance to the shrine.[52] The horse of the 1922 account, which stood to the left of the entrance, is a statue of a different style than the horses we have discussed (it stands at rest with all four feet on the ground). The one in the 1926 article, however, is the same style as the horse in the park. Upon detailed inspection, it is evident that although the horses are very similar, this one is not the same as the horse in the park: the clearest difference is that the horse in the park has its head turned slightly to its left, while the one in the photograph has its head turned to its right. Could there have been a third horse at Taiwan Shrine? The records for the shrine are particularly detailed, yet, in the last extant record (1935), it lists only these two horses among its donations.[53]

Finally, let's consider the blogger's not quite rhetorical question: "Could this horse have originally been in the park?" He notes that "after researching Japanese period maps of New Park, I discovered that there was a statue of the governor-general, but the park had no horse within it. And if one were to suggest that this horse was placed in the park as individual ornament [not associated with a shrine], then it should not have had a *sakura* crest on its torso."

Although I am not certain that his last statement is true, he is correct that there is no record (written, cartographic, or photographic) of a horse in the park. I do not find that unusual for the maps, but it seems that there should be something in the photographic record and media because the park was extensively photographed and reported on—how could the 1935 Exposition literature not include such evidence? Although the park was not the site of a Shinto shrine where the horse might have stood, there was in fact a Tenmangū shrine dating from 1931 in the park (these shrines are dedicated to the patron saint of study and calligraphy, Sugawara no Michizane). Ponsonby Fane describes it as "a small Temmangū-*sha*, in the south-east angle of the Shinkōyen [New Park]."[54] Ponsonby Fane was apparently slightly confused in his directions, however, for in the 1935 panoramic map of the city discussed in chapter 1, the Tenmangū temple is clearly marked in the south*west* corner of the park near the current playground area.[55] This Temmangū was not classified as a Shinto shrine, however, just as a shrine (*sha*).[56] Could the horse have been associated with this sort of shrine? Or could it have been in the park, not associated with any shrine? We do have some evidence that bronze horses were associated with lesser shrines. For example, there was a horse very much like the one in the park that was associated with the shrine in Hokutō (Beitou), established in 1930, about the same time as the Tenmangū; perhaps not coincidentally, this shrine also was located inside a public park.[57]

In fact, He Xunyao, who came to Taiwan in 1946 and worked at the Taiwan Provincial Museum, reports that there was a horse located next to the museum that was damaged by U.S. bombing at the end of the war and moved into the museum basement; he identified this as the horse currently held in storage.[58] This account cannot be entirely accurate, however (and one must remember that Mr. He had heard this from others and not actually seen the horse in situ).[59] There are two reasons for doubt. First, the site where He Xunyao understood that the horse had been located (where the statue of Confucius currently stands) was occupied by the statue of the first chairman of the Bank of Taiwan, Yagyū Kazuyoshi (see chapter 6). And second, the damaged horse currently held by the museum surely came from the Kenkō Shrine, given the nature of its crest.

Nonetheless, He Xunyao's account suggests that there may have been a horse in the park, at least at the end of the colonial period. If so, two possible ways to account for this come to mind. First, it could have been originally associated with the Tenmangū after 1935, and, if so, the horse would have been located very near to where it now stands. Or it could have been moved from the Kenkō Shrine along with the other horse, but installed in the park instead of going into storage, perhaps first in the stone alcove replacing Yagyū Kazuyoshi, then later in its current setting (the Confucius statue was installed in the alcove in 1976). The fact that the current base for the horse is a not a Japanese-era one (these are of a uniform type) and contemporary in design suggests the latter.

In the early postwar period, the Taiwan colonial experience was viewed by Nationalist authorities as a stigma to be eliminated and replaced with new symbolism, like the crests of the Taizhong and Hualian horses. In the post–martial law period, with cultural power shifting more to the Taiwanese majority, the colonial experience is being recast in a positive light and used to distance Taiwan from two cultural hegemonies: the martial law period and the People's Republic of China's designs for the island. The treatment of these horses and their shrines, from the early years of Japanese colonialism to the post–martial law period, marks them as sites where the politics of cultural displacement are performed. In this chapter, I have tried to move that cultural process one step further by recovering an earlier cultural context for the horse in Taipei Park, but the mystery remains—at least for now.[60]

Postface

THEORETICAL CONSIDERATIONS

Over the last ten years I have wandered Taipei City, sometimes purposefully in search of information related to this research, sometimes merely in search of noodles or a newspaper. In that wandering I have passed by and through a wide variety of built environments: shoddy and chic, informal and formal, vernacular and international, neoclassical and postmodern, hegemonic and resistant, anonymous and over-inscribed. And I have become increasingly aware that each place has a history, a story of contingencies and changes, layers of production and construction, often reaching back through the decades and centuries, that informed its contemporary condition. To understand those places, I also had to wander through the historic and academic materials that informed their stories, materials related both to Taiwan and to broader cultural conditions. I needed to understand not only aboriginal settlement patterns in Taipei basin but also the culture of world exhibitions, not only the workings of Japanese colonialism but also the history of cartography, not only the cult of Chiang Kai-shek but also the development of public statuary in Europe and Japan. This study is about the intersection of those two wanderings, one pedestrian and one intellectual.

As this project approached its later phases, a working title surfaced, awkwardly agglutinative but relatively well formed: "Signs of Displacement:

Representations of Cultural Space in Colonial and Postcolonial Taipei City."
Fortunately, the publisher helped craft a more graceful title; yet, in many
ways that old working title embodies the contours, intellectual and structural, that inform the current work. To provide a theoretical introduction
and rationale for this study, I propose to parse that earlier title into its con-
stituent key terms, assigning each an initial meaning: the title as a sign.

Signs

The sign is the focus of semiotic studies at all levels, from the dance of bees
to art criticism. It is the molecular unit of meaning: the process by which the
signifier is joined with the signified, linking the arbitrary and material form
to its biological, social, or cultural meaning. Language is not only the core
human semiotic system, it is also the heuristic model for all other semiosis,
human and nonhuman—the system of meaning that describes all others.

The "sign" and the "city" have had a long relationship, emerging from
the urban semiotics of the 1960s and 1970s and finding prominence in
Gottdiener and Lagopoulos's collection of essays, *The City and the Sign*. In
their introductory remarks, they argue that the city is not a true text, but
rather a "pseudo text," because it is produced by semiotic *and* nonsemiotic
processes.[1] The editors are here reflecting studies in which "functionality"
is highlighted as the nonsemiotic nature of the city's built space. Roland
Barthes, on the other hand, argues that the spatiality of the city *is* a "true
text," "an inscription of man in space"; in fact, he says, "the city is a poem."[2]
(Trained as I am in Chinese poetics, that formulation appeals to my sensi-
bilities.) Yet he adds that this textual metaphor should yield elements of the
urban tissue that generate meaning, not some simple "lexicon of significa-
tions"[3]; this he illustrates famously with a discussion of the city centers of
Paris and Tokyo.

For Umberto Eco, architecture is particularly challenging to semiotics
because of the high functionality of built space; it is designed to do, not to
communicate. Thus, he concludes that a code of architecture begins with
denotation, a communication of "the function to be fulfilled," which is its
primary ideology.[4] He illustrates this with a quirky speculation about Stone
Age man and the discovery of a cave, in which "the cave came to denote a
shelter function."[5] Of course, architectural forms are much more than function, especially in the development of their "language" of style. It is the "secondary [cognitive] functions" that are especially open to readings within

cultural codes: for the Stone Age code this might mean, according to Eco, that the cave came to "connote 'family,' or 'group,' 'security,' 'familiar surroundings,' etc."[6] Moreover, as these codes change, so do the object's connotations, even if its function does not; or conversely, the connotations can remain stable even as surrounding codes change. Eco's illustration is that of the Gothic cathedral, whose structure and details have been open to historically mutating codes (Neoplatonic, romantic, and medieval), while its divinity, expressed in its elevation and verticality, remains stable (at least for the faithful), even when surrounded by new architectural codes of the skyscraper, which so diminish the majesty of the church.

Many writers have absorbed these concepts of text and reading, function and communication into their views of the city to such an extent that they become nearly invisible, if nonetheless informing. When Akbar Abbas explores the "space of disappearance" that defines contemporary Hong Kong culture, he offers readings and typologies of its architecture that are entirely semiotic in nature, although far derived from the typologies of which Eco speaks. Even David Harvey's essay on the construction of the Basilica of the Sacred Heart, which is motivated primarily by considerations of historicity and materialist politics, shows an affinity with the architectural semiotics of Eco. This is first manifested in the different readings that the cathedral's space elicits from nineteenth-century French Republicans and their rivals; yet, we might argue that Harvey's own eloquent description of the building with which he opens the essay is also basically a semiotic reading.[7]

Following Pierce and Mitchell, the sign can be classified either as an "icon," where there is semblance in its representation (i.e., the statue); a "symbol," where the meaning is more arbitrarily coded (i.e., the insignia); or an "index," where the representation is captured in the physical presence or residual trace (i.e., the signature or fingerprint).[8] In my discussion, the Taipei city gates are represented as an icon in several cartographic codes, a symbol of various versions of political power (imperial, colonial, and nationalistic), as well as an index of the razed city wall. The distinctions between icon, symbol, and index are often ambiguous and fluid. Photography, which commands a good deal of our attention in the opening chapters, presents a particularly complex condition of representation. The photograph is iconic in the extreme, and it *is* indexical in the sense that the physical presence of its subject has been left in the medium of light and salts; yet, as many have argued, this medium is also produced and read within specific cultural codes and is thus "symbolic."

The early intersection of the photographic image and modern technology aligned photography with the evidential world of science: it was a "proof" of its subject's existence at a specific point in time and space. As the technology became widespread, manipulated, divergent, and theorized, its iconicity and indexical nature were challenged, in part because of what Roland Barthes calls the "connotation procedures" of photography: trick effects, pose, objects, photogenia, syntax, and aestheticism.[9] More importantly, this challenge comes from the power of the surrounding discourse to bring the image into specific significance: to move a photograph from one discursive system to another is to reform the representation of the image. John Tagg and James Ryan both make that argument for the constitutive, nonindexical nature of photography: Tagg describes how the photographs' evidential condition has been manipulated by nineteenth-century institutions of state control for their own purposes, while Ryan explores the photographic construction of the British Empire, where both colonizer and colonized are given "true form" through photography.[10] My understanding is that the tautological index of the photograph (as Barthes says, "a pipe, here, is always and intractably a pipe") and discourse systems in which the photograph is always embedded (whether explicitly present or not) are in a dialogue of signification, a dialogue that is always subject to revision.[11]

I now turn to the most literal sense of the sign: those physical entities that stand throughout the city, declaring street names, suggesting the function of a building, identifying the subject of a statue, and warning against eating on the subway. Since these signs circulate almost entirely in language, they are part of both the most obvious and the subtlest semiotic systems. Like architecture, these signs are grounded in function, and the function *is* denotation—to declare in a very clear voice; yet these signs also embody connotation. In fact, like architecture, connotation/implication may be stronger than denotation/intention in these signs. For example, one thinks of those "spoken signs" on the Taipei subway that announce the stations: in Mandarin, Taiwanese, Hakka, and English. The message from that array of languages enunciated every minute of the day throughout the city is not just an announcement of the next station, but also (and maybe more so) the declaration and instantiation of the linguistic complexity of the island, which was so long suppressed: it says, the subway is a space of our new multiculturalism.[12]

Is it significant that there is no Japanese spoken in the subway announcements, a language of many of the island's tourists? Is this a vestige of Nationalist resistance to all things Japanese? Of course, the Japanese tourist will often be able to *read* the Chinese that streams across the digital signboard. For this study, it is no small matter that the languages of the physical signs of the city were/are primarily Chinese and/or Japanese, which share a certain porous quality at the written level (especially in Meiji-period Japanese) but are deeply divided, even more than the local dialects, at the spoken level. This dual nature has allowed for a certain amount of ideological formation as well as practical exchange. This includes the argument for the inherent affinity of Japanese power in East Asia, with its shared script system (the so-called *dōbun* policy); simultaneously allowing colonized subjects to read the colonizer's signs in their own voices: 臺北市 as "Taipacchi" instead of "Taihokushi." This specific linguistic contingency of multiple dialects and different languages swirling around a shared script also affects the nature of the city's named spaces. The way in which one pronounces 西門町 is an ideological as well as a linguistic choice; in fact, the existence of the character 町 on a map of Taipei is itself a coded spatiality.

Displacement

In her review of the urban anthropology literature, Setha Low notes a series of metaphors that have been used for the city, based on social relations, economics, urban planning and architecture, and religion and culture.[13] From there, she creates a typology of twelve city types. We could easily place Taipei City in a number of these categories; it has already been described as a "world city" and a "global city," although perhaps Low's "contested city" is more fitting.[14] Here I offer another metaphor, "the displaced city."

This study is driven very much by the materiality of the city, especially as that materiality is transformed through time: like David Harvey, I am interested in space and time (but not so much in economics), and like Sharon Zukin, I am interested in "public spaces as places that are physically *there*" (but I am also interested in the place that is not there). When I began this "counting the cats in Zanzibar," I had no detailed plan or theoretical model to pursue, other than the methodology of "close reading" inherited from my literary training. The "texts" that drew my attention were not self-evident, but rather came to me from other scholarship, mundane contingencies, and, no doubt, hidden ideological drives (both social and personal).

First, there was the work related to Taipei and its environs. Early Chinese studies of the city (before the lifting of martial law) tended to focus on the historical conditions of the late Qing period, since this was a politically safe topic and materials were readily available. From these studies, the "wall" emerged as a special space for consideration. In the 1990s, in both scholarship and general reading, attention turned toward the Japanese period and the colonial city, and toward their graphic representations, especially maps and photographs, which were becoming available at the time. I, too, was drawn deeply into those materials. In addition, Roger Selya's sociological investigation of the city, *Taipei*, provided a deep and detailed social science background. Writings about the city during the last decade have been increasingly informed by cultural studies, especially the lineage of Lefebvre, Harvey, and Hayden, and the theoretical model of "contestation." I have come to that work often through studies by young scholars working under the mentorship of Professor C. J. Hsia (Xia Zhujiu) of National Taiwan University.

During the course of this research, a number of heuristic models for reading cultural space in Taipei City suggested themselves (or were suggested by others). Among them were inscription and erasure, text and fragment, pastiche and palimpsest, memory and amnesia, occupation and exile, hegemony and resistance, hybridity and multiculturalism— and undoubtedly there are others. Although I have used and continue to use several of these terms and concepts, another concept emerged that seemed especially useful in "sorting out the structures of significance" in Taipei City: *displacement*.[15] The concept of "displacement" offers an analytical tool that seems to fit particularly well the general spatial conditions of Taipei City. This is not to say that "displacement" can account for all of the dynamics of cultural space in Taipei, nor do I claim that it is the city's unique condition. I would argue, however, that the specific geographic, historical, and cultural contingencies in Taiwan make the island a particularly fertile ground for displacement's genesis. [16] This is similar to the way that specific conditions in Hong Kong made it susceptible to being analyzed as a "space of disappearance" by Akbar Abbas.

The term "displacement" has a wide range of meanings in disciplines such as chemistry, physics, geology, human geography, and Freudian analysis. (It has even been used to describe the post-symbolist poetics of that peculiar China hand, Victor Segalen.[17]) In part, my usage derives from these fields, sometimes in a straightforward manner, other times more metaphorically. First, I speak of various displaced peoples in the history of the island. On one level, this follows the common usage of designating people forced to leave their residencies or homeland and live elsewhere in compromised conditions, as in the encounter between Taiwan's aboriginal peoples and various colonizers, or in the massive influx of Mainlanders to the island in 1949–50. Other human displacements are more sociopolitical than physical, however: such as the displacement of local power centers that occurred in the formulation of the walled city of Taipei. Letty Chen has used the term in these two ways to characterize Taiwanese identity formation:

> The disconnection from native culture that is due to migration (e.g., the 1949 exodus from China to Taiwan) and the imposition of a foreign culture through the fifty-year Japanese colonial rule have created for the different groups of people in Taiwan a serious and complex problem in defining not only their own but also a collective Taiwanese cultural identity. It is a double-edged struggle to overcome *cultural displacement* and authenticate cultural hybridity.[18] (emphasis added)

While the concept of "cultural hybridity" is the central theoretical concern in Chen's essay (and her book), she uses "displacement" exactly as I do in several parts of this study. In my use, however, I have applied this relatively straightforward term far more broadly, encompassing different types of the social displacements long before and after that of Japanese/Nationalist rule; in fact, I would say that "native" (by which Chen means primarily Taiwanese/Min'nan) culture results from and is agent in other important moments of displacement.

The terminology of "neurotic displacement" as a psychological coping mechanism has often been translated into literary and cultural criticism, especially that with a psychoanalytical basis. For example, this is how Carlos Rojas uses the term "libidinal displacement" in his analysis of Tsai Ming-liang's film *Rebels of the Neon God*, which is set in Taipei.[19] Occasionally, I use the term in this explicitly Freudian fashion, such as in discussing family relationships in the film *Eat Drink Man Woman*, but more often I have sought to extend that use beyond individual behavior. I believe certain events in the colonial and postwar periods might also be considered "neurotic displacements" at a more sociological level. The inability of Taiwanese to "become Japanese" may have led to behavior in the elite population that displaced that frustration into the celebration of Chinese literary arts, which were also esteemed and practiced by the Japanese but were more authentically the cultural property of the Taiwanese. This implied that they did not *want* to become Japanese, because being Chinese was *more* East Asian.

My primary model for cultural displacement comes from the materiality of fluid mechanics: a certain volume of liquid is displaced by an object that enters it, such as the hull of a ship, and that becomes the measure of the object. In an argument derived from those physical properties, I speak of one cultural form or phenomenon displacing another in the sense of forcing it out of the center and to the side, where it becomes peripheral but not absent or partial. Thus, the "hull" of the new cultural work moves into the center, but is measured (and even known) from its periphery, where it no longer is. This presence-in-absence makes displacement different from the metaphorical conditions of erasure or amnesia, which have been common models in cultural theory.[20] In that vein, it is arguable that the Nationalist government sought to erase the Japanese experiences from the Taiwan landscape and rewrite them in the Taiwanese consciousness; yet, with the lifting of martial law, those experiences have regained visibility and power. They have returned from their displacement, in my view, not from their disappearance. Moreover, in its completeness and integrity, this form of displacement differs from the conditions of fragment, pastiche, and palimpsest, all of which have also been used to describe the urban cultural landscape—the last of these has been a particularly fecund metaphor for the materiality and meaning of the city.[21]

On occasion I have used each of these metaphors, although I was and am inclined most to "pastiche" to explain the urban landscape of Taiwan. The layered and partial inscriptions/messages found in many physical sites of the city appear not to have been "scraped away" (the meaning of palimpsest), but rather lightly "papered over." Exceptions to that general rule are the conditions of the Japanese and Nationalist insignias investigated in chapter 7. In one way, palimpsests (in their original, nonmetaphorical sense) are a "displacement," in that over time an erased inscription can reappear and is often fully legible; and it is that once-lost *scriptio inferior* that attracts the attention of classical scholars, just as the effaced Japanese insignia attracted my attention.

Extending this understanding of cultural displacement we might argue that while the peripheral position of the displaced cultural material is maintained by the force (symbolic value) of the new material at the center, conversely, the object at the center holds its position against the resistance of the displaced material. Resistance is what "floats the boat." One example of this phenomenon has been discussed by Sue-Ching Jou[22] (although she does not use these terms): the emergence in the 1990s of the new "city center" (*shizhongxin*) in the Eastside (Dongqu), which has come to occupy a central position both politically and economically in the post–martial law period. With the emergence of a new city center, the old government and entertainment centers in the downtown area were pushed aside, but not replaced— they continue to function but have lost social and economic force. Yet, the old areas also continued to apply pressure/resistance against the Eastside, principally in their claim of cultural authenticity in the *bentuhua* (localization) ideology. In the end, conditions in the Eastside led to modifications of the old downtown area, such as the opening of public squares and pedestrian ways for which Eastside is noted; this in turn applied more pressure on the Eastside, keeping it "afloat."

Another condition of cultural displacement that mimics fluid mechanics happens when the center is vacated or weakened; a new displacement will naturally occur in that space. Sometimes this is a reversal of an earlier displacement; that is to say, the once-displaced is often prepared to return to the center. Dynamically, this is like water flowing back into its displaced space as the ship pulls away. This metaphor begins to break down when the center is not reoccupied by what was originally displaced: thus, in my first example, intramural Taipei originally displaced the port settlements of Mengjia and Dadaocheng, but when the downtown weakened, it was replaced by the new Eastside, not by resurgent old areas. Moreover, I would argue that even if it appears that the displacement is reversed (i.e., the water flows back when the ship passes), the object or phenomenon returning to the center is always qualitatively changed by having occupied a peripheral position; it never regains its original condition. In fact, the repositioning is often accompanied by new nomenclature: the Shinto shrine is restored, but as a "cultural object."

One area in which the dynamics of displacement approach those of memory is in the question of agency: in both cases, absence exists only through the agency of consciousness. After all, amnesia is not a phenomenon of pure forgetting but rather a disparity of memories. It is a type of subtle irony in which one knows something is missing but does not know what. Complete memory loss would be self-erasing: the ignorance of ignorance. Similarly, displacement must be somehow visible in order to exhibit its condition. But visible to whom? This question can be manifested in very concrete, mundane forms: for example, in the rotunda of the National Taiwan Museum (Guoli Taiwan Bowuguan) stand two towering Chinese vases that have displaced the statues of Japanese colonial rulers, which were moved into basement storage at the end of the colonial period. This is clearly a cultural displacement for those to whom the displaced objects are visible (through memory, photography, or the curator who actually knows where they are located and can bring them into view). But for those who do not know about the displaced object or who, when seeing it, do not recognize its original condition, there is no absence, there is no displacement—the two vases in their current positions look fine.

These various forms of displacement and recovery often involve practices of nostalgia. Svetlana Boym says that nostalgia is "a sentiment of loss and displacement, but it is also a romance with one's own fantasy." The layers of loss, displacement, and fantasy that are woven into Taiwan's history make its nostalgia particularly complicated. One place where nostalgia, which literally means a longing for a return home, is most obviously manifested in Taiwan is in the desire of postwar Chinese immigrants to return to their continental homes: not under communism but rather under displaced conditions of the Republic of China. This is a type of nostalgia that Boym calls "restorative," which emphasizes the rebuilding of a lost home (*nostos*) and is often associated with rightwing nationalism and its "truth projects."[23] That certainly describes the postwar policies of the Nationalist government. In their case, the rebuilding of that home was transformed into the neoclassical architecture, a type of cultural fantasy, that populated Taipei City during the martial law period. We see an even more fantastical version of this restorative nostalgia with the post–martial law invocations of the lost Republic of Taiwan (Taiwan Minzhuguo), which had barely existed in the first place—in this case, that sentiment is manifested in the display of its "national" flag in the National Taiwan Museum. The other type of nostalgia Boym describes is "reflective," emphasizing the "longing and loss" (*algia*), not the home. She writes: "*Re-flection* suggests new flexibility, not the reestablishment of stasis. The focus here is not on recovery of what is perceived to be an absolute truth but on the meditation on history and passage of time."[24] This sentiment, which can contain irony and humor, is associated more closely with the individual, not the national, narrative, although both narratives can be constructed around similar displacements. We can see this type of reflective nostalgia in the personal essays that fill the *Returning to Sun Yat-sen Hall* (Huidao Zhongshantang) volume.

In recent years Taiwan has displayed a third kind of nostalgia, one that does not want to rebuild a lost home per se but does want to return (or at least to bring attention) to some cultural conditions associated with that time and place. When this nostalgia takes the form of public display then it becomes more politically and ethnically driven, escaping the individual narrative of longing. We see this most clearly in the nearly obsessive recovery and display of cultural materials from the Japanese colonial period. In this case these materials have been stripped of their negative colonial associations and have become emblems of an anti-Nationalist fantasy: a rhetorical return to an imaginary past. I would call this a "refractive nostalgia." Here the intent is neither to restore nor to reflect but to use these memories, as reified in recovered objects, to cast light (focused in its refraction) on contemporary conditions of displacement.

Acts of cultural recovery and the promotion of nostalgia can in effect be mechanisms for making such displacements visible or for sharing that visibility more broadly. This is a form of cultural power related to what Sharon Zukin in *The Culture of Cities* describes as "decisions about what—and who—should be visible [in the city]."[25] My intent is similarly driven: to reveal cultural displacements that have occurred, suggesting the ideological work that both motivated and comes from them; at the same time, I hope to make visible displacements that are happening now, or that might happen in the future—not as prescriptions for or against such displacements, for they are unavoidable, but simply to increase awareness of them. The various phenomena of cultural displacement may be structurally quite similar, but their ideological work is not.

Representations

Ideology (in the sense of those assumptions by which we order reality so as to render it intelligible) remains central to the question of representation in its many forms. In its most obvious application, representation is a conscious use of a semiotic system to construct a cultural product, whether a painting or a mathematical formula, that is meant to stand for another level of reality. This is the form of representation explored in depth by Edward Casey in his *Representing Place* and, closer to home, in Sylvia Lin's *Representing Atrocity in Taiwan*. I, too, have used the materials at hand in this way, especially in the consideration of maps, photography, and statuary. Yet, even in these most mechanical forms of representation, meaning is still culturally produced and is neither wholly controlled nor stable. The meaning of a representation is in a chronic state of change, both synchronically and diachronically, as it passes through different codes and different agents of interpretation.

On occasion, I have discussed representation at a meta-level (that is, the representation of representation), especially when I have engaged exhibitions, publications, and other displays. Exploring sites of public display, one always exposes at least two, and often more, levels of presentation. On the first level is the primary sign, let us say a photograph, with all its necessary complications of denotation and connotation; then there is a re-deployment level, where the photograph is recontextualized in a broader narrative frame. Later this re-presentation can once more be brought forth in yet another context. We can see this multilayered representation in the recent reissuing of materials from the Japanese period, which are now tied closely to the current *bentuhua* rhetoric and strategies of refractive nostalgia. This new representation can occur with overt modifications, such as *huaijiu* (nostalgia) anthologies that gather together the old photographs into new semantic groups. Sometimes, however, the original representational context is left largely intact, such as in the reissue of the 1907 translation of Takekoshi Yosaburō's *Japanese Rule in Formosa,* with its original photographs. This is a facsimile edition with minimal comment, but its ideological underpinnings have radically changed with its reissue, as has its meaning.

Finally, this study is not just a consideration of different types of representation; it is also itself essentially representational. First are the graphic materials I have embedded in the narrative to illustrate my arguments, including my own photographs. In addition, I have sought to place different forms of representations in a new semiotic structure: in this case, the spatiality of Taipei City. Thus, maps are viewed not just as representations of urban space produced by cartography's specific conventions, but also as ideological manifestations of cultural power; in this sense, the maps are both iconic and symbolic. Beyond that reading of cartography, which follows closely the work of Norman Thrower and others, I have also often sought to draw the maps into the central rationale of this study through the dynamics of displacement. At certain times, I have sought to engage urban space directly in my own representational terms without the filter of earlier forms, verging more toward ethnography. My discussion of the plaza in front of Sun Yat-sen Hall (Zhongshantang) as a space of occupation is an attempt to "represent" my personal experience in the space.

In these different levels of consideration, I have paid little explicit attention to that other important area of representation, governmental forms and identity politics. In part, this is practical; these are huge topics that have been amply explored by others, such as Shelly Rigger and Melissa Brown.

Moreover, I am principally interested in sites where ideology is embedded in the mundane world and ironic in nature. This is not to say, however, that representational politics do not inform the sites I consider here; the interweaving of these different forms of representation is in fact a critical part of production and construction of space in the city. It is my goal to consider cultural space as both informed by and producing these social conditions, but I remain attached to the material world.

Cultural Space

Since all humanly known space is essentially culturally (or socially) produced and constructed (this probably includes even outer space and nano space), the term "cultural space" is perhaps redundant. In various studies, other analysts have used the terms "social space," "public space," and "symbolic space," and Edward Soja claimed "space" alone as a critical term.[26] I use those terms, but more often "cultural space," by which I here mean urban sites (and their representations), where particularly large amounts of symbolic value have accrued over time. These spaces can be formal and elite, such as museums and exhibitions, or casual and mundane, such as subway stations and city streets. In several instances, these sites are more objects than spaces (this is especially so for the civic statuary that I discuss in chapter 6); still, the objects typically occupy or create space around them, often public space, although such sites might be better called "cultural emplacements."

Sharon Zukin's various essays on specific sites in North America (city parks, regional museums, and local restaurants) have inspired me to find similar spaces in Taipei where the "symbolic economy" is fast at work. While Zukin is primarily interested in recent social politics of these spaces, I want to include the chronologically layered meanings of a site. In this, I follow Setha Low, who is interested in both "the historical emergence and political and economic formation of urban space," which is at the heart of its production, and the "phenomenological and symbolic experience of space," which is in its construction.[27] A major difference in our approaches is that Low's work is principally ethnographically driven, while my use of ethnography is rather limited. Here I want to use the spatial-temporal lenses of various visual and verbal media to observe how the selected sites generate their ever-shifting meanings.

Most spaces that I discuss are public and their representations widely disseminated, but not always: the storage facilities of the National Taiwan

Museum featured in chapter 7 are hidden from the public eye, and the 1945 U.S. Army bombing map of Taipei City discussed in chapter 1 has had very restricted distribution. In fact, some cultural spaces I discuss are physically absent or even imagined: the contemporary importance of the city's nonextant West Gate finds its way into several chapters; and in chapter 3, the discussion of the vertical displacement of the city wall, boulevard, and subway involves both absent and imaginary space. Occasionally, I have even sought to create (or make visible) new cultural spaces in the city. I have "found" a heretofore unnoted pathway in Taipei Park that passes by a small Earth God Shrine (Tudigongmiao), making it a site of increased civic and spiritual activity in the park. In that case, I have even produced its iconic representation: a modified map of the park.[28]

Colonialism and Postcolonialism

The scholarship on colonialism is vast, but not without lacunae. In 2001 Leo Ching wrote that "a conspicuously missing element in the burgeoning critique of colonialism is the lack of any concerted reference to Japan, the only non-Western colonial power that, even in this postcolonial era, still situates itself ambivalently in the West/non-West divide."[29] As if to drive home that point, a five-hundred page collection of essays published two years later— "intended to be an introduction to the history of decolonization in Africa and Asia"[30]—has only one essay tangentially related to Japanese colonialism (in Burma) and barely a mention of Taiwan and Korea. If Japan, Taiwan, and Korea have anything to add to the debate, their experiences in decolonization (or lack of it) are particularly pertinent. Although the discussion of Japan in the theoretical literature on colonialism is thin, when addressed, it seems no one doubts that it practiced a full-fledged form of colonialism; in his categorization of colony types, Jürgen Osterhammel places Taiwan in the group of "exploitation colonies."[31]

The volume of essays edited by Ramon Myers and Mark Peattie established a strong baseline for the work on Japanese colonialism in the 1980s, and there has been a steady stream of related work since then.[32] Many of these studies share an intellectual agenda that seeks to situate the Japanese colonial efforts within a larger, comparative historical and global frame, especially to find the points of distinction for Japan therein. Leo Ching addresses this at some length, but he warns against fetishizing the differences between Japanese and other colonial efforts: "What we need to be mindful of is how the insistence on the differences of Japanese colonialism conceals the structural sameness of its colonial/imperialist practice compared with all other workings of imperialism and colonization."[33]

Keeping those structural continuities firmly in mind, I would like to note what might be distinctive and significant in Japanese colonialism in Taiwan as it relates to the materials studied here. I recognize four interrelated issues: (1) along with Germany, whom it emulated, Japan entered the colonialist community late and was very self-conscious about its position therein; (2) there were cultural materials, especially associated with the literary world, shared between the Japanese and the colonized Han elite; (3) "raciality" was used in ways quite different from its use by European colonialists, for example, Japan claimed affinity with, as well as differences from, the colonized people; and (4) the indigenous peoples of Taiwan formed a "third class" of colonized subjects, which not only affected their status but also that of the "second class" Han population. We see various manifestations and legacies of these conditions, either separately or in some combination, in different aspects of the spatiality of Taipei city introduced in this study.

When we speak of colonialism in Taiwan, we naturally think of the Japanese period, 1895–1945. Yet, Taiwan might also be seen as continually colonized for nearly the last three hundred and fifty years. The earlier colonial period would include not only the brief Dutch and Spanish efforts but also Chinese expansionist programs of the late Qing period. This period would ask us to see the Chinese in Taiwan not as colonized but as colonizers, bringing the displaced indigenous peoples of the island back into the center of consideration. This is, in part, the very point of Emma Teng's study, whose subtitle boldly announces *Chinese Colonial Writing and Pictures, 1683–1895*. Echoing Leo Ching, Teng offers a direct challenge to Chinese colonial studies:

> The presumption that colonizers were European and the colonized non-European is deeply entrenched both inside and outside the academy. The very notion of studying "Chinese colonialism" thus seems alien to many. . . . The idea that "imperialism" is essentially a Western phenomenon has also been reinforced by scholars of modern China's "postcoloniality," who have tended to focus on China's historical experiences with Western imperialism while ignoring China's own history as an imperialist power. . . . I seek to remedy this situation by asserting that China's postcoloniality must also be understood in terms of the legacy of Qing expansionism.[34]

As Teng notes, this is certainly true from the viewpoint of the indigenous peoples of Taiwan, who experienced the presence of Han Chinese on the island as a direct result of colonization, first as part of the Dutch system, then as part of their own. Teng believes that much of this elision of China's colonial past results from the rhetoric of "national unity" that emerges from the Peoples' Republic of China, whose argument is retrofitted to include Qing expansionist history: to wit, the "autonomous regions/provinces" of Tibet, Xinjiang, and Taiwan. If we accept her arguments (and I do), then another special condition of the Japanese colonial period is that the former Chinese colonialists were transformed by the Japanese presence into the colonized, yielding the doubled colonization of the aboriginal peoples.

A more difficult question related to Teng's argument is whether there was also a Han-on-Han colonization involved in the incorporation of the island into Qing imperial rule. That is, were the local Han Taiwanese also colonized by the Qing or were they part of the general imperialized Chinese population? The local Chinese population in Taiwan had come to the island independently (and often illegally) from the southeast coast of China and certainly represented subethnic identities far removed from Beijing. But was the sense of "domination" and "cultural dissimilarity" in this relationship adequate to meet the criteria of colonial rule?[35] At one point Teng notes a "multilevel hierarchy of colonial officials (both Manchu and Han), Han settlers, and indigenous peoples" that challenged the simple dichotomy between colonizer and colonized;[36] yet it is clear that she also feels colonization in Taiwan was principally a Han-on-indigenous phenomenon. While that may be true, and it is significant to her arguments regarding the problem of postcoloniality in China, there was also enough cultural disparity and ethnic tension between the imperial representatives and local Chinese during the late Qing period to affect the trajectory of political and cultural politics. And when the imperial government abruptly abandoned the local population in 1895, that disparity became even clearer. At that point, they truly became "islanders."

What about the years after 1945? Were they, too, part of the "colonial period"? Leo Ching has argued that the specific conditions of the collapse of the Japanese empire meant that the Japanese did not experience decolonization in any significant way; they never had to confront the "other" in their colonial past, but rather only themselves in defeat. In a similar way, the Taiwanese did not experience any sustained period of decolonization after 1945; they did not have the opportunity to confront their colonial condition.

With the arrival of the Nationalists, especially with the retreat of the central government to the island in 1949, the potential postcolonial condition of the Taiwanese was displaced by what could be argued as a neocolonial (or internal colonial) one—although oddly formed since the "colony" was temporarily the "metropole." This condition continued and even intensified for several decades.[37]

When opportunities did come to decolonize (if we accept that that is what happened with the lifting of martial law in 1987), then the experience of Japanese colonization of the island (which had yet to be recognized fully and openly in the decolonization process) was instrumentalized in a peculiar way: the earlier colonial experience was used to legitimize decolonizing the present, especially through the discourse of multiculturalism that challenged the political and cultural hegemony of the martial law period under the Nationalists. This is a very telling formation of cultural displacement that we encounter often in this study. I have generally reserved the term "postcolonial" to refer to the post-1987 period, and I refer to the period between 1945 and 1987 with variations of "postwar," "martial law," or occasionally "neocolonial" period.

Taipei City

Naming of the city has its own special complications. Historical and common renderings included Mengjia, Dadaocheng, Taibeifucheng, Taibeicheng, Taihoku, Taipeh, Taipei, Taibei, Taipak, and even the current PRC-sanctioned "Chinese Taipei," where the city stands for the nation. Before these, there were also aboriginal terms for the region, probably at the village level, which have been largely displaced (if not erased) by the various Chinese, Japanese, and English renderings—Mengjia (or in Taiwanese "Banka") takes its name from the approximation of an aboriginal term for a dugout canoe, which was used as a ferry at this location on the river (Mengjia Zhoudutoujie). Throughout the study, I use the old common spelling "Taipei," but "Taibei (shi)" in transliterations and annotations. Yet even the spelling "Taipei" involves peculiarities in its necessary romanization: technically, the name should be either "T'ai-pei" (in the older Wades-Giles romanization) or "Taibei" (in current standard Hanyu Pinyin, which now is used in Taipei, although not other parts of Taiwan), both of which are tacit acceptances of Mandarin as the official language of the island (no small issue). By whatever spelling, the name first means "the northern part of Taiwan," the area named as a prefecture in 1876, creating the bifurcation of the island into north and south. The city created to govern that region was Taipei Prefectural City (Taibeifucheng), with the common abbreviation Taibeicheng. When the term now rendered "Taipei City" (Taibeishi in Hanyu pinyin) became official, it was actually pronounced "Taihokushi," the Japanese reading of these characters. For fifty years, the city was officially Taihoku/shi, a term I use when referring specifically to the Japanese colonial city, although in the local dialect, both historically and currently, it was and is pronounced "Taipakchhi." Nonetheless, the designating signs have always been written 臺北市, or their simpler version 台北市, allowing one to pronounce them in these various, not necessarily innocent, ways.

The cultural demarcations of the city do not always align well with its political boundaries. Thus, the original Grand Hotel was technically not in the city, nor was the former Taiwan Shinto Shrine, but culturally these two institutions could not have been more representational of the city's respective centers of power. Conversely, in the 1950s and 1960s, the eastern suburbs that were technically within the city limits were still largely rice paddies and bamboo groves, *in* but not *of* the city. The Taipei City to which I refer is what is commonly called Greater Taipei (Da Taibei): from Danshui to Nangang, from Banqiao to Neihu. Nonetheless, this study sometimes strays from even that broad definition of the city. In two significant instances, considerations take us beyond the Taipei basin area: to a sculpture park in the town of Daxi in the countryside south of Taipei (chapter 6), and then on an island-wide tour of former Shinto shrines and their remnants (chapter 7). These sites are definitely *of* but not *in* the city.

Notes

Prologue: Naming the Island

1   Various essays in David Blundel's *Austronesian Taiwan* review those linguistic/cultural ties. John Shepherd's *Statecraft and Political Economy* has the most detailed overview of the aboriginal cultures on the eve of colonization. Tonio Andrade's recent study *How Taiwan Became Chinese* provides a detailed discussion of the status of the island before and during the seventeenth century, primarily from a European perspective.

2   Yu Yonghe, *Small Sea*, 10.

3   Emma Teng has an extensive and eloquent investigation of this "off the map" phenomena in *Taiwan's Imagined Geography*.

4   Some Japanese powers were also interested in control of the island but their colonization efforts were haphazard and short lived, see Andrade, *How Taiwan Became Chinese*, 6–9.

5   Hsu, "From Aboriginal Island," 10.

6   Davidson, *Island of Formosa*, 10.

7   *Shiqi shiji Helanren*, vol. 1, 72–73. While the labeling on the map is in Dutch, the title in the elaborate banner uses the Portuguese name. The indigenous name "Pakan" or "Packan" first appears on a 1625 map (ibid., 17).

8   The name, meaning something like "terraced bay," is probably derived from the old, indigenous term Dayuan, rendered "Tayouan" by the Dutch, which

referred to the sandy islands of the southwest coast near the early settlement area; see Chou Wan Yao, *Taiwan lishi tushuo*, 52.

9   Shepherd, *Statecraft and Political Economy*, 7.

10   Emma Teng, in *Taiwan's Imagined Geography*, calls this the "Chinese colonial period."

11   Ibid., 54–56. Teng covers this period in detail in her chapter 1 (whence comes much of the following).

12   A review of those policies can be found in Mark Peattie's "Japanese Attitudes."

13   The Japanese census noted the Hoklo/Hakka distinction, but not the Quanzhou/Zhangzhou identities within the Hoklo group.

14   Ching, *Becoming "Japanese,"* 211.

15   Ming-Cheng M. Lo has a detailed study of these doctors and the complex and ambiguous position they held as "mutually embedded" in their ethnicity and profession; the "in-between position" is Lo's term (*Doctors within Borders*, 7).

16   Lau, *The Unbroken Chain*, 17; trans. Jane Parish Yang, romanization adjusted.

17   Bhabba, *The Location of Culture*, 86.

18   See Steven Philips's *Between Assimilation and Independence* on those tensions.

19   Lai, Myers, and Wou have the most detailed and reasoned account of this incident in *A Tragic Beginning*.

20   Ibid., 113.

21   Most notably by Chen Fangming in terms of literary production of this period; he uses the terms *zaizhiminshiqi* (28) and *xinzhiminzhuyi*(40); see his *Houzhimin Taiwan*, 23–46.

22   Thomas Gold's *State and Society* has the standard account of the policies and conditions surrounding this economic transformation.

23   This is the term Allen Chun uses to describe the third phase of the postwar period in Taiwan ("Discourses of Identity").

24   Weller, *Discovering Nature*, 2.

25   Ching, *Becoming "Japanese,"* 174–75.

26   Brown, *Is Taiwan Chinese?* 14.

27   Yip, *Envisioning Taiwan*, 7.

28   *Chiang Kai-shek Memorial Hall.*

One: Mapping the City

1   *Taibei guditu zhan.*

2   Allen Chun provides a critique of this social policy in "The Coming Crisis of Multiculturalism."

3   Author's translation; for catalogue, see Wei and Gao, *Chuanyue shikong*.

4   Ibid., 3.

5   Ibid., 4.

6   For a collection of Japanese maps of the island, see Wei et al., *Celiang Taiwan*.

7   Ibid., 239, map no. NMTH2004.042.0011

8   For an analysis of the inherent ideological weight of colonial photography (in this case British), see James Ryan, *Picturing Empire*; in our case that ideological weight is doubled by the reassertion of the photography into the contemporary discourse of multiculturalism.

9   Compare June Yip on this strategy of "rejecting the mainland Chinese heritage imposed by the KMT in favor of a more local identity" (*Envisioning Taiwan*, 7). Caroline Ts'ai discusses this discursive strategy in the postcolonial construction of a Taiwanese identity in *Taiwan in Japan's Empire*, 228-31.

10   The Spanish maps of northern Taiwan focused on settlements in the Jilong and Danshui harbor and did not detail the Taipei basin area; see Mateo, *Spaniards in Taiwan*, xliii, reproduced in Allen, "Mapping Taipei," fig. 1.

11   Casey, *Representing Place*, 58.

12   From Yu Yonghe's late-seventeenth-century travelogue; he is quoting a common disparagement, although he does not agree (*Small Sea*, 99). Emma Teng has detailed the Chinese authorities' pre-1684 vision of the island as "beyond the seas" [*haiwai*]—a term perhaps equivalent to the English "at the ends of the earth." (*Taiwan's Imagined Geography*, chap. 1).

13   The Dutch originally wanted to establish a base in China and repeatedly attempted to take the Portuguese position in Macao, but they were finally forced back to the Penghu (Pescadores) Islands in 1622. From there, they negotiated with Fujian authorities and obtained trading rights under the condition that they repair to Taiwan (the Penghus were then part of Fujian province, while Taiwan was not) (Davidson, *Island of Formosa*, 12).

14   Tonio Andrade provides a detailed description of this complicated web of trade and competition in the area in which Dutch, Spanish, Chinese and Japanese entrepreneurs were engaged (*How Taiwan Became Chinese*).

15   *Shiqi shiji Helanren*, I, 88.

16   Wen-hsiung Hsu reviews the presence of the Dutch, with a map on page 13 ("From Aboriginal Island"). A review of the Dutch maps is found in *Shiqi shiji Helanren*.

17   This map has been reproduced in a number of sources, including Wei and Gao, *Chuanye shikong*, 10; and Allen, "Mapping Taipei," fig. 3.

18   The relative blankness of the land beyond the river may reflect Dutch ignorance more than actual settlement patterns; a Chinese map one hundred years later suggests that aboriginal settlement in the basin was quite uniformly distributed.

19   Wei and Gao, *Chuanye shikong*, 10.

20 Weng, *Da Taibei*.

21 Wang and Hu, *Taiwan de guditu*, 111.

22 Shouhuangshe is identified by Weng on the Dutch map as Sirongh, in the present-day Yonghe area (*Da Taibei*, 59).

23 Chinese settlement of the basin is usually dated to 1709, when the first land deed in the area was issued to Chen Laizhang of Quanzhou, Fujian; see Shepherd, *Statecraft and Political Economy*, 170.

24 We can see a hint of that local mapping in the 1859 map of the Jin Mountain area outside of Xinzhu (Lai, Wei, and Gao, *Zhuqian guditu*, 103).

25 Teng, *Taiwan's Imagined Geography*, 54.

26 Ibid.; Wei and Gao discuss the latter in *Chuanyue shikong*. Wang and Hu summarize the Chinese studies of the former, referring to it as "the finest representative of the [Qing] Taiwan maps using the traditional landscape techniques" (*Taiwan de guditu*, 14).

27 The flooding occurred following a major earthquake of 1694 that obstructed the Danshui river, creating a tidal lake in the northwest part of the basin; this lasted until the eighteenth century, when the lake receded due to the "uplift of the Taipei Basin, accumulation of sediment, a decrease in rainfall, and human activies" (Xie Yingzong 85). Yu Yonghe describes the lake as he found it in 1697 (*Small Sea*, 77–79); a Chinese map of 1734 clearly depicts this lake, perhaps in exaggerated terms (Wang and Hu, 144–45).

28 For details, see Allen, "Mapping Taipei," figs. 5 and 6.

29 John Shepherd offers a detailed examination of the conflict and contractual relationship between the Chinese settlers and the indigenous population (*Statecraft and Political Economy*).

30 A general outline of these events is found in Gardella, "Treaty Ports"; on Shen Baozhen's role, see Pong, *Shen Pao-chen*.

31 Cited in Zhang M, *Yuesheng de chengshi*, 119.

32 Yin Z, *Taiwan Kaifashi*, 410.

33 Lamley, "Formation of Cities," 177.

34 For an analysis of the rise of the port city Takao/Gaoxiong in the Japanese period, see Taylor, "Colonial Takao."

35 An overview of this period, with accompanying sources, is available in Lamley's "Taiwan under Japanese Rule."

36 Morris's "Taiwan Republic" details these events.

37 Ibid., 17–18.

38 See Yang, *Taiwan lishi*, 111, for a copy of the painting. Sources quoted in Morris's "Taiwan Republic" suggest that the Japanese were invited to pacify the city after weeks of chaos and violence. Some Chinese studies also suggest this, for example, Zhuang Z, *Taibei gucheng*, 27 (note that his photograph of Japanese troops "entering the city" is from a much later period). How wide-

spread and warm that welcome might have been is somewhat problematic since the sources (principally British diplomatic and media documents) have their own ideological agenda.

39 The map exists in two known versions, one held by Wei Dewen, reproduced in Wei and Gao, *Chuanyue shikong*, 28; the other by the Qiu Jiang Museum Prepatory Office, as seen in Liu, *Guditu Taibei*, 4–5. Both sources date the map, without clarification, to 1896. I have used the Wei and Gao version, which has a cartouche, written in what appears to be a slightly Japanese infused classical Chinese, giving the size, dimensions, and population of the city. The Qiu Jiang map has handwritten notes by the famous Japanese scholar of Taiwan, Inō Kanori, but no cartouche. Liu Wenjun has printed the map "upside down," with north at the top and has inverted the title cartouche to match. Both reproductions have added contemporary place names.

40 Compare, for example, the map of Danshuiting (now Xinzhu) in *Danshuiting zhi*, 20–21; Lai, Wei, and Gao discuss this map and compare it to an 1899 planimetric map of the city (*Zhuqian Guditu*, 100–101).

41 Some early Japanese maps also display this shifting point of view, although not with the regularity seen in the Chinese maps—for example, it is not used in the popular Japanese "town-plan" or travel itineraries of the seventeenth century. Kazutaka Unno describes a property map from 1230 with "multiple perspectives" ("Cartography in Japan," 364–65).

42 In Wei Dewen's copy of the map used here, this is labeled as a field hospital; while in the Qiu Jiang copy, it is labeled as a railway office.

43 Numerous publications, both academic and popular, describe and often celebrate the Japanese colonial railway system; for example, see Hong, *Taiwan Tiedao*.

44 The earlier map is dated August 10, 1895, just four months after the Japanese had arrived; the other is from 1897 (reproduced here). There is no substantial graphic difference in the depiction of the city between these two maps, other than that the 1897 version is in color and its legend more developed. The only overt Japanese addition is in the 1897 map, where the label "location of the central government headquarters and official residence" (*Sōtokufu kansha no chi*) appears in the lower center. In addition, there is a dotted red line that sweeps across the map near this label, although its significance is unclear to me.

45 See Harley and Woodward, *Cartography in the Traditional East*, chap. 11. Marcia Yonemoto explores the relatively "modern" cartography of the Tokogawa period, including north-top maps ("Spatial Vernacular," 656).

46 This awkward transition was common to most new colonial enterprises (see Osterhammel, *Colonialism*, 42–43); yet as Mark Peattie emphasizes, the Japanese were especially without a coherent colonial policy as they lurched

into the role of colonial power after the Sino-Japanese War ("Japanese Attitudes"). Takekoshi Yosaburō provides a contemporaneous (1904) reflection on the directionless earlier years before Governor-General Kodama's arrival (*Japanese Rule*, especially 17–18).

47 These culminate in an 1898–1905 survey producing the *Taiwan Baotu*. For an analysis of this mapping and its importance to the colonial state, see Yao J, "Japanese Colonial State."

48 Seidensticker, *Tokyo Rising*, 10–11; Buck, "Railway City," 82–83. Caroline Ts'ai critiques the "modernization myth in the person of Gotō Shimpei," although she also discusses his role in initiating key forms of social control (*Taiwan in Japan's Empire*, 70-71).

49 Peattie, "Japanese Attitudes," 83.

50 Ibid., 88.

51 Estimates of the percentage of undeveloped land in the intramural area vary. Ye Suke quotes an 1895 Japanese source suggesting 30 percent (*Riluo Taibeicheng*, 77), while Yang Mengzhe suggests as much as 75 percent for the same year (*Taiwan lishi*, 120). Judging from the maps, my estimation is about 50 percent.

52 *Taikoku kenhō* 64, item 188, August 23, 1900, 113–14; reproduced in Allen, "Mapping Taipei," fig. 13.

53 *Taikoku kenhō* 90, item 276, June 1, 1901, 94–95; see discussion in Huang W, *Rizhi shidai*, vol. 3, 73.

54 There are two versions of this map: the original, used here, issued in March; and a December revision held by the National Taiwan Library. The later version contains an expanded map of the southern suburbs; for that version, see Allen, "Mapping Taipei," fig. 12.

55 *Taikoku kenhō* 200, item 425, October 7, 1905, insert. This map/plan has slightly different titles, but here it is called *Taipei City Area Planning Map* (Taihokushiku kaikaguzu). See Allen, "Mapping Taipei," fig. 15.

56 Su, *Kanbujian*, 241–42.

57 For a review of that policy, see Peattie, "Japanese Attitudes." Leo Ching argues that "assimilation" was always a policy of contradiction by which the Taiwanese never could become Japanese, even if they wanted to (*Becoming "Japanese"*).

58 The details of that recovery plan are reviewed by Huang W., *Rizhi shidai* (vol. 3), 86–87. Some of the earliest modernization efforts were in public sanitation, including extensive sewer and drainage systems, designed and supervised by William Burton, an American engineer from Japan; see Su, *Kanbujian*, 184–92.

59 Huang Wuda gives the population at 244,244 in 1930, and 266,066 in 1932 (*Rizhi shidai* [vol. 3], 82, 96).

60 *Taihoku shūhō*, no. 765, March 7, 1932, public notice no. 54. This plan is reviewed in Huang W, *Rizhi shidai* (vol. 3), 95–101.

61 There are numerous post-1932 Japanese maps of the city, including a 1939 planning map (Taipei City Archives [Taibeishi Wenxianhui], map no. 50) that seems to be a replica of the 1932 map.

62 I discuss the concept of "refractive nostalgia" in the Postface. *Zijigai zong-tongfu* was designed in consultation with the prominent historian of Taiwan architecture Li Qianlang, who also provided an introduction to the history of the building.

63 Compare, for example, the controversy surrounding the Sōtokufu in Korea, which was razed in 1996; see Jin, "Demolishing Colony." The reasons for the different fates of the Japanese building are intertwined with the trajectories of national identity in the two colonies, especially as related to the postwar conditions; see Ts'ai, *Taiwan in Japan's Empire*, 237.

64 *Taihoku kyōchō*. An example of this photography is found in Allen, "Mapping Taipei," fig.17.

65 See Wei and Gao, *Chuanyue shikong*, 140–50, for a series of these photographic comparisons; one of the most elaborate displays of such materials is in the Discovery Center of Taipei City Hall.

66 The map, *Saishin Taihoku shigai hikōki chōmoku zenzu*, is reproduced and discussed in Wei and *Gao, Chuanyue shikong*, 33–36; for select details, see Allen "Mapping Taipei," figs. 18 and 19.

67 From the cartouche on the map reproduced most clearly in Wei and Gao, *Chuanyue shikong*, 35–36.

68 Thrower, *Maps & Civilization*, 163.

69 The term *chōmoku/niaomu*, which literally means "bird's eye," is not the standard term for "bird's-eye view" (*chōkan/niaokan*) that would be used later.

70 A collection of these maps is reproduced in Zhuang Y, *Taiwan chōkanzu*; samples are found in Allen "Mapping Taipei," figs. 20, 21.

71 Paul Barclay discusses the flourishing tourist industry in Taiwan during the 1930s, as seen through the medium of picture postcards ("Japanese Postcards").

72 Li Qinxian discusses the maps and the important painter Yoshida Hatsuzo, who was trained in both Japanese and Western painting techniques ("Hua Taiwan," 236–37).

73 Edward Casey describes similar Japanese maps from the pre-Meiji period as "*Ukiyoe*" maps that "were at once cartographic and painterly, equally and fully both" (*Representing Place*, 209). Depth, encompassability, partial exaggeration, and density of composition are all qualities he identifies on these maps (210–11).

74 *Dai Taihoku chōkanzu*; this map has been widely reproduced since the early

1990s. The 1994 copy from SMC Publishing (Nantian shuju) has extensive information about the city and exhibition on the reverse side, taken from *Shisei yonjisshūnen kinen*. The map and a series of details can be found in Allen, "Mapping Taipei," figs. 21–26.

75 Cannon, *Leyte*, 43–45; Zhong, *Taiwan hangkong*, 273–82.

76 The 1945 U.S. Army map, *Taihoku-Matsuyama, Formosa (Taiwan)*, provides information on the reconnaissance flights whose photographs, along with Japanese maps, were used to construct the map. I want to thank Robert Andrew Edmondson for making a copy of this map available to me.

77 "Formosa Interim Report."

78 This labeling is most complete on the *Taihoku-Matsuyama, Formosa (Taiwan)* map.

Two: Picturing the City

1 Roger Selya discusses postwar urban planning in detail (*Taipei*, 138–47); Huang Li-ling reviews the ineffectualness of urban planning during this period ("Urban Politics," 82–84).

2 *Taibei huakan*, 1.1 (1966), 14; caption in English.

3 I discuss the "Jieshou" term (and park) in chapter 3.

4 Yi-wen Wang and Tim Heath compare the "pseudo Western" building style of the newly constructed provincial capital with the "Sinic" (what I call neoclassical) style of Taipei ("Constructions of National Identity"). Charles Musgrove discusses the Nationalist plans for their mainland capital, Nanjing ("Dreaming a Dream").

5 Abbas, *Hong Kong*, 82.

6 Tardio, *Sees Taiwan*, 99–100.

7 Chih-Hung Wang reviews these changes on the social cityscape, suggesting that Chen Shuibian's administration sought to consolidate its support "through cultural governance" ("Modernization Ideoscape," 201).

8 Ting, "The Political Architecture," 15.

9 The Taipei Photographic Association (Taibeishi Sheyinghui) was founded in 1954 by Li Mingdiao and others. It has presided over a range of amateur activities, including serial publications of *Taipei Salon* (Taibei shalong) and *Taipei Photo* (Taibei sheying) and numerous photo exhibits. There is a detailed record of that history at http://www.photo.org.tw.

10 *Deng Nanguang*, 193.

11 Chen S, "Xu," 6; Chen S, "Shizhang xu," 3; Ma Y, "Yongxin," 5. Ma is quoting from Wu Zhuoliu's 1947 remark that the task of the Taiwanese people is to establish a Taiwan "free and tolerant in body and mind" (*shenxin kuanrong er ziyou*).

12   Wu Y, "Renzhende" 7.

13   Ibid., 7–8.

14   Braester, "If We Could Remember," 53.

15   Chen Ru-shou and Liao Jinfeng suggest the essays in *Xunzhao dianyingzhong* are dealing with the city as the films' "main character" ("Focus on Taipei," 17).

16   Jameson, "Remapping Taipei," 154.

17   For June Yip's discussion of the *Son's Big Doll*, see *Envisioning Taiwan*, 54–55. The Nativist Literature Movement and Huang's role in it are fully explored by Yvonne Chang in *Modernism and Nativist Resistance*.

18   In the short story, the car is a Mercedes sedan (*binzihao jiaoche*) ("Taste of Apples," 27), but the filmic translation into a Ford Mercury is more accurate. Having the colonel drive his car is, however, completely out of character for the time.

19   Huang C, "Pingguo," 53; translation, Goldblatt, *Taste*, 154.

20   Yip, *Envisioning Taiwan*, 35.

21   Ibid., 140.

22   All dialogue (Mandarin, Taiwanese, and English) is subtitled with Chinese characters, providing another layer of "translation."

23   These and other terms cited are from the short story.

24   Yomi Braester describes this shot as the "vulnerability of the slum as well as the blood debt it might exact in the future" (*Painting the City Red*, 200).

25   In the film the police officer reads off the addresses and asked directions to the residence at "Lane 28, Xinsheng North Road," which is the address for the formerly planned (and now restored) park. A full history and description of the area is found in Tang Jiyong and Zhou Yuhui, *Taibeishi shisi shiwu hao*, 13–74.

26   Ibid., 21.

27   Technically, this flashback and background are inventions of the film, but they actually draw on another of Huang's short stories, "Ringworms," (Xuan) in which Afa's family appear before their move to Taipei; see Huang C, *The Taste of Apples*, 125–34.

28   The first two films in the series are *Pushing Hands* (Tuishou, 1992) and *Wedding Banquet* (Xiyan, 1993). Whitney Crothers Dilley reviews the economics of these three films; she discusses the relative commercial success of *Eat Drink Man Woman* in U.S. theaters (*Cinema*, 74–75).

29   Chow, *Sentimental Fabulations*, 138–43. Here the second film, *Wedding Banquet*, is her primary topic for discussion, but the father in all of these films (played by Lung Sihung) is nearly identical.

30   Yip, *Envisioning Taiwan*, 237.

31   Dilley has described the oft-noted relationship between food and sex in this film, but she is clear that despite the film's extravagant food scenes, the few sexual scenes are relatively modest and understated (*Cinema*, 77–78).

32 Lee and Schamus, *Two Films*, 8.

33 Yip, *Envisioning Taiwan*, 235.

34 Dilley discusses the house in some detail, noting that it is a "Japanese style house" (*Cinema*, 76).

35 Ibid., 77.

36 I leave that question for others, but clearly an issue surrounds the missing mother and the father's attraction to a woman his daughter's age.

37 Lee and Schamus, *Two Films*, 46; romanization has been adjusted throughout

38 Ibid., 41.

39 Ibid., 43.

40 The film script translates these terms as "daughter" and "father," but that certainly loses the sense of affection here.

41 Although this portrait of the city is filled with pornographic elements of consumption, it is very different from that described by Tani Barlow in her condemnation of the new Chinese city ("The Pornographic City"). Here the depiction is not "smutty" but rather naively romantic. It coincides with what Wang Ban calls the city's "consumerist mode" ("Rechanting the Image," 375).

42 Jou, "Domestic Politics," 134.

43 Ibid., 121

44 Ibid., 122; see her fig. 6.2

45 Bonnie Adrian describes the importance of these outside spaces in the pursuit of young romance (*Framing the Bride*, 82–89), but in the movie there is hardly a nod to the familial home.

46 On MTV's influence on visual culture, see Mirzoeff, *Visual Culture*, 96–98.

47 At the time the movie was shot, Taipei 101 had not been built; instead, the film uses long shots of the cityscape and the Mitzukoshi tower in transitions between sequences. On the "placeless" architecture of the globalized city, see Abbas, *Hong Kong*, chap. 4.

Three: Traffic in the City

1 Lamley, "Formation of Cities," 155.

2 This idealization is traced to the archaizing *Zhou li* of the Han period; see Wright, "Cosmology," 46–51.

3 The circular walled city was formed when placed over an already existing "market" town, which naturally evolved from some node of commerce; irregularities of landscape would deform the natural circle into specific demographic shapes. This is seen even in imperial cities, such as the southern capital cities of Hangzhou and Nanjing; see Arthur Wright, "Cosmology," for a comparison of these two different city shapes and F. W. Mote, "Transformation," on the evolution of Nanjing.

4   For a review of walled cities in Taiwan, see Chiang, "Walled Cities."

5   It turns out that the Taipei city wall was never needed for these protective uses—the feared French attack was thwarted and the Chinese did not defend the city against the Japanese. The only time walls were used for defense was when the Japanese defended themselves against a local insurrection led by Chen Qiuju in 1896; see Li Qianlang, *Taibei guchengmen*, 14, including a photograph of Japanese soldiers on the wall.

6   Yin Zhangyi has refuted claims that Shen Baozhen's memorial named a specific location for building the new prefectural city (*Taiwan Kaifashi*, 404–6); not until the imperial edict of December 20, 1875 (which reached Taiwan in February 1876), was the "area of Mengjia" (Mengjia difang) mentioned (ibid., 407).

7   Harry Lamley reviews the development of Xinzhu City in "Formation of Cities" (158–64).

8   Ibid., 168; Huang F, *Taibei jiancheng*, 25; Yin Z, *Taiwan Kaifashi*, 410.

9   Lamley, "Formation of Cities, 180.

10   There was apparently a loss of documents related to the planning and work on the wall of Taibeifu. Yin Zhangyi speculates that these documents were removed from the Danshui-Xinzhu archives by Japanese researchers in the early colonial period, perhaps by Inō Karnori, who published several articles on architecture of the island around 1900; Yin Z, *Taiwan Kaifashi*, 402–3, 419.

11   The most important works on the wall's history are Huang Deshi's early "Chengnei de yange," Yin Zhangyi's best reasoned and documented in *Taiwan Kaifashi*, chapter 7, and Zhang Mingxiong's recent *Yuesheng de chengshi* (derivative, often without citation, of Yin). In English, Lamley's "Formation of Cities" is most complete, citing Huang.

12   Lamley discusses the cooperative nature of this work by the managers ("Formation of Cities," 197); Su Shuobin has a list of these managers with the sub-ethnic and locale affiliations (*Kanbujian*, 115).

13   Huang F, *Taibei jiancheng*, 25–28; Li Qianlang, *Taibei guchengmen*, 52–59.

14   For dating the gates, I follow Yin Zhangyi's revised evaluation—conventionally, it has been thought that the wall was begun in 1879 and finished in 1882, but Yin clearly shows that the wall was not begun until 1882 and completed in late 1884 (*Taiwan Kaifashi*, 418). Between 1879 and 1882, officials were busy planning and raising funds; at the same time, the tract of land upon which the wall was to be built was planted with bamboo to solidify the loose paddy soil and provide a solid foundation for the wall (ibid., 413–15).

15   For details, see Huang D, "Chengnei de yange," 22–23, including the names and addresses of these merchants.

16   The announcement is cited variously, most completely in ibid., 22.

17   The plot was 1.8 *zhang* wide by 24 *zhang* deep (approximately 21 x 280 feet); this width and depth allowed for elaborate storerooms and residential quarters in the back of the shop, a graphic description of which is available in *Taibei lishi sanbu*, 110–11. Cheng Zhengxiang's detailed 1956 land-use maps for the downtown business center show the modern condition of these old plots very clearly (*Taibeishi zhi*, 108–11). Typically the width of the lot has been maintained, although the depth has often been subdivided when possible, such as in the Starbucks in figure 3.1.

18   In Jeffrey Meyer's analysis of geomancy and the building of Beijing, he notes that "the basic symmetry of the north-south axis is present as well as the relentless grid-work pattern of the streets" (*Feng-shui*," 141).

19   Schinz, *Magic Square*, 379. Schinz also addresses the anomalous south wall, which is slightly convex and irregular in its footprint, writing: "The bend in the south wall . . . follows a river further south." I am not clear as to which river he is referring (certainly not the moat just south of the wall, and Xindian xi is too far removed and circuitous to provide alignment). My suspicion is that the curve in the south wall may represent the original misalignment of the two south gates, which the wall had to accommodate retroactively.

20   Liao Chunsheng cites an article by Schinz from 1976, which includes the same map (*Taibei zhi dushi*, 107). Also Shih-wei Lo (reproducing a version of Schinz's map) argues that the wall was "slightly rotated to be more in tune with Feng-sui [fengshui] requirements" ("Palimpsest," 68).

21   Liao Chunsheng, who first offers this explication, states that the initial plans for the city were made in consultation with the governor of Fujian, Cen Yuying, who subscribed to a school of geomancy that took the "unmovable axis" (particularly the north star) as primary; this yields the orientation of the streets that Chen Xingju first planned in 1879. Subsequently, when responsibility for construction of the city fell to the Intendant for Taiwan, Liu Ao, he changed the orientation of the wall to reflect his own geomantic beliefs, which took topography, particularly mountains, as the primary criterion. By the time Liu did this (around 1882), the streets had already been laid out and were partially populated, which explains the two orientations (*Taibei zhi dushi*, 111–18).

22   Lo S, "Palimpsest," 68.

23   See chapter 1; photographs in Yang, *Taiwan lishi*, 114, 129.

24   As mentioned above, the *yamen* was reconstructed in the Botanical Garden as a public monument; see chapter 5 for a discussion of the Civic Hall.

25   Todd Henry discusses the contestation between city planners and residents, both Korean and Japanese settlers, in building central Seoul ("Respatialization").

26   Jinnai, *Tokyo*, 22–23.

27   This is Spiro Kostof's term for Haussmann's radical urban plan for Paris; Kostof

provides a relatively harsh critique of this process (*City Assembled*, 266–79); David Harvey, offers a more sympathetic reading, based on the financial pressures of the time and the constraints of the old city (*Consciousness*, 73–76). For the Japanese administrators, particularly Gotō Shimpei, Paris of 1890 would have been seen as a model of modern urban planning.

28 Jinnai, *Tokyo*, 160.

29 These colonial buildings have been studied extensively by scholars of history and architecture, perhaps most so by Li Qianlang in his *Taiwan jindai*, and Fu Chaoqing in *Rizhishidai*; C. J. Hsia takes a more theoretical approach to the analysis of the architecture ("Theorizing Colonial Architecture").

30 As mentioned in chapter 1, these renovations are recorded in detail in *Taihokushi Kyōchō*; also see Li Qianlang, *Taiwan jindai*, 104–8.

31 These facades seem to have been built to integrate the fourteen-story Century Building (Shiji Luofu Dalou) at 51 Hengyang Road into the smaller streetscape.

32 Su, *Kandejian*, 199; here my remarks are similar to those of Su, 196–203. Su's work has been very valuable to me, and I have been able to incorporate it at several points, but most of the thinking about the wall and these early plans was plotted before I had the opportunity to read his book. I take his analysis as an authoritative confirmation of my earlier thoughts (see "Mapping Taipei").

33 *Taikoku kenhō* 64, item 188 (August 23, 1900), 113–14, reproduced in Allen, "Mapping Taipei," fig. 13. The 1901 map (see fig. 1.3) clarifies exactly how that was to be done: two sections of the wall (one in the north wall and one in the west wall) were to be removed to make room for the track, leaving North Gate and the very far corner of the wall intact.

34 E Chen, *Gotō Shimpei*, 33.

35 This is seen especially in the cross-section elevations drawn to illustrate the two street designs. Compare, e.g., the "profiles de voies publiques" illustrations in Francois Loyer with those in Huang W, *Rizhi shidai* (vol. 3), 85. These streets were also obsessively photographed; see *Taibeishi dushi jihua*, 65, figs. 1.6d, 3.2.

36 Lo S, "Palimpsest," 72–73.

37 Li Qianlang describes the special architecture of the South Gate (*Taibei guchengmen*, 38–45); C. J. Hsia claims that the Chinese city was south-facing ("Theorizing Colonial Architecture ," 11); in my reading, South Gate was only nominally the orientation of the city. Each gate has a traditional formal name, but I use these common designations throughout.

38 Li Qianlang, *Taibei guchengmen*, 58–59. Li speculates that the wall should have eight gates (four principal [*da*] ones and four small [*xiao*] ones), like the wall in Tainan, but that because of financial or other restraints, the other three small gates were not built (ibid., 53)—while the location of South and North Gates toward the corners of their walls would allow for a second gate, the central location of West and East Gates would not.

39　There is some confusion regarding exactly when the wall was dismantled. Huang Wuda says the wall was torn down between 1904 and 1906, with the boulevards finished in 1911 (*Rizhi shidai* [vol. 3], 54).

40　Li Qianlang, *Tabei guchengmen*, 60.

41　Ibid.; see also Huang D, "Chengnei de yange," 21.

42　C. J. Hsia suggests that in building the Sōtokufu "all historical traces had been demolished and completely restructured" ("Theorizing Colonial Architecture," 11), but the space where the Taipei Sōtokufu was built had almost no "historical traces." Compare this to conditions in Korea, where the Kyongbok Palace was largely destroyed to make room for the Sōtokufu (Jin, "Demolishing Colony," 41).

43　Yang Mengzhe says that East Gate was chosen by the Japanese as the "main gate" (*zheng men*) because it faced east toward the rising sun, a symbol of the nation (*Taiwan lishi*, 132). C. J. Hsia suggests that this reorientation "violently changed the directions of the building into facing east, i.e., worshiping the 'rising sun,' a very Japanese symbol" ("Theorizing Colonial Architecture," 11). While I do not deny the important change this reorientation brought to the city (in fact, that is my point) and the orientation toward the rising sun certainly *looks* ideologically instructive, I see it as having been determined by the configuration of intramural space rather than the result of overt ideological policies.

44　Li Qianlang discusses the unusual architectural style of the original Taipei gates compared with those of most Chinese cities in *Taibei Guchengmen* (22–26). Li "credits" architect Huang Baozhen with the 1965 renovation of the gates (*Taiwan jianzhu*, 179).

45　In 2009, during repair of the gates, these emblems drew the ire (and the paintbrushes) of DDP city councilors, who noted, with no small sense of irony, "the KMT symbol did not appear on the gate during the Qing dynasty. What we are doing today is restoring the monument to its original appearance" (*Taipei Times*, May 27, 2009, 4).

46　Li Qianlang, *Taibei Guchengmen*, 44; *Discover Taipei*, no. 2, November 1997, 15 (for the full quote, see chapter 2).

47　The 1920 system for the intramural city did retain some Qing terms, such as Wenwu/Bunbu (Civil Martial) and Shuyuan/Sho'in (Academy) as ward names. For details, see Huang D, "Chengnei de yange," 30. Zhu Wanli gives the names of sixty-four wards for the entire city issued in 1922 (*Taibeishi dushi*, 8–9).

48　See Phillips, *Between Assimilation and Independence*, especially chap. 3.

49　*Shengbu guanguang ditu*; see Allen, "Mapping Taipei," fig. 29.

50　There are a few overt signs of the new Chinese presence: somewhat confusingly, the old Beimenjie (North Gate Street) was renamed Guangfulu (Retrocession Road), which is today's Bo'ailu (Brotherhood Road); and Fuhoujie

(Prefecture Back Street) was renamed Bo'ailu, which is today's Chongqing-nanlu (Chongqing South Road).

51   *Taibeishi diming*, 402.

52   Ibid.

53   In their narratives, both *Taibeishi lujie* and *Taibeishi diming* elide the restored Chinese names seen on the 1946 map and jump directly from the Japanese names to the current usages.

54   These maps are *Taibei ditu*, April 15, 1949, and *Zuixin Taibeishi*, March 10, 1949.

55   For example, the legend records that the new Hengyang Street (Hengyangjie), which was in the Japanese Eichō ward, had the interim name Civil-Martial Street, which was ultimately derived from Qing practice; yet Chongqing South Road, which was in the Japanese Hon ward, was called Bo'ai Road in the interim period, and not Fuhoujie of the Qing nomenclature.

56   One wonders if there is a connection between this second, more mainland-based conversion and the tragic February 28th Incident a few weeks before. Note that in 1947, this street was called Hengyanjie (street), but in April 1948, the name was recorded as Hengyanglu (road), which has remained in con-tinual use since that time.

57   It is also possible to read this address all in Chinese.

58   Riep, "Renaming Taipei Streets," 1.

59   In 1963, when the boulevard was widened, the park was added on its southern side, across from Taipei Park (*Taibeishi diming*, 259).

60   *Ziji gai*, 4. On the renaming of Chiang Kai-shek Road in the 1970s, see Riep, "Renaming Taipei Streets," 4.

61   *Ziyou shibao* (March 22, 1996), 6.

62   Although Mayor Chen publicly claimed that this change was not meant to be disrespectful to Chiang Kai-shek, this certainly could be read as part of the implicit de-Chiang Kai-shek (qu Zhongzheng) program of the Chen adminis-tration. Proof came under Chen's presidency when he proposed the renaming of Chiang's largest monument, the Chiang Kai-shek Memorial Hall, as the National Taiwan Democracy Memorial Hall (Guoli Taiwan Minzhu Jinnianguan).

63   "Establishment of the Anti-Graft."

64   *Taibei huakan*, 1.1 (1966), 14; see chapter 2 for a discussion.

65   The MRT deviated from the old boulevards in one place: the Red Line from Xin-dian did not, as might be expected, trace the route of Zhongshan South Road on the way to the train station but instead followed its parallel, intramural street, Gongyuan Road, in order to bring the line closer to downtown civic center.

66   Anru Lee's discussion of the MRT system, "Subways as a Space," provides a critical review of the changes during this period, to which I am indebted.

67   Braester, "Tales," 168.

68 Anru Lee, "Subways as a Space," 54.

69 Ibid., 35.

70 The archaeological site report is Li Qianlang, *Taibeifu chengqiang*; the exhibition catalogue is *Qiang*.

Four: A Park in the City

1 This park is known by a variety of names. Officially, it was called Taipei Park (Taihoku Kōen/Taibei Gongyuan), but it was informally and most commonly known as New Park (Shin Kōen/Xin Gongyuan)—the "newness" because it came after the first park, Murayama Park, which was built in 1897 in the northern suburbs (*Taihoku meishō*, 523–24). In 1996 the name was changed to February 28th Peace Park (Ererba Heping Gongyuan). I will refer to it by its colonial/official name in its common Chinese spelling, Taipei Park. *Toushi Xingongyuan* gives the size of the park as 60,600 square meters; *Taibei Ererba* has it at 71,530 square meters (17.6 acres).

2 The term *gongyuan* originally referred to official lands dedicated to public agriculture (*Zhongwen daci dian*, no. 1480.613/1, citing a third-century CE text). In China, public parks became part of the urbanization plans beginning around 1914 (e.g., Central Park in Beijing) and gained momentum throughout the early twentieth century; see Dong, "Defining Beiping."

3 Cai Hounan reviews the history of the term *kōen*, suggesting that it may be derived from a contraction of the pre-Meiji term *kō teki yūen*, or public recreation/amusement area ("Taiwan dushi," 42–43).

4 Seidensticker, *Low City, High City*, 116. Akira Sato calls it "the first park in Tokyo primarily in Western style, with a portion in the traditional Japanese garden style" (*Landscape Planning*, 1).

5 Wyke, "Marginal Figures," 86. In part, Terry Wyke is reprising George Chadwick's seminal study on the function of the early European park, *The Park and the Town* (50–51). This is not to say that Victorian parks lacked a civil purpose (Wyke called them "agents of citizenship" [Wyke, "Marginal Figures," 86]), but rather that the Japan/Taiwan parks were more driven by a civic rationale, which was closely associated with modernization.

6 Henry, "Respatializing," 23.

7 There were also Civil, Military, and City God temples built in the city in 1880, 1889, and 1881, respectively. According to Stephan Feuchtwang, all four of these official temples were destroyed by the Japanese ("City Temples," 282). The City God Temple has been restored, however.

8 Lamley, "Subethnic Rivalry," 295; Feuchtwang, "City Temples," 261, 268–70.

9 Li Qianlang describes the Tianhougong as unique in Taiwan temple architecture; he calls it a "large-scale, government-constructed [official]" temple"

(*Taiwan gujianzhu,* 289). Stephan Feuchtwang discusses the adoption of Mazu into state rites, with this temple as the principal example in Taipei ("Domestic and Communal," 281).

10 The examination hall was built in 1880 on land donated by Hong Tengyun, a wealthy merchant from Mengjia (Zhuang Z, *Taibei gucheng,* 78).

11 The 1977 edition of *Taibeishi zhi* (vol. 8, 30) reports that the idols were moved by the Japanese to the Longshan Temple of Mengjia and then later moved to a small Mazu temple in Jilong. The 1988 edition elides this information and merely says (incorrectly) that the temple was torn down in 1906. Another source says the idol was stored by the Japanese in the Taibei District Office (Taikokuchō), where it was discovered by gentry elite from Sanzhi; when the Fuchenggong temple at Sanzhi was built in 1919, they had the idol installed there (http://blacky.scjp.idv.tw/252goldenfacemazu_temple.html).

12 Taipei City Government, News Release, no. 45.248. Stephan Feuchtwang describes these anniversary *jiao* circuits of the local gods: "The god's procession past every household in the territory is a sweeping away and warding off of malicious spirits " ("City Temples," 272).

13 Taipei City Government, News Release, no. 45.249.

14 While temples were relatively untouched for most of the colonial period, the status of specific temples during the *kōminka* (Japanization) period of the late 1930s is unclear. Stephan Feuchtwang says, "Temples were to be destroyed or transformed into Japanese style Buddhist or state (Shinto) places of worship, and their land and other property confiscated. Local Japanese officials pursued the policy with varying degrees of vigour, in some places hardly at all, in others quite thoroughly" (*Popular Religion,* 234). Wan Yao Chou reports that one-third of local temples were destroyed before the policy was halted in late 1940 ("*Kōminka* Movement," 46). According to Yin Jianyi, an information officer of the Longshan Temple in Mengjia (who lived through the *kōminka* period), that temple continued to operate without interruption during that period (interview, August 2003).

15 See Allen, "Mapping Taipei," fig. 14. Wei and Gao list a set of uses (as medical school, barracks, etc.) for the building between 1901 and 1911 (*Chuanyue shikong,* 101). In the 1911 map the building is labeled as the Taiwan Association of Chinese Studies (Taiwan Chūgakukai)

16 *Sōtokufu ho,* no. 644, November 21, 1900, 23, Ordinance 13; *Taihoku kenho,* no. 88, August, 23, 1900, Public Announcement 64, 113–14. See Allen, "Mapping Taipei," fig. 13.

17 Li L, "You dushi gongyuan," 40. Both Li and Cai Hounan ("Taiwan dushi," 70) give the pending visit of the Crown Prince as impetus for building the park—this would have been the future Taisho Emperor, not the future Showa Emperor, as they say. If so, that visit apparently did not take place. The *Tai-*

wan Meishō, 511, gives September 9, 1896, as the date for the establishment of the park; it does not mention the visit.

18 An exception might be the bund in Shanghai, which was called both a garden (*huayuan*) and a park (*gongyuan* [*kōen* in Japanese]), although this was clearly not an indigenous East Asia construction; see Bickers and Wasserstrom, "Shanghai's Dogs and Chinese," 445.

19 *Taibeishi dushi jihua*, 78.

20 Seidensticker, *Low City, High City*, 123.

21 Hsia, "Theorizing Colonial Architecture," 17.

22 The two parks will come to share many features, but their small size, location in the center of the city, and general shape sets the pattern; Cai Hounan makes this explicit comparison (*Taiwan dushi*, 44–46).

23 The club appears on a 1905 map reproduced in Wei and Gao, *Chuanyue shikong*, 76. A drawing in the Taiwan Historica Archives (Guoshiguan Taiwanwenxianguan) in Nantou (document no. 7.5476.2, August 1, 1912) provides a detailed ground plan and surroundings.

24 An announcement of plans for the building appears in the *Taiwan nichinichi shimpō*, July 8, 1902, 2, giving the address as Wenwu/Bunbu Street near the sanitation works office, but also mentioning that it is within the site of the proposed park. The Taiwan Historica Archives document no. 2.852.3 (March 13, 1903) contains various materials related to the establishment and design of the club, including a sketch of the building and grounds (19) and a text on the construction of the club, citing Ordinance no. 3675 of November 10, 1902 (28). I have not been able to locate studies or descriptions of the club; oddly, even Takekoshi Yosaburō does not mention it, although he is most interested in such amenities of colonial life (*Japanese Rule*).

25 Also seen in photographs in the album commemorating the departure of Gotō Shimpei from the island in 1906 (*Gotō danshaku*); in the background of a photograph of Kodama's statue in the 1911 *Taihoku shashinchō*; and in the background of a photograph of the memorial arch in the park, reproduced in *Taiwan huixiang*, 290.

26 In fact, the 1912 drawing of the building marks the site line to the south side of the governor-general's compound (see note 23).

27 Takekoshi, *Japanese Rule*, 315–16. In the 1905 map, a gymnasium in this compound is so labeled, but the track that encircles it is not. In the 1911 map, it is referred to as a bicycle track (*jidensha torakku*) and must be the same one mentioned by Takekoshi, as attested by the photographs of a bicycle race in *Kodama Sōtoku*, 56–60.

28 *Kodama Sōtoku*, 56–60. I assume the "Athletic Society," which appears in the passage by Takekoshi, is the same entity as the "Athletic Club" mentioned here and is associated with the Taipei Club.

29 Jürgen Osterhammel says that "the club became the center of British social life in India and other Asian colonies during the Victorian era. In clubs, one could feel like a gentleman among gentlemen while being served by the native staff" (*Colonialism*, 87). He goes on to describe the racial exclusiveness of the European clubs. It is not clear, however, whether the Taipei Club maintained such strong racial barriers for its duration.

30 *Shashin kurabu*, n.p.

31 See Allen, "Taipei Park," fig. 10.

32 Ryan, *Picturing Empire*, 99. Note that the *Kodama Sōtoku* (61–63) has photographs of skeet-shooting competitions, and that the *Taiwan nichinichi shimpō* of this time often carried advertisements for hunting rifles and equipment.

33 Hundred of notices of club activities appear in the *Taiwan nichinichi shimpō* up through 1937. The club house was finally replaced by a guesthouse constructed for the Taiwan Exposition of 1935—an announcement of the club's move is made in *Taiwan nichinichi shimpō*, March 27, 1935, 7. Currently, this site is occupied by the offices of the Municipal Department of Street Lighting and Parks.

34 From a cartouche on the map; reproduced most clearly in Wei and Gao, *Chuanyue shikong*, 35–36. For a translation of the entire passage, see chapter 1.

35 See Allen, "Taipei Park," fig. 8. The cartouche appears to read "Kodoma sōtoku oyobi Gotō minkan kinen zōeibutsu shikichi" (site of the buildings of the Governor-General Kodama and Civil Administrator Gotō memorial). The memorial was conceived in 1906 by Civil Administrator Hirō Tatsumi but was not completed until 1915 (*Taibeishi dushi jihua*, 78).

36 The police were originally part of the military, but in 1901 Gotō reorganized them into a separate civil unit and upgraded their status (Ye, *Riluo Taibeicheng*, 39). Caroline Ts'ai has a detailed discussion of the special role that the civil police played in the colonial government of Taiwan, including Gotō's important initial work, in *Taiwan in Japan's Empire* (see especially chapter 4).

37 *Taibeishi lujie*, 244.

38 Li Qianlang, *Taibeishi: Guji*, 28. The arch now stands astride a walkway near the National Taiwan Museum. During the construction of the MRT station, the arch was moved and restored to its present condition; see *Taibei Huangshi*.

39 In 1915, when the old prefectural office (Taibeifu yamen) was torn down, the stone lions that fronted the building were moved to this site and used to frame the arch. The arch is now next to the band shell and amphitheater. In a pre-1915 photograph (*Taiwan huixiang*, 290), and the 1911 map, it appears that the arch's location and orientation differed somewhat from the current ones. Lin Hengdao provides a transcription of the engraved texts of these two monuments ("Taibei gongyuan," 256–57).

40 Peattie, "Introduction," 40.

41 *Gotō danshaku,* n.p.

42 Takekoshi, *Japanese Rule,* 17.

43 Khemir, *Orientalisme,* 24–25. As evidence of the reporter's serious attitude, there is another portrait of him similarly attired in the 1900 commercial directory, *Taiwan shishō meikan.*

44 See Allen, "Taipei Park," fig. 8.

45 A photograph of this pavilion is first seen in an announcement of its construction, *Taiwan nichinichi shimpō,* October 26, 1908, 5; the earliest located record of a performance at this pavilion is from *Taiwan nichinichi shimpō,* June 25, 1912, and includes both Western and Japanese music: a march, a waltz, a polka, the "Crown of Victoria Overture," an "Irish Fantasy, "New Aborigines (Shin Takasago)" played on a koto, popular songs on the samisen, and a traditional Kabuki theater piece put to music.

46 Leo Ching, *Becoming "Japanese,"* discusses the inherent contradictions of the *dōka* policy, wherein the Taiwanese moved toward cultural integration at the same time that they remained forever economically and politically unequal. Compare Caroline Ts'ai's recent reexamination of the concept and Ching's understanding (*Taiwan in Japan's Empire,* 190-92).

47 A list of these activities, ranging from billards to family hygiene, is found in Ye, *Riluo Taibeicheng,* 300–307.

48 Photographs of these three pavilions are in *Taiwan huixiang,* 234; a photograph of the earliest is in *Taiwan huaijiu,* 54 (also see note 45); a photograph of the Hibiya Park pavilion is in Maejima, *Hibiya Kōen,* 65.

49 Maejima , *Hibiya Kōen,* 69.

50 The stage can be rented by any organization for formal programming, but as long as the group is not large and does not use electronic equipment, the space is available free (interview with park office staff, July 2005).

51 Lai Zhengzhe identifies this as a place for making "blind dates" (*Zai gongsi shangban,* 114)

52 Scott Simon's essay on gay life in Taiwan, "From Hidden Kingdom," also contains numerous references to the park, including lengthy comments by Lai.

53 Lai, "Zai gongsi shangban," "Thesis Abstract," np.

54 Bai, *Niezi,* 3.

55 Damm, "Same Sex Desire," 68–69.

56 Chang and Wang, "Mapping Taipei's Landscape," 120.

57 The name of Lai's bookstore seems to have gone through a cross-cultural translation process: Jingjing, which means "crystal," seems to be derived from Howard Goldblatt's translation of the title of Bai Xianyong's novel as *Crystal Boys,* which in turn is derived from the slang term *boli* (glass) for boy prostitutes.

58 Lai, "Zai gongsi shangban," 151.

59 Ibid., 153.

60 See Feuchtwang, "Domestic and Communal Worship in Taiwan."

61 Interview with caretaker, December 8, 1999.

62 This narrative is contained in a brochure/calendar obtained in 2005 from the office of the shrine; the narrative was written by Huang Abei in 2003. Subsequently, I spoke at length with committee member Huang Ruiyu (2005), who provided more details, including the opinion that there had been a small shrine during the Japanese period.

63 Lai Zhengzhe gives 1980 as the date of the construction of the temple ("Zai gongsi shangban," 49).

64 Interview with Huang Ruiyu (2005) and official certificate no. 09232697000.

65 I insert that path over the official map in Allen, "Taipei Park," fig. 5.

66 Li L, "You dushi gongyuan," 44.

67 In later years, Taipei Park also included a baseball diamond and tennis courts, which stayed in place until the 1970s. However, the primary sports facilities, including the baseball stadium, were in the northern suburbs within Murayama Park.

68 Li L, "You dushi gongyuan," 42.

69 Cai H, "Taiwan dushi gongyuan," 78.

70 *Tabeishi dushijihua cankaotu.*

71 Chang and Wang, "Mapping Taipei's Landscape."

72 For example, the 1992 pamphlet from the Taipei City Department of Public Works was titled *Taibeishi Da'an qihaogongyuan jianjie* (Brief introduction to No. 7 Park of Da'an Ward, Taipei City); cited in Braester, "Tales," 170n22.

Five: Display in the City

1 Details of the holdings and an outline of the history of the museum are available at http://www.npm.gov.tw/en/home.htm. Jeannette Shambaugh Elliott's *Odyssey of China's Imperial Art Treasures* puts the museum in historical and cultural perspective. More details, especially regarding the historical conditions of the museum, are found in the essays collected in Cai Meifang's *Bazheng maonian.*

2 "Beijing curator."

3 Shambaugh Elliott, 69–70.

4 The Web site of the Palace Museum in Beijing contains several annotated (and animated) itineraries for visitors; see "Ways to Explore the Museum," http://www.dpm.org.cn/English/default.asp. Shambaugh Elliott describes the limited and poor exhibition space (*Odyssey,* 141–42).

5 The curators studied the packing techniques of shipments from the imperial kiln (Jingdezhen) by dismantling and analyzing crates of ceramics in the trea-

sury that had theretofore not been unpacked (Chen X, "Lao zhuang laoyun hao," 9).

6   Shambaugh Elliott, *Odyssey*, 94.

7   Cahill, "Place of the National Palace Museum." Here Cahill recalls a series of increasingly important visits to the museum, including his involvement in the three-month photography project in 1963–64, in which almost the entire collection was photographed.

8   Cai F, "Beigou de gugong," 47.

9   Ibid., 54.

10   Wang and Heath, "Constructions of National Identity," 35.

11   Chun, "Discourses of Identity," 55.

12   We should note that the Palace Museum in Beijing was one of the institutions that was almost completely isolated from the machinations of the Cultural Revolution, protected by the direct authority of Chairman Mao and Premier Zhou Enlai (Shambaugh Elliott, *Odyssey*, 125–32).

13   Yi-wen Wang and Tim Heath argue for the significance of the role that the Cultural Revolution played in legitimizing the work of the "cultural renaissance" policies of the Nationalist government in Taiwan ("Constructions of National Identity," 75).

14   Lu X, "You shenqian,"186.

15   Vickers, "Re-writing Museums," 77.

16   "Taiwan Museum Director."

17   "China to Lend."

18   Karp and Lavine, *Exhibiting Cultures*, 1.

19   Ibid., 16.

20   The history of this museum is detailed in Lü S, *Taiwan zhanshi*, 296–304.

21   Li Z, *Taiwan shengli bowuguan*, 306–11. On these statues, see chapter 6.

22   Wei Z, *Guoli Taiwan bowuguan*, 13. Note that the Chinese text is more formal and does not include any pronoun subjects, although at least "one" can be assumed.

23   Mitchell, *Colonizing Egypt*, 7.

24   Peattie, "Japanese Attitudes," 84–86.

25   The History Museum also participated actively in the narrative of a displaced China. Housed first in the Japanese Commodities Exhibition Hall next to the botanical garden, in 1956 the History Museum was brought physically closer to the Nationalist story when it was renovated in a five-floor traditional palace-style structure. The materials and activities of the History Museum were overwhelmingly connected to conditions of mainland/traditional China. Edward Vickers reviews the status of this museum, including its tilt toward local culture in the post–martial law period ("Re-writing Museums," 78–80).

26   Li Z, "Linian dashiji," 313.

27   Wei Z, *Guoli Taiwan bowuguan*, 9.

28   Ibid., 7.

29   The enormity of the project is recounted in detail in the 1939 publication *Shisei Yonjisshūnen Kinen*, reviewed by Lü Shaoli in *Taiwan zhanshi* and by Cheng Jiahui in *Diyi dabolanhui*. Cheng's richly illustrated volume contains a vast amount of information about the exposition, for which I am indebted to the author.

30   Cheng, *Diyi dabolanhui*, 52.

31   *Shisei Yonjisshūnen Kinen*, 563. The data contain details of daily ticket sales but do not include information on the visitors. This number must have included numerous multiple visits by individuals, thus Cheng Jiahui's estimate that a third of the island's population visited the exposition is perhaps not quite accurate (*Diyi dabolanhui*, 32).

32   Lau, *Unbroken Chain*, 30–31; translated by James C. T. Shu, romanization adjusted. Also cited by Lü Shaoli, along with other sources on the Taiwanese response to the exposition (*Taiwan zhanshi*, 282–91).

33   Chen F, "Zhaohe jiyi," 32.

34   Lau, *Unbroken Chain*, 25.

35   See Yamaguchi Masao, "The Poetics of Exhibition," for a discussion of this new view.

36   Japanese authorities were well aware of this neither-nor role, which they exploited in their own self-positioning; see Rydell, *All the World's a Fair,* 50, 51, 181.

37   Cheng, *Diyi dabolanhui*, 40–42.

38   Shih-wei Lo describes Exposition Site No. 1, which centered on the Civic Hall (Kōkaidō) and the West Gate Park, extending down the boulevard (currently Zhonghualu) ("Palimpsest," 71–72).

39   For a discussion of the "white city" phenomenon, see Rydell, *All the World's a Fair*.

40   Lo, "Palimpsest," 72.

41   For a detailed description and analysis of this massive reservation (twelve hundred Filipinos on a forty-seven-acre site), see Rydell, *All the World's a Fair*, 167–78.

42   Andrew Morris speaks of a "Gallery of Savages" featuring 6,450 aborigines (*Taiwan nichichi shimpō*, October 8, 1935, 7), but I believe that that refers to the various performances and not to a specific site (*Colonial Project*, 46).

43   An exception to this general rule seems to be the Monopoly Bureau's display of modern packaging equipment, which appears to be operated by Taiwanese women.

44   Karp, "Other Cultures," 375.

45   *Toushi Xinggongyuan* (75) explains the symbolism of this construction and

dates it to 1961, while the calligraphy panels flanking the pavilions are dated from 1964.

46 Taylor, "Discovering a Nationalist Heritage," 6.

47 Borrowing the term from Jeffrey Brooks's study of Stalin, Jeremy Taylor describes the traditional hagiography (where authorship is elided) as a "theft of agency" ("Discovering a Nationalist Heritage," 9n34).

48 On the original motivation for the construction, see Yin D, "Yuanjin Zhongshantang," 75 ; on the Civic Hall in Hibiya Park, see Maejima, *Hibiya Kōen*, 71–74.

49 Chen F, "Zhaohe jiyi," 31.

50 Steven Phillips describes the special and complicated position of Chen Yi in Taiwan's transition from colony to province (*Between Assimilation and Independence*, 52–55).

51 Chen F, "Zhaohe jiyi," 33.

52 Huang X, "Zhongshantang dashiji," 218; although the name was changed immediately, it is unclear when the signage was added.

53 Yao Qizhong mentions the removal of these imperial crests but does not give dates; he also describes the installation of the plum blossom insignia (national flower of the Republic of China) during renovations in the 1970s ("Zhongshantang fenzhan," 175).

54 Again it is not exactly clear when these rooms adopted the new names. In Japanese, they are simply called assembly and banquet rooms: detailed architectural drawings of the building, including of these spaces, are in *Shisei Yonjisshūnen Kinen*, plates following page 76.

55 Jiang, "Longfeng chenxiang," 47.

56 Li Qingzhi, "Taibei xin leyuan," 165.

57 Guo Guanying says, "On the east side of China Market (Zhonghua Shichang) in the area between Sun Yat-sen Hall and the New Life Newspaper was the place where the young people met" ("Xiashi," 123–24).

58 Long, "Xu."

59 After the lifting of martial law, the National Assembly became a quick target of the new reforms. The student demonstrations of 1990 were directed at this institution, which was reconstituted in 1991 and abolished in 2005. Denny Roy reviews this history (*Taiwan*, 190–95).

60 Hsia, "Gonghuitang," 157.

61 Yin Di names a Baolei Ting (Fortress Chamber) and mentions a restaurant from the early postwar years, but it is not clear whether these are the same place ("Yuanjin Zhongshan tang," 75). In the original Japanese drawings, this space is labeled *raihindō* (reception room).

62 Li Qingzhi, "Taibei xin leyuan," 166.

63 A photo caption for the monument in *Returning* says, "In facing Sun Yat-sen Hall, [the Retrocession Monument's] function carries certain historical implications" (Long, *Huidao Zhongshantang*, 41). The monument seems to be an attempt to recast the Japanese legacy of the space into a more Nationalist narrative.

64 Barthes, "Semiology," 96.

65 Long, *Huidao Zhongshantang*, 65, 67.

66 See Kun-hui Ku, "Rights to Recognition," for a discussion of post–martial law politics and aborigine identity formation. This is a theme that Edward Vickers also explores in the formation of these museums ("Rewriting Museums," 86–96).

67 Rudolph, "The Quest for Difference."

68 *Ketagalan Culture Center Guide.*

69 The Mongolian and Tibetan Affairs Commission of the Executive Yuan was established in China in 1912 and lives on in Taiwan as a tattered vestige of that old condition; the Council for Hakka Affairs was established in 2001.

70 Hsieh, *Collective Rights*, 47–49.

Six: Statues in the City

1 This space was originally planned as Park No. 3 in the Japanese park system of 1932. The term Xinsheng (New Life) refers to a Nationalist-led social program, New Life Movement (Xingshenghuo yundong), devised in the 1930s to counter Communism with a mixture of Confucianism and nationalism.

2 "Flying Tigers" (Feihu jun) was the nickname originally given by the Chinese to the "American Volunteer Group," a small company of several hundred American airmen and support staff that was sent under secret orders of President Roosevelt in early 1941 to assist Chiang Kai-shek against the Japanese. The same name was applied later to the much larger 14th Air Force, which Chennault commanded after the United States entered the war.

3 The Chennault family did not know exactly where the bust was located, and Cynthia Chennault had asked me to give her a description of the new setting if I found it. Much of the information on the Chennault family is from her personal correspondence.

4 *Zhongyang ribao* (Central Daily News), April 15, 1960, 1. One source says the base for the Chennault statue was originally built for the statue of Yagyū Kazuyoshi, first president of the Bank of Taiwan, which stood elsewhere in the park, although I have not been able to compare them; http://zh.wikipedia.org/wiki/偉人銅像 (臺北市). The installation of the Yagyū statue is recorded in *Taiwan nichinichi shimpō*, September, 17, 1918, 7.

5   "Jiang furen." Mayor Huang's remarks conclude with an elegant twelve-line, four-character panegyric for Chennault, which was cast in bronze and attached as one of the panels to the side of the pedestal.

6   Ibid.

7   The site is now occupied by a large Chinese bell, named the Peace Bell (Heping Zhong), which was donated by the Taipei Lions Club and installed about the same time as the building of the February 28th Monument.

8   The museum, located near Marco Polo Bridge (Lugouqiao), where Japan's full-scale invasion of China began, was opened on the fiftieth anniversary of that incident, July 7, 1987.

9   Wu H, *Remaking Beijing*, 69–72. In a personal communication, Wu Hung clarifies that the portrait has been installed on national holidays beginning in 1958.

10 "Anti-Japan War Museum."

11 "Founder of 'Flying Tiger.'"

12 Segalen, *Great Statuary*, 23.

13 Note that Richard Vinograd's study of portraiture of the late imperial period, *Boundaries of the Self*, is limited to painting. When bureaucratic figures appear in statuary, they are typically of a "type," not an individual.

14 Anna Paludan describes the divergent histories of sculpture in China and the West in these terms ("Introduction," 15–34).

15 Michalski, *Public Monuments*, 8.

16 Wyke, "Marginal Figures."

17 Fujitani, *Splendid Monarchy*, 124, quoting Ubukata Toshirō at the turn of the century.

18 Ibid., quoting an 1881 newspaper article.

19 Schiermeier and Forrer, *Wonders of Imperial Japan*, 86.

20 On the introduction of landscape (watercolor) painting to Taiwan, see Yen, "Colonial Taiwan." Carlos Rojas discusses the circulation of the photographic portraiture of Sun Yat-sen in the late 1920s, although this phenomenon was clearly preceded in Japan during the Meiji period, including the circulation of important portraits of the emperor (Rojas, "Abandoned Cities," 222–23).

21 Li Z, "Linian Dashiji," 306. Su Shuobin notes that a bronze statue of the first civil administrator of the colony was installed in Murayama Park in 1903 (Shuobin, "Kongjian shijuehua," 37). The only image I have seen is undated in *Taiwan meishō*, 511.

22 Wyke, "Marginal Figures," 93.

23 The club building predates this installation, which also has a civic nature, although more coincidental.

24 The blueprint is located in the Taiwan Historica Archives, document no. 1188.32 (July 17, 1906).

25 I have yet to find details on the destruction of the statue or the site during the fifteen intervening years.

26 Su Shuobin has a summary chart of fourteen public statues in the city dating from 1903 to 1935 ("Kongjian shijuehua," 37).

27 Compare *Taiwan huaijiu*, 55, 63. The animated pose of this larger-than-life figure is clearly borrowed from early photographic portraiture, especially its three-quarter profile.

28 According to *Taiwan huaijiu* (126), this is also a statue of Kodama, but I follow Su Shuobin on this ("Kongjian shijuehua," 37). Zhuang Yongming compares the two statues and says that the Chiang statue was moved when the Zhongshan North Road overpass was built (in 1955, according to *Taibeishi lujie*, 313) (*Taibei laojie*, 181). I have not yet identified the subsequent location of this statue. There was a similar exchange in the installation of Sun Yat-sen's bronze figure on the base where the statue of Hirō Tatsumi, the fourth Japanese civil administrator, once stood. See Allen, "Taipei Park," fig. 9.

29 One source says the Sun Yat-sen statue (see note 28) was cast by Fu Tiansheng (1912–1966), who studied sculpture in Japan, and was installed October 10, 1949; http://zh.wikipedia.org/wiki/偉人銅像 (臺北市).

30 In *Colonial Project*, Andrew Morris discusses both baseball and tennis as part of colonial and Nationalist policies.

31 Interview, December 4, 2004.

32 *Toushi Xinggongyuan* (75) dates this to 1961; the calligraphy panels flanking the pavilions date from 1964 (when dated). Note that this complex is the area called the "lily pond" in the materials from Lai Zhengzhe (A'zhe) describing gay activities in the park, cited in chapter 4.

33 Xu Shiying (1873–1964) was actually a Qing official who, late in life, became associated with the Nationalist government and came to Taiwan in 1951. He died apparently shortly after writing this inscription.

34 A picture from 1970 shows the pavilions without their bronze busts (*Taibei huakan*, 26, 28–29). The accompanying plaques are dated variously from 1976 to 1982.

35 Significantly, a stone statue of Wang Tiandeng stands in the entryway to the February 28th Memorial Hall, the museum in the park; Wang Tiandeng was a businessman and newspaper editor who authored the "Outline of Thirty-two Articles of Management" (Sanshiertiao Chuli Dagang) that was presented to the Nationalist authorities during the February 28th Incident. After the brutal conclusion of the incident, Wang was burned alive and his body thrown into the Danshui River. A review of the political implications of the Memorial Museum can be found in Edward Vickers, "Re-Writing Museums," 86–87.

36 *Taibeishi ererba heping gongyuan.*

37 Wu J, "Guozu jiangou," 101. I have very much relied on Wu Jinyong's detailed

account of these proceedings; I have not acknowledged him at every occurrence but, when possible, I cite original sources that his study provides.

38   The first monument to be completed (in 1988) was a private one outside of Taipei in memory of Lin Maosheng, one of the most socially prominent victims of the carnage that followed the incident (Wu J, "Guozu jiangou," 18). But more important memorials were built in Gaoxiong in 1991 and 1992; the latter of which was placed in a park renamed "February 28th Park."

39   Ibid., 20.

40   Phillips, "Fighting," 12.

41   Li S, "Ererba Jianbei nabian," 14; Feng, "Ererba Jianbei yizai," 14.

42   Feng, "Ererba Jinianbei jianli," 3.

43   Wu J, "Guozu jiangou," 24; it is unclear in this account if the train station plaza remained in consideration.

44   Ibid.

45   Xiao, "Xinsheng gongyuan."

46   The memorial was opened in 1996, but the official ceremonies, including the unveiling of the commemorative plaque, were in 1997; Phillips, "Fighting," 14.

47   Original English, *Liang Jiang wenhua*, 15.

48   http://zh.wikipedia.org/wiki/偉人銅像 (臺北市).

49   Michalski, *Public Monuments*, 66, 74.

50   Quoted in Ross, "Taiwan Sculpture Wars."

51   Ibid.

52   On the post-1989 fate of this statuary in Eastern Europe, see Michalski, *Public Monuments*, 148–53.

53   Conversation with Fan Huancai of the Daxi Cultural Community Center, May 31, 2008.

54   Michalski, *Public Monuments*, 152. Svetlana Boym also describes this museum, including its later transformation into the "Park of Arts" where the old statuary was largely restored and presented as fully historicized art (*The Future of Nostalgia*, chapter 8).

55   Jeremy Taylor mentions that the park was designed by local artists, but I do not have information on their identities or motivations ("Discovering a Nationalist Heritage," 5).

56   *Kinen hakubutsukan.*

57   Ouyang and Li, "Bowuguan de yanjiu," 136.

58   Li Zi'ning, interview, 1999.

Seven: A Horse in a Park in a City on an Island in the Sea

1   Until the summer of 2005, there was a set of small steps on the base that encouraged the children's approach. Over the years, however, there seems

to have been a decline in the practice of climbing on the horse; children still gaze at and fondle it, but parents seem more reluctant to allow the children to sit on it. This change in behavior may be part of a larger social change that David Schak has identified as a new civility of the post–martial law period (Schak, "Development").

2 Professor Dai Baocun suggested that the flower might not be a *sakura*, which is quite rare, but rather a *kiri* (paulownia) blossom, which it resembles. The effacement makes the design ambiguous, but it appears to be the *sakura* as illustrated in Dower, no. 238. I would note that the travel blogger Binbin (see p. 177) also identifies it as a *sakura*, reconstructing the complete design from the traces.

3 This photograph was provided by Cai Jintang just as I was finishing the manuscript and contributes to some rethinking of the crest, as accounted below. For another photograph of the horses in front of the Xinzhu Shinto shrine, see Allen, "Taiwan de shenma," fig 4.

4 I have identified seven such sites: (1) In Taizhong Park, a pair of horses on their original bases, where the Shinto shrine has been converted into one for Confucius. (2) In Tainan, a similar pair that has been moved, with original bases, to the city's *zhonglieci* (shrine for Chinese martyrs). (3) In Taoyuan, a single horse where the Shinto shrine architecture (within its *zhonglieci*) has been recently restored. (4) In Hualian, a single horse at the *zhonglieci* (site of the former Shinto shrine). (5) In Zhongli, a horse that has been moved to the courtyard of the city high school. (6) In a temple in Yilan, an original horse, with a reproduction near the entrance of the former old Japanese shrine, converted into a *zhonglieci* in 1958. (7) In Xinying, near the playground area, one of the original pair of horses from its shrine, with two reproductions of this horse in different locations around the city. Since completing my survey, an on-line source has produced images of three other extant horses, all from small shrines (Douliu, 1929; Yunlin, 1931, and Beidou, 1938). http://web.hach. gov.tw/hachweb/blog/kypo809/myBlogArticleAction.do?method=doListAr ticleByPk&articleId=12786. I have not yet had a chance to visit these sites.

5 Two prominent pairs of horses that have apparently been lost are from the shrines in Xinzhu (see fig. 7.2) and Gaoxiong; photographs are found in *Taiwan Huaijiu*, 249, 246. There is also a newspaper account of the installation of a pair (?) of horses at the shrine in Pingdong; *Taiwan nichinichi shimpō*, April 24, 1940, 5.

6 Todd Henry has confirmed their presence in Colonial Korea (personal communication); for the Dalian shrine; see http://homepage2.nifty.com/ liondog/douraku/kaigai_mansyu_dairen.htm, reproduced in Allen, "Taiwan de shenma," fig. 6.

7 I measured the Taipei Park horse at 190 cm from hoof to ear and 257 cm

from tail to nose; compare the Taoyuan horse at 205 cm tall by 270 cm long (*Taoyuan zhonglieci*, 2).

8 As we shall see, the Xinying horse also was placed unlabeled in a park, but its provenance is well attested.

9 Benedict Read discusses in detail Victorian equestrian statuary, reproducing images of eighteen different examples (in stone and bronze), which share many obvious similarities with the Japanese bronze horses (*Victorian Sculpture*). However, the Japanese horses have distinctive stylistic elements, most notably in the rendering of the mane and tail. Almost all the Japanese horses have a streaming tail and many have a relatively stylized mane, conventions shared with the Kusunoki Masashige statues but not with any of the European examples. The European equestrian statue that most resembles the Japanese horses is that of Joan of Arc at the Place des Pyramides, Paris (1874), although it, too, lacks the streaming tail (Michalski, *Public Monuments*, 15).

10 The Taiwan Kusunoki Masashige statue stood on the site of the first public school in Taiwan, currently the Shilin Elementary School; the statue was destroyed at the end of the war, but a photograph of it and its accompanying temple is found in *Jianzheng*, vol. 1, 221; see Allen, "Taiwan de shenma," figs. 8, 9.

11 Hardacre, *Shintō*, 3.

12 Ibid., 24.

13 Ibid., 38.

14 *Kitashirkawa*, frontispiece and 621, standing in front of the Imperial Guard Troop Headquarters (Kone Sotsuton Shireibu). In 1977 the headquarters were converted into the Craft Gallery, the National Museum of Modern Art, Tokyo, where the statue still stands. There was a similar statue displayed in Taiwan during a 1917 industrial exhibition (*Taiwan hangyō*).

15 Ponsonby Fane, *Vicissitudes*, 318.

16 Ibid., 353. Note that there was also a Zheng Chenggong temple in Tainan that was converted, at least in name, to a Shinto shrine in 1897 (Cai J, Zhanzheng tizhi, 24–25).

17 *Jianzheng Taiwan* (vol. 2), 19. This illustration is probably a representation of Prince Kitashirakawa.

18 Chen Yijun explained this use of the wrappings, December 2006.

19 *Taiwan jinja shashinchō*, front cover, reproduced in Allen, "Taiwan de shenma," fig. 11

20 The record provides a composite list of military and police officers, educators, officials, firemen, and leaders of community organizations (*hokō*). (*Kenkō jinja*, 2).

21 Ponsonby Fane, *Vicissitudes*, 344.

22 Ibid., 345.

23 *Kenkō jinja*, 2.

24 This was one of the few shrine buildings used by the postwar Chinese Nationalist government (as the site for the National Central Library, relocated in 1949); the very "non-Shinto" look of the building may have masked its origins well enough to allow this reuse for some years.

25 *Taichu jinja*, 59.

26 *Taiwan jinja shi*, 122.

27 *Tainan jinja*, 34; *Taiwan jinja shi*, 125. Iwahashi Tei may be a woman, since the given name is written in hiragana; in the 1935 overview of the shrine (*Taiwan jinja ryakushi*, 19), this name is not on the donor list, only that of Furuya Seisaburo. There is also a newspaper account of a group of firefighters donating a horse or horses to the Tainan shrine; *Taiwan nichinichi shimpō*, March, 30, 1924, 4.

28 The donation of the horses is recorded in *Taiwan nichinchishimpō*, December 2 and 7, 1921 (7, 4), while the dedication plaque dates from November. Recent additional on-line information identifies the artist as Asada Ritarō of Osaka. http://tw.myblog.yahoo.com/hank1980-blog/article?mid=8746&sc=1. Unfortunately, I have no records on donations to the Taoyuan shrine. The two site restoration reports for these temples (see Huang J, *Taoyuanxian* and *Shiding guji*) are also silent on the horses.

29 Baoyi Daifu (Official Protecting Righteousness) is identified as the heroic military figure of the Tang dynasty (*Caituan faren*).

30 The temple's civil administrator, Xie Binqi, in consultation with a temple elder, dated the horses to the 1950s (interview, June 2009).

31 Kawahara Isao details the beginning of these policy changes in 1937 with the appointment of Governor-General Kobayashi Seizō ("State of Taiwanese Culture"). The term "make Japan and Taiwan as one" is from Kobayashi's memoir, quoted in ibid., 130. Caroline Ts'ai has detailed investigation of these changes in social policy, which she dates to beginning as early as 1931 (*Taiwan in Japan Empire*, especially chapter 7). Cai Jintang has data on Shinto shrine attendance activities during this period; for example, in 1941 there were more than 12 million visits island-wide, with 7.6 million of them by Taiwanese (*Nihon teikoku shugi*, 159; compare *Zhanzheng tizhi*, 31).

32 *Taihokushi seishi*, 414–15, 418.

33 *Taoyuan zhonglieci*.

34 The exact forms of the effacements in the horses I have seen vary and include (1) cutting away the crest from the outer layer of bronze (one of the two Taizhong horses); (2) covering the crest with a bronze plate welded to the body (one of the two Tainan horses and the Hualian horse); (3) making the design illegible through complete effacement (one of the Tainan horses, the Xinying horse, and Zhongli horse); and (4) partially erasing the crest, such that it can still be read (the Taipei Park horse, the Taoyuan horse,

and one of the Taizhong horses). In contrast, we should remember that there are two cases of completely intact crests: the horse in storage at the museum and the Yilan horse held by the temple (as well as its copy). Based on the photograph posted on-line, the crest on the horse in Douliu has been cut away, leaving a distinct hole in its torso (http://web.hach.gov.tw/hachweb/blog/kypo809/myBlogArticleAction.do?method=doListArticleByPk&articleId=12786).

35 In other sites, the Japanese associations of the horses remain part of public memory. For example, older men who take their leisure in the Confucian shrine of Taizhong Park know the Japanese origins of those horses very well, but this memory may be aided by the surrounding remains of the Shinto shrine (interview, January 30, 2005).

36 Fu, *Rizhi shiqi*, 61. Details (and sources) for this history are available in Huang J, *Taoyuanxian*, 1.2-1.3.

37 Zhuang Weicheng of the Xinying City cultural office explained the relationship between the original, the reproductions, and the new public statue (interview, November 24, 2006).

38 Chen Y, "Yuanshan zhonglieci," 170–71. I want to thank Chen Yijun for clarifying the relationship between the original horse and its replica. I have relied very much on his thesis and sources here, though not acknowledging them at every occurrence.

39 Ibid., 167.

40 *Faxian Xinying*, 38.

41 Chen Y, "Yuanshan zhonglieci," 167.

42 According to the official records, the Yilan Shinto Shrine was built in 1906, but moved to this location in 1919 (*Jinja oyo sha*, 2).

43 Lin Hengdao, "Taibei gongyuan" introduces the "valuable relics" in the park and has photographs of many objects, including Japanese lanterns and the like, but does not mention the horse. Similarly, the official 1999 handbook for the park covers many small details of the park's materials and history but contains no mention of the horse (*Toushi Xingongyuan*). Neither the official map nor the tourist brochure produced by the city government (*Taibeishi Ererba*) marks the site, although other sites are well labeled, including the restrooms.

44 The blog, "My Barefoot Travel," is by a young man who goes by the name of Binbin and focuses on historic sites in Taiwan. Although I began my investigations of the horse before I happened upon this Web site, Binbin's information and clarifications were very useful to me. I have never been able to make contact with him, however, so allow me to thank him here; http://www.barefoot.idv.tw/messages/notebook/20060205/20060205.htm. As late of 2007, another blogger, Tong Huang, responding to Binbin, says that he does not

know if the horse comes from the Taiwan shrine or not (http://www.tonyhuang 39.com/tony0519/dbtt0519.html).

45 Ponsonby Fane, *Vicissitudes of Shintō*, 346. It appears to have been a popular shrine (hosting 161,984 visitors in 1938), perhaps because of its location in the downtown area (*Taihoku seishi*, 419–20).

46 *Taiwan huixiang*, 321; reproduced in Allen, "Taiwan de shenma," fig. 16.

47 Richard Ponsonby Fane mentions another Inari shrine in Taipei, the Daian Inari, but I cannot identify the location or nature of this shrine (*Vicissitudes of Shintō*, 346).

48 *Taiwan nichinichi shimpō*, June 22, 1937, 4.

49 This horse was located and photographed for me by Li Zi'ning (January 2005); see Allen, "Taiwan de shenma," figs. 7, 17.

50 The *Taiwan jinja ryakushi* records these statues as part of the Taiwan Shrine materials (19). He Xunyao relates that these oxen and other materials (he does not mention a horse) were moved to the museum in 1949 from the old Taiwan Shrine, which had been converted into the Taiwan Provincial Civil Education Hall (Taiwansheng Minzheng Jiaoyuguan) for a short time (He, "Wo zai bowuguan," 284).

51 *Taiwan jinja shi*, 122, 125.

52 *Taiwan nichinichi shimpō*, September 26, 1922, and June 2, 1926; *Gochinza sanjū*, reproduced in Allen, "Taiwan de shenma," figs. 18, 19.

53 *Taiwan jinja ryakushi*, 19; we should note that horses were added to shrines well after 1935; for example, for the Taoyuan shrine built in 1938.

54 Ponsonby Fane, *Vicissitudes of Shintō*, 346.

55 For a detail of that map with the shrine, see Allen, "Taiwan de shenma," fig. 20.

56 *Jinja oyo sha*, 9.

57 The photograph of this horse comes from a postwar snapshot in which two young Chinese men playfully, or perhaps mockingly, mount the horse for the camera. The source, *Guojia wenhua ziliaoku*, says that the photo was taken at a Shinto shrine (*shenshe*), but I believe this to be a technical error; *Jinja oyo sha* lists this as only a temple, or *sha* (9), and Cai Jintang does not include it in his comprehensive list of Shinto shrines (*Nihon teikoku shugi*, 351-55).

58 Interview, January 27, 2005.

59 He Xunyao was only fifteen when he arrived in Taiwan, but he often visited the museum (through the office of the museum director, whom he had known in Guizhou) and joined the staff around 1948 (He, "Wo zai bowuguan).

60 After I completed work on this chapter, the blogger Kai Zhang suggested that the Taipei Park horse had come from the Gokoku *jinja* (Huguo *shenshe*), but he gave no evidence (http://web.hach.gov.tw/hachweb/blog/kypo809/myBlogArticleAction.do?method=doListArticleByPk&articleId=12786).I first doubted that possibility because the shrine was built very late (1942).

Although I have yet to find direct evidence, I now believe this could very well be the original location of the horse. A newspaper photograph of the shrine's opening ceremonies (*Taiwan nichnichi shimpō*, May 23, 1942, 1) shows a drapery with what must be its *shinmon*; it is that of a *sakura* surround with the stlyized *tai* in the center, just as seen on the horse. There is certain logic to this, since the Gokoku *jinja* was next to the Taiwan *jinja*, whence came the bronze oxen mentioned above. Why this horse was moved and not the ones from the Taiwan *jinja* is perplexing. A final mystery remains: on the horse's lower abdomen, just forward of the genitalia, is a small casted cartouche that reads: Made by Jō'un/Xiangyun 祥雲作. I now wonder if other horses have such small, unnoticed markings? And who is this Auspicious Cloud artist?

Postface: Theoretical Considerations

1   Gottdiener and Lagopoulos, "Introduction," 17.

2   Barthes, "Semiology," 90, 97.

3   Ibid., 93–94.

4   Eco, "Function and Sign," 59.

5   Ibid., 64.

6   Ibid.

7   Harvey, *Consciousness*, chapter 4.

8   This derives from C. S. Pierce's "The Icon, Index, and Symbol," although I have come to the usage of the terms via W. J. T. Mitchell's *Iconology*.

9   Barthes, "Photographic Message," 20–25.

10   John Tagg critiques the concept of the photograph's "evidential force" developed in Barthes's "The Photographic Message" and *Camera Lucida* (*Burden of Representation*, 1–5). See also Ryan, *Picturing Empire*.

11   Barthes, *Camera Lucida*, 5.

12   Emma Teng notes the missing aboriginal languages from this list, calling the omission "a symptom of the preoccupation in Taiwanese nationalist discourse since 1949 on the ethnic conflict between 'mainlanders' and 'Taiwanese'" (*Taiwan's Imagined Geography*, 253).

13   Low, "Introduction," 5–21.

14   Roger Selya calls it a "world city" in his *Taipei*; Reginald Kwok's volume *Globalizing Taipei* is one place where Taipei is considered a global city.

15   Geertz, "Thick Description," 9.

16   Although I came to this idea of displacement as a spatiality particular to Taipei through my own meandering logic, I was not the first to use the term. In 1996 Shih-wei Lo completed a dissertation titled "Figures of Displacement: Modes of Urbanity in Taipei, 1740–1995." I was not able to obtain a copy of this study, but I did benefit very much from Lo's derived article, "A Palimpsest

of '*Fait Urbains*' in Taipei."

17 Clifford, "Poetics of Displacement."

18 L Chen, "Mapping Identity," 301.

19 Rojas, "'Nezha Was Here,'" 85.

20 These concepts are well represented in the essays in Iain Borden et al., *Unknown City*. For Taipei, similar metaphors are used by Yomi Braester in "If We Could Remember."

21 Sarah Dillon discusses the metaphor in literary criticism (*Palimpsest*); Andreas Huyssen uses the palimpsest metaphor to describe broadly urban space (*Present Pasts*), and Lo Shih-wei uses it to describe Taipei City specifically ("Palimpsest").

22 Jou, "Domestic Politics."

23 Boym, *Nostaglia*, xiii. I want to thank Tze-Lan Sang for bringing Boym's work and its relationship to Taiwan to my attention.

24 Boym, *Nostalgia*, chapter 4; quote from 49.

25 Zukin, *Culture*, 7.

26 Soja, *Postmodern Geographies*.

27 Low, "Spatializing Culture," 112.

28 Allen, "Taipei Park," fig. 5.

29 Ching, *Becoming "Japanese*," 29–30

30 La Sueur, *Decolonization Reader*, 1.

31 Osterhammel, *Colonialism*, 11.

32 The essays in Ramon Myers and Mark Peattie's collected volume, *Japanese Colonial Empire*, provide general overviews, especially the two by Peattie, as well as small, telling details of the period and colonial processes. In addition, there have been several monographs on a subset of Japanese colonial conditions, especially in history and the social sciences; Patricia Tsurumi's *Japanese Colonial Education* and Chih-ming Ka's *Japanese Colonialism* are examples. Recently more theoretical work on the conditions of Japanese colonialism have added to the discussion, not only Leo Ching's *Becoming "Japanese"* and Ming-Cheng Lo's *Doctors within Borders* but also essays in Liao and Wang's *Taiwan under Japanese Rule* and Caroline Tsai's recent *Taiwan in Japan's Empire Building*, which also offers a thorough review of the recent scholarship in Chinese and Japanese, which has been substantial.

33 Ching, *Becoming "Japanese*," 27.

34 Teng, *Taiwan's Imagined Geography*, 7.

35 These are terms Jürgen Osterhammel uses as two "decisive elements" in defining colonialism (*Colonialism*, 15).

36 Teng, *Taiwan's Imagined Geography*, 11.

37 This is essentially the argument made by Chen Fangming in *Houzhimin Taiwan*, 25–30.

Chinese and Japanese Glossary

NOTE: *Hanyu pinyin and Hepburn romanization are used, except where Taiwanese (T) dialect is indicated. Common terms are in lower case unless they begin with a proper noun. All personal names appear in Chinese and Japanese style and order; personal names appearing in Works Cited are not included here.*

Afa　阿發
Aihe 愛河
Akashi Motojirō　明石元二郎
Ang Lee.　See Li An
Asada Ritarō 浅田利太郎
A'zhe 阿哲.　See Lai Zhengzhe
Azuma　吾妻
ba　爸
Bai Xianyong (1937–)　白先勇
Baigong　白宮
bajun　八駿
banjin　番人
Banqiao　板橋
baobing　薄餅
Baolei candian　堡壘餐店
Baoyi daifu　保儀大夫
Bei'yi'nü　北一女
beifang gongdianshi　北方宮殿式
Beigou diqu　北溝地區
Beimenjie　北門街
Benmusho/banwushu　辦務署

bentuhua　本土化

Binbin　斌斌

binzihao jiaoche　賓字號轎車

bo'ai　博愛

Bo'ailu　博愛路

boli　玻璃

Cai Mingliang (1957–)　蔡明亮

Cen Yuying (1829–1889)　岑毓英

Chang'an　長安

Chen Jinchuan　陳進傳

Chen Laizhang (fl. 1709)　陳賴章

Chen Limei　陳麗美

Chen Qiuju (fl. 1896)　陳秋菊

Chen Shuibian (1950–)　陳水扁

Chen Xiangmei (1925–)　陳香梅

Chen Xiasheng　陳夏生

Chen Xingju (1817–1885)　陳星聚

Chen Yi (1883–1950)　陳毅

Chen Zhenyu　陳振瑜

Chenghuangmiao　城隍廟

chengqian chengwan　成千成萬

chengshi　城市

Chiang Ching-kuo.　See Jiang Jingguo

Chiang Kai-shek.　See Jiang Jieshi

chō　町

chōkanzu　鳥瞰圖

chōme　町目

chōmoku　鳥目

Chongqinglu　重慶路

Chou Kung-hsin.　See Zhou Gongxin

Cihu　慈湖

Cihu diaosu jinian gongyuan　慈湖雕塑紀念公園

da　大

Da'an senlin gongyuan　大安森林公園

Dadaocheng　大稻埕

Da'nanmen/Da Nanmen　大南門

Dai Baocun　戴寶村

Dai Liren (1966–)　戴立忍

Dai Taihoku chōkanzu　大臺北鳥瞰圖

Dai'ichi bunga shisetsukan　第一文化施設館

daimyō　大名

Danshui　淡水

Danshui cheng　淡水城

Danshuiting　淡水廳

Daqian shanren　大潛山人

Daxi　大溪

Deng Nanguang (1907–1971)　鄧南光

diaobao　碉堡

dōbun　同文

dōka　同化

Dongmen　東門

Dongmenjie　東門街

duoyuanhua　多元化

Dusi jianpan　都司剪盤

Edward Yang.　See Yang Dechang

Eichō　榮町

ema　絵馬

er shishi cangsang ze nanyan yi　而世事滄桑則難言矣

Ererba guanhuai lianhehui　二二八關懷聯合會

Ererba heping gongyuan　二二八和平公園

Ererba jinianbei　二二八紀念碑

Ererba jinianguan　二二八紀念館

Ererba shijian　二二八事件

Ererba shijian jianbei weiyuanhui　二二八事件建碑委員會

Erzi de da wan'ou　兒子的大玩偶

Fan Huancai　范煥彩

fangong dalu　反攻大陸

Fantanfu minzhu guangchang　反貪腐民主廣場

Feihujun　飛虎軍

fengshui　風水

fu　府

Fude　福德

Fuhoujie/Fukōkai　府後街

Fujian tongzhi　福建通志

Fuqianjie　府前街

Furuya Seisaburō (fl. 1926)　古矢正三郎

gaichi　外地

Gaidagelan dadao　凱達格蘭大道

gainian diaosu　概念雕塑

gaixiang weigui　改相為櫃

Gaoxiong　高雄

goka ni toka　五瓜に唐花

Gongfei renminshe zuixing ziliaozhan　共匪人民社罪行資料展
gonggong　公共
gongsi　公司
gongyuan　公園
gōsha　鄉社
Gotō Shimpei (1857–1929)　後藤新平
Guan Songsheng　関頌聲
Guangfujie　光復節
Guangfulu　光復路
Guangfuqian diming　光復前地名
Guangfuting　光復廳
Guanqianjie　舘前街
Guanqianlu　舘前路
Guanyin　觀音
Gufengcun　古峰村
Gugong bowuyuan　故宮博物院
guji　古跡
Guofu jinianguan　國父紀念館
Guojia tushuguan　國家圖書館
Guojia wenhua ziliaoku　國家文化資料庫
Guoli gugong bowuyuan　國立故宮博物院
Guoli lishi bowuguan　國立歷史博物館
Guoli Taiwan bowuguan　國立臺灣博物館
Guoli Taiwan minzhu jinianguan　國立臺灣民主紀念館
Guomin dahui　國民大會
Guomindang　國民黨
Guoshiguan Taiwan wenxianguan　國史館臺灣文獻舘
guoyu　國語
Guting cun　古亭村
haiwai　海外
Hakka.　See Kejia
Hanxue zhongxin　漢學中心
hao　號
Hao Longbin　郝龍斌
hashutsujo　派出所
hebian　河邊
Heluo　河洛 (also written 福佬)
Hengyangjie　衡陽街
Hengyanglu　衡陽路
Heping zhong　和平鍾
Hepingdonglu　和平東路

Hirō Tatsumi (1865–1908)　祝辰巳
Hoklo (T.).　See Heluo
hokō　保甲
Hokutō/Beitou　北投
Honchō　本町
Hong Tengyun　洪滕雲
Hontōjin　本島人
hōō　鳳凰
Hou Hsiao-hsien.　See Hou Xiaoxian
Hou Xiaoxian (1947–)　侯孝賢
Hsiao Tsung-huang.　See Xiao Zonghuang
Hualian　花蓮
Huang Abei　黃阿北
Huang Boji (1931–)　黃伯驥
Huang Ruiyu　黃瑞魚
huguo/gokoku　護國
huigu　回顧
huishou　回首
Huishou Taiwan bainian sheying youguang　回首臺灣百年攝影幽光
Hutoubpi　虎頭埤
Hwang Pai-Chi.　See Huang Boji
Inari　稻荷
Inō Kanori (fl. 1900)　伊能嘉矩
Iwahashi Shōzan (fl. 1911)　巖橋章山
Iwahashi Tei (fl. 1926)　巖橋てい
ji　驥
jian cheng　建城
jiangong　建功
Jiang Jieshi (1887–1975)　蔣介石
Jiang Jingguo (1910–1988)　蔣經國
Jiang Xun　蔣勳
jiaotong heianqi　交通黑暗期
jidensha torakku　自電車トラック
Jieshou　介壽
Jieshou gongyuan　介壽公園
Jieshouguan　介壽舘
Jieshoulu　介壽路
jieyunzu　接運族
Jilong/Kirū　基隆
Jing Caifeng (ob. 1948)　荊彩鳳
Jingdezhen　景德鎮

Jingjing　晶晶

jinian　紀念

jinja　神社

jōnai　城內

juancun　眷村

Kainan shanggong　開南商工

kami　神

kamon　家紋

kanpeisha　官幣社

kandejian de Taibei　看得見的臺北

Kang Peide　康培德

Kangri zhanzheng shengliji Taiwan guangfu jinianbei　抗日戰爭勝利暨臺灣光復
　　紀念碑

Ke Jintie　柯金鐵

Keelong.　See Jilong

Kejia　客家

Kenkō　建功

kiri　桐

Kitashirakawa Yoshihisa (1847–1895)　北白川宮能久

kō teki yūen　公的遊園

Kodama Gentarō (1852–1906)　兒玉源太郎

Kodoma Gotō kinenkan　兒玉後藤紀念館

Kodoma sōtoku oyo Gotō minkan kinen zōeibutsu shikichi　兒玉総督及後藤民官
　　紀念造営物敷地

Kodomo no kuni　子供の國

kōen　公園

kōen michi　公園道

Kōkaidō/ Gonghuitang　公會堂

kōminka　皇民化

Kone sotsuton shireibu　近衛師團司令部

Kongbu fenzi　恐怖分子

Koxinga.　See Zheng Chengong

Kusunoki Masashige (1294–1336)　楠木正成

Kyō　京

kyū/jiu　舊

Lee Teng-hui.　See Li Denghui

Li An (1954–)　李安

Li Denghui (1923–)　李登輝

Li Mingdiao (1921–)　李鳴鵰

Lian Yatang (1878–1936)　連雅堂

Liao Xianhao　廖咸浩

Lin Daquan　林達泉 (ob. 1878)

Lin Maosheng (1887–1947)　林茂生

Lin Muchuan　林木川

Lin Weiyuan (fl. 1885)　林維原

Lin Zhengren　林正仁

Lin Zongyi　林宗義

lingluan　凌亂

Liu Ao (ob. 1889)　劉璈

Liu Mingchuan (1836–1896)　劉銘傳

Lo Ching (Luo Qing)　羅青

Longshansi　龍山寺

Lu Gouqiao　盧溝橋

Lü Xiulian (1944–)　呂秀蓮

ma dao chenggong　馬到成功

Ma Ying-jeou.　See Ma Yingjiu

Ma Yingjiu (1950–)　馬英九

Matsuyama/Songshan　松山

Mazu　媽祖

Meiji　明治

meilidao　美麗島

Mengjia　艋甲

Mengjia difang　艋甲地方

Mengjia zhoudutoujie　艋甲孟渡頭街

mihunzhen　迷魂陣

Min'nan　閩南

Mingshenglu　民生路

Minquan donglu anquandao　民權東路安全島

Minquanlu　民權路

Minzhu jinbudang　民主進步黨

mukakusha　無科社

Muyangtong　牧羊童

na jiushi ji　那就是雞

naichi　內地

naichijin　內地人

Nangang　南港

Nanputuo　南普陀

Neihu　內湖

neko demo shakushi demo　猫でも杓子でも

niaokantu　鳥瞰圖

no　ノ

nü'er　女兒

nuhua jiaoyu　奴化教育

Ochi Torachi (fl. 1921)　越智寅一

Omotemachi　表町

Ōmura Masujirō　大村 益次郎 (1824–1869)

ongakudō　音樂堂

Ōshima Kumaji　大島久滿次 (1865–1918)

paifang　牌坊

patoron no kamon　パトロンの家紋

Penghu　澎湖

Pingguo de ciwei　蘋果的滋味

Qiang　牆

Qianlong Taiwan yutu　乾隆臺灣輿圖

Qiguishe　奇龜社

qiji　奇跡

qilin　麒麟

Qin Shihuang　秦始皇

Qingnian gongyuan　青年公園

Qiu Chuanghuan　邱創煥

Qiu Fengjia (fl. 1895)　邱逢甲

Qiu Xieyou　邱燮友

Qiu xin　秋信

qu ribenhua　去日本化

qu Zhongzheng　去中正

Quanzhou　泉州

raihindō　来賓堂

Saigo Takamori　西鄉隆盛 (1827–1877)

Saishin Taihoku shigai hikōki chōmoku zenzu　最新臺北市街鳥目全圖

sakura　櫻

san jianke　三劍客

Sanmin zhuyi　三民主義

Sanminlu　三民路

sansenro　三線路

Sanshiertiao chuli dagang　三十二條處理大綱

Sanyi　三邑

Sanzhi　三芝

Sasaki Noritsuna (fl. 1921)　佐々木紀綱

seiban　生番

sha/she　社 (shrine)

shaku/chi　尺

Shanghen zaisheng　傷痕再生

she　社 (village)

Shen Baozhen (1820–1879)　沈葆禎

shenghuo pinzhi　生活平直

shenxin kuanrong er ziyou　身心寬容而自由

Shida Denzaburō (fl. 1920)　志田傳三郎

Shiji luofu dalo　世紀儸伕大樓

Shili zhongxue　市立中學

Shilin　士林

shimme　神馬

shimmon　神紋

Shin kōen /Xin gongyuan　新公園

Shinto　神道

Shisei yonjisshunen Taiwan hakurankai　始政十四年記念臺灣博覽會

shizhongxin　市中心

Shoudu wenhua yuanqu　首都文化園區

Shouhuangshe　首晃社

Shuyuan/Sho'in　書院

siren　私人

Sishili gongyuandao　四十理公園道

Soeda Rōichi (fl. 1900)　添田朗一

Song Meiling (1896–2003)　宋美齡

Songshan/Matsuyama　松山

Soong May Ling.　See Song Meiling

Sōtokufu　總督府

Sōtokufu hakubutsukan　総督府博物館

Sōtokufu kansha no chi　総督府官舎の地

Sōtokufu toshokan　総督府圖書館

Sugawara no Michizan　菅原道真

suiran　雖然

Sumiyoshi Hidematsu (fl. 1921)　住吉秀松

Sun Yatsen.　See Sun Zhongshan

Sun Zhongshan (1866–1925)　孫中山

tai 台　(in stylized form)

Taibei, dongqu, xiexie　臺北 東區 謝謝

Taibei dazhong jieyun xitong　臺北大眾捷運系統

Taibei gongyuan ludeng guanlichu　臺北公園路燈管理處

Taibei gongyuan　臺北公園

Taibei gu ditu zhan　臺北古地圖展

Tabei jiancheng yibaiershi zhounian　臺北建城一百二十周年

Taibei shalong　臺北沙龍

Taibei sheying　臺北攝影

Taibei wanjiu chaowu　臺北晚九潮五

Taibeicheng　臺北城

Taibeifu　臺北府

Taibeifucheng　臺北府城

Taibeishi　臺北市

Taibeishi sheyinghui　臺北市攝影會

Taibeishi wenxianhui　臺北市文獻會

Taibeishi zhengfu yuanzhumin shiwu weiyuanhui daidagelan wenhuaguan　臺北市
政府原主民事務委員會凱達格蘭文化館

Taichū mokkuto ukeo kumiai　臺中土木建築請負組合

Taiheichō　太平町

Taihoku　臺北

Taihoku Inari jinja　臺北稻荷神社

Taihoku kōen/Taibei gongyuan　臺北公園

Taihoku kurabu　臺北俱樂部

Taihoku shiku keikaku: Gairo yo ko'en zu　臺北市區計劃：街路與公園

Taihoku ukeo kumiai　臺北請負業組合

Taihokuchō 臺北廳

Taihokushi　臺北市

Taihokushiku kaikaguzu　臺北市區計畫圖

Taihokushū　臺北州

Tainan　臺南

Taipacchi (T)　臺北市

Taipak (T)　臺北

Taishō　大正

Taiwan　臺灣

Taiwan Chūgakukai　臺灣中學會

Taiwan fanjie tu 臺灣番界圖

Taiwan guangfu nianqi zhounian　臺灣光復廿七周年

Taiwan jinja　臺灣神社

Taiwan lishi yanjiusuo　臺灣歷史研究所

Taiwan minzhuguo　臺灣民主國

Taiwan nichinichishimpō　臺灣日日新報

Taiwan shengli bowuguan 臺灣省裏博物館

Taiwan sōtokufu minseibu shokusankyoku fuzoku hakubutsukan　臺湾総督府民
正部殖産局付属博物館

Taiwan tongshi　臺灣通史

Taiwan xinsheng ribao　臺灣新生日報

Taiwan zonghui　臺灣總會

Taiwanfu　臺灣府

Taiwanjin　臺灣人

Taiwan sheng minzheng jiaoyuguan　臺灣省民政教育館

Taiwansheng　臺灣省

Taizhongxian　臺中縣

Takao　打狗/打鼓

Takasago zoku 高砂族

Tamsui. See Danshui

Tang Jingsong (1841–1903) 唐景崧

Taoyuan/Tōgen　桃園

Tenmangū　天滿宮

tian　田

Tian Zaimai　田在勱

Tianhougong　天后宮

Ti'iku kurabu　体育俱樂部

Tongan　同安

Tongzhi　同治

Tsai Ming-liang.　See Cai Mingliang

tsubo　坪

Tudigongmiao　土地公廟

Tuishou　推手

Ubukata Toshirō (1882–1969)　生方敏郎

Waishengren　外省人

Wanhua　萬華

wenhua daguo　文化大國

Wenmiao　文廟

wenwu/bunbu　文武

Wenwujie　文物街

wo yao ji　我要雞

Wu Boxiong (1939–)　吳伯雄

Wu Jiawu　吳甲午

Wu Jing-jyi.　See Wu Jingji

Wu Jingji　吳靜吉

Wu Zhuoliu (1900–1976)　吳濁流

Wudedian/Butokuden　武德店

Wufengxiang　霧峰鄉

Wumiao　武廟

Xiahai chenghuangmiao　霞海城隍廟

Xiamen　廈門

Xiangtu wenxue yundong　鄉土文學運動

Xiao　小

Xiao Zonghuang　蕭宗煌

Xiaonanmen　小南門

Xie Binqi　謝秉錡

Xie Dongliang　謝棟梁 (1949–)

xili　洗禮

Ximending　西門町

Ximenjie　西門街

xin anju gucheng; meng hangxiang shijie　心安居古城: 夢航向世界

Xin gongyuan 新公園

xin Taiwanren 新臺灣人

xinjieluming　新街路名

Xinsheng(bei/nan)lu　新生(北/南)路

Xinshenghuo yundong　新生活運動

Xinyi qu　信義區

Xinyilu　信義路

Xinying　新營

Xinying zhi ji　新營之驥

xinzhimin zhuyi　新殖民主義

Xinzhu　新竹

Xinzhuangjie　新莊街

Xiyan　喜宴

Xu Shiying (1873–1964)　許世英

Yagyū Kazuyoshi (1864–1920)　柳生一義

Yamanaka Shō (1882–1947)　山中樵

yamen　衙門

Yan Bicong (fl. 1948)　顏必從

Yang Dechang (1947–)　楊德昌

Yang Jiu　楊玖

Yang Weizhong　楊維中

Yang Yingfeng　楊英風

yansu　嚴肅

Yata no kagami　八咫鏡

yejiche　野雞車

yi baoliu zhenxiang he weihu yishu qianti, zuo houxiandai zhuyi fenge de biaoxian
　　以保留真相和維護藝術前提，做后現代主義風格的表現

Yilan/Giran　宜蘭

Yin Jianyi　鄞建義

ying　營

Yinshi nanü　飲食男女

yinyuetai　音樂台

Yoshida Hatsusaburō　吉田初三郎

youxin renshi　有心人士

yuan　園

Yuanshan dafandian　圓山大飯店

yuanyou luming　原有路名

Yunmen wuji　雲門舞集

zaizhimin shiqi　再殖民時期

Zeng Rongjian　曾榮鑑

zhang 丈

Zhang Cai (1916–1994)　張才

Zhang Zhonghe　張忠和

Zhangzhou　漳州

Zheng Chenggong　鄭成功

zheng men　正門

zhong　鍾

Zhongguo renmin kangri zhanzheng jinianguan　中國人民抗日戰爭紀念館

Zhongguohua　中國化

Zhonghua shihchang　中華市場

Zhonghua wenhua　中華文化

Zhonghualu　中華路

Zhongli　中壢

zhonglieci　忠烈祠

Zhongshan　中山

Zhongshan bowuyuan　中山博物院

Zhongshantang　中山堂

Zhongtai binguan jungonghou de zhouwei jingguan　中泰賓館竣工後的周圍景觀

Zhongxiaolu　忠孝路

Zhongxing xincun　中興新村

Zhongxunmiao　忠訓廟

Zhongzheng　中正

Zhongzheng Guoxiao　中正國小

Zhongzheng jiniantang　中正紀念堂

Zhongzheng ting　中正廳

Zhongzhenglu　中正路

Zhou Changzhen　周長楨

Zhou Danlong　周丹龍

Zhou Gongxin　周功鑫

Zhou li　周禮

Zhu Dianren (1903–49)　朱點人

Zhu shifu　朱師傅

zhuang　莊

Zhuang Weicheng　莊維誠

Zhuang Yan　(1899–1980) 莊嚴

zhuangyan dianya　莊嚴典雅

zhuangzhi yishu　裝置藝術

Zhuqian 竹塹
Ziyou guangchang 自由廣場
Ziyou yingzhan 自由影展
zongli 總理
Zongtongfu 總統府

Works Cited

NOTE: *Original bilingual titles are treated as part of the work's title and placed in parentheses. Translated titles are not treated as part of the title; they are placed in parentheses in sentence style. Characters are provided for names if the author has works here in either Chinese or Japanese.*

Abbas, Ackbar. *Hong Kong: Culture and the Politics of Disappearance*. Minneapolis: University of Minnesota Press, 1997.

Adrian, Bonnie. *Framing the Bride: Globalizing Beauty and Romance in Taiwan's Bridal Industry*. Berkeley: University of California Press, 2003.

Allen, Joseph R. "Exhibiting the Colony, Suggesting the Nation: Taiwan/Japan 1935." Modern Language Association, Society for Critical Exchange; www.cwru.edu/affil/sce/MLA_2005.htm.

———. "Mapping Taipei: Representation and Ideology." *Studies on Asia* II, no. 2.2 (2005): 5–80, plus illustrations; www.isp.msu.edu/studiesonasia.

———. "Taipei Park: Signs of Occupation." *Journal of Asian Studies* 66, no.1 (2007): 159–99.

———. "Taiwan de shenma yu yishi xingtai" (Divine horses and ideology in Taiwan). In *Taiwan yu Dongya sikao* (Taiwan and East Asian thought), edited by Chen Fangming, 332–58. Taipei: Cheng-chi University, 2007.

Andrade, Tonio. *How Taiwan Became Chinese: Dutch, Spanish, and Han Colonization in the Seventeenth Century*. New York: Columbia University Press, 2008.

"Anti-Japan War Museum in Shenyang to add KMT military leaders to exhibit." http://en.beijing2008.cn/news/olympiccities/beijing/n214237336.shtml.

Bai Xianyong 白先勇. *Niezi* (Crystal boys). Taipei: Yucheng wenhua, 1983.

Barclay, Paul D. "Japanese Postcards and the Selling of the Empire: Image Making in Taiwan under Japanese Colonial Rule." *Japanese Studies* 30, no. 1 (2010): 81–110.

Barlow, Tani. "The Pornographic City." In *Locating China: Space, Place and Popular Culture*, edited by Jing Wang, 190–99. London: Routledge, 2005.

Barthes, Roland. *Camera Lucida: Reflections on Photography*. Translated by Richard Howard. New York: Hill and Wang, 1981.

———. "The Photographic Message." In *Image, Music, Text*, translated by Stephen Heath, 15–31. New York: Hill and Wang, 1977.

———. "Semiology and the Urban." In Gottdiener and Lagopoulos, *City and the Sign*, 87–98.

"Beijing Curator Visits Taiwan." *The Straits Times* (Singapore), Associated Press, March 1, 2009; http://www.straitstimes.com/Breaking+News/Asia/Story/STIStory_344608.html.

Bhabha, Homi. *The Location of Culture*. London: Routledge, 1994.

Bickers, Robert A., and Jeffrey N. Wasserstrom. "Shanghai's Dogs and Chinese Not Admitted Sign: Legend, History, and Contemporary Symbol." *China Quarterly* 142 (1995): 444–66.

Blundel, David, ed. *Austronesian Taiwan: Linguistics, History, Ethnology, Prehistory*. Berkeley: Phoebe A. Hearst Museum of Anthropology, University of California, 2001.

Borden, Iain, Joe Kerr, Jane Rendell, and Alicia Pivaro, eds. *The Unknown City: Contesting Architecture and Social Space*. Cambridge, MA: MIT Press, 2002.

Boym, Svetlana. *The Future of Nostalgia*. New York: Basic Books, 2001.

Braester, Yomi. "If We Could Remember Everything, We Would Be Able to Fly: Taipei's Cinematics of Demolition." *Modern Chinese Literature and Culture* 15, no.1 (2003): 29–61.

———. *Painting the City Red: Chinese Cinema and the Urban Contract*. Durham, NC: Duke University Press, 2010.

———. "Tales of a Porous City: Public Residences and the Private Streets in Taipei Films." In Laughlin, *Contested Modernities*, 167–70.

Brown, Melissa. *Is Taiwan Chinese? The Impact of Culture, Power, and Migration on Changing Identities*. Berkeley: University of California Press, 2004.

Buck, David. D. "Railway City and National Capital: Two Faces of the Modern Changchun." In Esacherick, *Remaking*, 65–89.

Butler, Ruth. *Western Sculpture: Definitions of Man*. Boston: New York Graphic Society, 1975.

Cahill, James. "The Place of the National Palace Museum in My Scholarly Career." www.jamescahill.info, CLP 117. Published in Chinese in *Gugong wenwu*, National Palace Museum Monthly 23, no.8 (2005): 93–99; reprinted in Cai M, *Bazheng miaonian*, 57–64.

Cai, Fangwen 蔡玫芳. "Beigou de Gugong: Cong yifeng weiji jichu de xin shuoqi" (The Palace Museum of Beigou: Speaking about a letter that was never delivered). In Cai M, *Bazheng maonian*, 39–56.

Cai, Hounan 蔡厚男. "Taiwan dushi gongyuan de zhidu licheng, 1895–1987 (The institutionalization of urban parks in Taiwan, 1895–1987)." Master's thesis, National Taiwan University, 1991.

Cai, Meifang蔡玫芳, ed. *Bazheng maonian: Guoli gugong bowuyuan bashinian de diandi huainian* (Individual remembrances: Detailed recollections on eighty years of the National Palace Museum).Taipei: Gugong, 2006.

Cai Jintang (Tsai Chin-tang) 蔡錦堂. *Nihon teikoku shugika Taiwan no shūkyō seisaku* (Religious policy in Taiwan under the Japanese imperialism). Tokyo: Dohsei Publishing, 1994.

———. *Zhanzheng tizhixia de Taiwan* (Taiwan under wartime rules). Taipei: Guoli bianyiguan, 2006.

Caituan faren Taibeishi Muzha Zhongxunmiao jianjie (Brief introduction to the Zhongxun Temple of Muzha, Taipei City). N.p., n.d.

Cannon, M. Hamlin. *Leyte: The Return to the Philippines, United States Army in World War II, the War in the Pacific*. Washington, DC: Department of the Army, 1954.

Casey, Edward S. *Representing Place: Landscape Painting and Maps*. Minneapolis: University of Minnesota Press, 2002.

Chadwick, George F. *The Park and the Town: Public Landscape in the 19th and 20th Centuries*. New York: F. A. Praeger, 1966.

Chang, Hsiao-hung, and Chih-hung Wang. "Mapping Taipei's Landscape of Desire: Deterritorialization and Reterritorialization of Family/Park." In Chen and Liao, *Xunzhao diangyingzhong*, 115–25.

Chang, Sung-Sheng Yvonne. *Modernism and Nativist Resistance: Contemporary Chinese Fiction from Taiwan*. Durham, NC: Duke University Press, 1993.

Chatterjee, Partha. *The Nation and Its Fragments: Colonial and Postcolonial Histories*. Princeton, NJ: Princeton University Press, 1993.

Chen, Edward I. "Gotō Shimpei, Japan's Colonial Administrator in Taiwan: A Critical Reexamination." *American Asian Review* 13, no.1 (1995): 29–59.

Chen, Fangming 陳芳明. *Houzhimin Taiwan: Wenxueshilun ji qizhoubian* (Postcolonial Taiwan: Essays on Literary History and Beyond). Taipei: Maitian, 2007.

——— "Zhaohe jiyi: Minguo yanse" (Memories of Showa: Shadows of the Republic). In Long Y, *Huidao Zhongshantang*, 30–35.

Chen, Jie. "Civil Society, Grassroots Aspirations and Diplomatic Isolation." In *China's Rise, Taiwan's Dilemna and International Peace*, edited by Edward Friedman, 110–29. London: Routledge, 2006.

Chen, Jinchuan 陳進傳. "Shenshe yu Yilan ren de shenghuo" (The Shintō shrine in the life of the people of Yilan). *Yilan wenxian zazhi* 51 (2001): 3–60.

Chen, Lingchei Letty. "Mapping Identity in a Postcolonial City: Intertextuality and Cultural Hybridity in Zhu Tianxin's *Ancient Capital*." In Wang and Rojas, *Writing Taiwan*, 301–23.

————. *Writing Chinese: Reshaping Chinese Cultural Identity.* New York: Palgrave McMillan, 2009.

Chen, Ru-shou, and Liao Jinfeng. "Focus on Taipei." In Chen and Liao, *Xunzhao dianyingzhong,* 17–19.

Chen, Ru-shou (Robert) 陳儒修, and Liao Jinfeng 廖金鳳, eds. *Xunzhao diangyingzhong de Taibei* (Focus on Taipei through cinema). Taipei: Wanxiang, 1995.

Chen, Shuibian 陳水扁. "Shizhang xu" (Mayor's preface). *Lao Taibeiren,* 3.

————. "Xu" (Preface). *Nianqing Taibei,* 6.

Chen, Xiasheng 陳夏生. "Lao zhuang laoyun hao: Chonghui Zhuang Shangyan xiansheng sui wenwu qiantu xi'nan de lishi xianchang." (All's well with old packages and old shipments: A retrospective on the historical situation of Mr. Zhuang Shangyan's southwest travel with the archives). In Cai M, *Bazheng maonian,* 7–32.

Chen, Yijun 陳逸駿. "Yuanshan zhonglieci tongma shitan" (Investigation of the bronze horse of Yuanshan shrine for Chinese martyrs). *Proceedings of Shuiwenfengtuyu renjian yishu,* 161–72. Yilan: Foguang University, 2005.

Chen, Zhengxiang 陳正祥. *Taibeishi zhi* (Record of Taibei City). 1957. Reprint, Taipei: Nantian shuju, 1997.

Cheng, Jiahui 程佳惠. *Diyi dabolanhui: 1935 nian meili Taiwan Show* (The first great exposition: The beautiful 1935 Taiwan Show). Taipei: Yuanliu, 2004.

Chiang, Tao-chang. "Walled Cities and Towns in Taiwan." In Knapp, *China's Island Frontier,* 117–41.

Chiang Kai-shek Memorial Hall. Taipei: National Chiang Kai-shek Memorial Management Office, n.d.

"China to Lend Treasures to Taiwan." *BBC News,* February 16, 2009. http://news.bbc.co.uk/2/hi/asia-pacific/7892178.stm.

Ching, Leo T. S. *Becoming "Japanese": Colonial Taiwan and the Politics of Identity Formation.* Berkeley: University of California Press, 2001.

Chou, Wan Yao (Zhou Wanyao 周婉窈). "The *Kōminka* Movement in Taiwan and Korea: Comparisons and Interpretations." In *The Japanese Wartime Empire, 1931–1945,* edited by Peter Duus, Ramon Myers, and Mark Peattie, 40–70. Princeton, NJ: Princeton University Press, 1996.

————. *Taiwan lishi tushuo* (Illustrated History of Taiwan). Taipei: Lianjing, 1998.

Chow, Rey. *Sentimental Fabulations, Contemporary Chinese Films: Attachment in the Age of Global Visibility.* New York: Columbia University Press, 2007.

Chun, Allen. "The Coming Crisis of Multiculturalism in "Transitional" Taiwan." *Social Analysis* 46, no. 2 (2002): 102–22.

————. "Discourses of Identity in the Changing Public Culture in Taiwan, Hong Kong and Singapore." *Theory, Culture & Society* 13, no. 1 (1996): 51–75.

Clifford, James. "A Poetics of Displacement: Victor Segalen." Chapter 5 in *The Predicament of Culture: Twentieth-Century Ethnography, Literature, and Art.* Cambridge, MA: Harvard University Press, 1988.

"Dai Taihoku chōkanzu" (Bird's eye view map of greater Taipei). Shisei yonjisshūnen kinen Taiwan hakurankai. 1935. Reprint, Taipei: Nantian, 1994.

Damm, Jens. "Same Sex Desire and Society in Taiwan, 1970–1987." *China Quarterly* 81 (2005): 67–81.

Danshuiting zhi (Gazette of Danshui Subprefecture). 1869. Reprint, Taipei: Taiwan yinhang, 1963.

Davidson, James W. *The Island of Formosa Past and Present.* London and New York: Macmillan & Company, 1903.

Diancang shouhuifeng (Postcard Drawing: The Rare Collection). Taipei: Lihong chubanshe, 1996.

Dilley, Whitney Crothers. *The Cinema of Ang Lee: The Other Side of the Screen.* London and New York: Wallflower Press, 2007.

Dillon, Sarah. *Palimpsest: Literature, Criticism, Theory.* London: Continuum Literary Studies, 2007.

Discover Taipei. Taipei: Department of Information, Taipei City Government, 1997–.

Dong, Madeleine Yue. "Defining Beiping: Urban Reconstruction and National Identity, 1928–1936." In Escherick, *Remaking,* 121–38.

Dower, John W. *The Elements of Japanese Design: A Handbook of Family Crests, Heraldry, and Symbolism.* New York: Weatherhill, 1971.

Eco, Umberto. "Function and Sign: Semiotics of Architecture." In Gottdiener and Lagopoulos, *City and the Sign,* 55–86.

Escherick, Joseph W., ed. *Remaking the Chinese City: Modernity and National Unity,* 1900–1950. Honolulu: University of Hawai'i Press, 2000.

"Establishment of the Anti-Graft Democracy Plaza." http://english.taipei.gov.tw/tupc/index.jsp?recordid=9902.

Exhibition Guide: Taipei 228 Memorial Museum. Taipei: Taipei City Department of Cultural Affairs, n.d.

Fane. See Ponsonby Fane, Richard

Faxian Xinying: Xinyingshi, nanying caihong wenhuashi (Discovering Xinying: Xinying City, a city of colorful southern culture). Xinying: Xinying shigongsuo, 2005.

Feng, Jinheng 馮金桁. "Ererba Jianbei yizai yuanshi fashengdi" (The 228 Memorial will probably be built at the site of the original event). *Lianhebao,* February 13, 1992, 14.

———. "Ererba Jinianbei jianli didian chubu xuanze, Beishi Xinsheng Gongyuan diyi youxian kaolü, Jiancheng Gongyuan juci, xiayue sanri Jianbeiweiyuan kancha jueding" (The first step in selecting the 228 Memorial Site, Taipei's New Life Park has priority, followed by Jiancheng Park, the Memorial Committee will consider and decide on the third of next month). *Lianhebao,* February 27, 1992, 3.

Feuchtwang, Stephan. "City Temples in Taipei under Three Regimes." In *The Chi-*

nese City between Two Worlds, edited by Mark Elvan and G. William Skinner, 263–301. Stanford, CA: Stanford University Press, 1974.

———. "Domestic and Communal Worship in Taiwan." In *Religion and Ritual in Chinese Society*, edited by Arthur Wolf, 241–81. Stanford, CA: Stanford University Press, 1974.

———. *Popular Religion in China: The Imperial Metaphor*. Richmond, Surrey, UK: Curzon Press, 2001.

"Formosa Interim Report." United States National Archives II, RG 38, box 32.

"Founder of `Flying Tiger' Unit Honored." *Taipei Times*; http://www.taipeitimes. com/News/taiwan/archives/2006/08/13/2003323002.

Fu, Chaoqing 傅朝卿. *Rizhi shiqi Taiwan jianzhu, 1895–1945* (Taiwan architecture during the Japanese period, 1895–1945). Taipei: Dadi dili, 1999.

Fujitani, Takashi. *Splendid Monarchy: Power and Pageantry in Modern Japan*. Berkeley: University of California Press, 1996.

Gardella, Robert. "From Treaty Ports to Provincial Status, 1860–1894." In Rubinstein, *Taiwan*, 163–200.

Geertz, Clifford. "Thick Description: Toward an Interpretive Theory of Culture." Chapter 1 in *The Interpretation of Cultures: Selected Essays by Clifford Geertz*. New York: Basic Books, 1973.

Gochinza sanjū shūnen kinen Taiwan jinja shashinchō (Photo album of the thirtieth anniversary of the establishment of the Taiwan Shinto shrine). Taipei: Taiwan jinja, 1931.

Gold, Thomas B. *State and Society in the Taiwan Miracle*. Armonk, NY: M. E. Sharpe, 1985.

Gotō danshaku sōbetsu kikenchō (Commemorative photo album of Baron Gotō's departure). N.p., n.d.

Gottdiener, M., and Alexandros Ph. Lagopoulos. *The City and the Sign: An Introduction to Urban Semiotics*. New York: Columbia University Press, 1986.

———. "Introduction." In *The City and the Sign*, 1–22.

Guo, Guanying 郭冠英. "Xiashi de qipaoxian" (Erased starting line). In Long Y, *Huidao Zhongshantang*, 122–27.

Hardacre, Helen. *Shintō and the State (1868–1988)*. Princeton, NJ: Princeton University Press, 1989.

Harley, J. B., and David Woodward. *Cartography in the Traditional East and Southeast Asian Societies: The History of Cartography*, vol. 2, pt. 2. Chicago: University of Chicago Press, 1994.

Harvey, David. *Consciousness and the Urban Experience: Studies in the History and Theory of Capitalist Urbanization*. Baltimore, MD: Johns Hopkins University Press, 1985.

Hayden, Dolores. *The Power of Place: Urban Landscapes as Public History*. Cambridge, MA: MIT Press, 1997.

He, Xunyao 何勛堯. "Wo zai bowuguan de huiyi" (Rememberence of my time at the museum). In Li Z, *Taiwan shengli bowuguan*, 282–85.

Heiman, Grover. *Aerial Photography: The Story of Aerial Mapping and Reconnaissance*. New York: Macmillan Company, 1972.

Henry, Todd. "Respatializing Chosŏn's Royal Capital: The Politics of Japanese Urban Reforms in Early Colonial Seoul, 1905–1919." In Tangherlini and Yea, *Sitings*, 15–38.

Hong Zhiwen 洪致文. *Taiwan tiedao chuanqi* (Taiwan railway history monograph). Taipei: Shibao wenhua, 1992.

Hsia, C. J. (Chu-joe) (Xia Zhujiu 夏鑄九). "Gonghuitang yu Dadaocheng Nanjie" (Civic Hall and South Street, Dadaocheng). In Long Y, *Huidao Zhongshantang*, 156–63.

———. "Theorizing Colonial Architecture and Urbanism: Building Colonial Modernity in Taiwan." Translated by Ip Iam Chong. *Inter-Asia Cultural Studies* 3, no.1 (2002): 7–23.

Hsieh, Jolan. *Collective Rights of Indigenous Peoples: Identity Based Movements of Plains Indigenous in Taiwan*. New York: Routledge, 2006.

Hsu, Wen-hsiung. "From Aboriginal Island to Chinese Frontier: The Development of Taiwan before 1683." In Knapp, *China's Island Frontier*, 4–29.

Huang, Chunming 黃春明. *Shayounala, zai jian* (Sayonara, goodbye). Taipei: Yuanjing, 1974.

———. "Pinguo de ziwei" (The taste of apples). In *Shayounala zai jian*, 27-57.

———. *The Taste of Apples*. Translated by Howard Goldblatt. New York: Columbia University Press, 2001.

Huang, Deshi 黃得時. "Chengnei de yange he Taibeicheng" (The development of downtown and the Taipei City wall). *Taibei wenwu* 2, no. 4 (1954): 17–34.

Huang, Fusan 黃富三. *Taibei jiancheng bainianshi* (Hundred-year history of Taipei City). Taibei: Wenxianhui, 1995.

Huang, Li-ling, "Urban Politics and Spatial Development: The Emergence of Participatory Planning." In Kwok, *Globalizing Taipei*, 78–98.

Huang, Wuda 黃武達. *Rizhi shidai (1895–1945) Taibeishi zhi jindai dushi jihua zhi yanjiu (Studies of the Contemporary City Planning of Taiwan in the Japanese Colonial Age)*. 3 vols. Taipei: Dushi jihua yanjiu shi, 1998.

Huang, Xiuhui 黃秀慧. "Zhongshantang dashiji" (Major events for Sun Yat-sen Hall). In Long Y, *Huidao Zhongshantang*, 216–21.

Huang Junming 黃俊銘. *Shiding guji Xinzhu shenshe diaocha yanjiu ji xiufu jihua* (Investigative study and renovation plans for the metropolitan historic site Shinto shrine of Xinzhu). Xinzhu: Xinzhu city government, 2003.

———. *Taoyuanxian zhonglieci wenhuaguan xiushan gongcheng shigong jilu ji gongzuo baogaushu* (A work report on the engineering and construction for the renovation of the Shrine for Chinese Martyrs in Taoyuan county). Taoyuan: Taoxian wenhuaju, 2007.

Huishou Tawian bainian sheying youguang (Retrospective of One Hundred Years of Taiwan Photography). Taipei: Guoli lishi bowuguan, 2003.

Huyssen, Andreas. *Present Pasts: Urban Palimpsests and the Politics of Memory*. Stanford, CA: Stanford University Press, 2003.

Jameson, Fredric. "Remapping Taipei." Chapter 2 in *The Geopolitical Aesthetic: Cinema and Space in the World System*. Bloomington: Indiana University Press, 1992.

Jiang, Xun 蔣勳. "Longfeng chenxiang: Zhongshantang de zuizao jiyi" (Dragon and phoenix omens: Earliest memories of Sun Yat-sen Hall). In Long Y, *Huidao Zhongshantang*, 44–48.

"Jiang furen zuo zhuchi dianli" (First Lady Jiang presides over ceremony). *Zhongyang ribao* (Central Daily News), April 15, 1960

Jianzheng Taiwan zongdufu (Witness—the Colonial Taiwan). 2 vols. Taipei: Lihong, 1996.

Jin, Jong-Heon. "Demolishing Colony: The Demolition of the Old Government-General Building of Chosŏn." In Tangherlini and Yea, *Sitings*, 39–58.

Jinja oyo sha sōran (Overview of Shintō and other shrines). Taipei: n.p., 1930.

Jinnai, Hidenobu. *Tokyo: A Spatial Anthropology*. Translated by Kimiko Nishimura. Berkeley: University of California Press, 1995.

Jordan, David K., Andrew D. Morris, and Marc L. Moskowitz. *The Minor Arts of Daily Life: Popular Culture in Taiwan*. Honolulu: University of Hawai'i Press, 2004.

Jou, Sue-Ching, "Domestic Politics in Urban Image Creation: Xinyi as the 'Manhattan of Taipei.'" In Kwok, *Globalizing Taipei*, 120–40.

Ka, Chih-ming. *Japanese Colonialism in Taiwan: Land Tenure, Development, and Dependency, 1895–1945*. Boulder, CO: Westview Press, 1995.

Kaishi xunji (Strolling the Old Trails). Taipei: Lihong, 1997.

Karp, Ivan, and Steven D. Lavine, ed. *Exhibiting Cultures: The Poetics and Politics of Museum Display*. Washington, DC: Smithsonian Institution Press, 1991.

Katz, Paul R., and Murray A. Rubinstein, eds. *Religion and the Formation of Taiwanese Identities*. New York: Palgrave Macmillan, 2003.

———. "The Many Meanings of Identity: An Introduction." Chapter 1 in Katz and Rubinstein, *Religion*.

Kawahara Isao. "The State of Taiwanese Culture and Taiwanese New Literature in 1937: Issues on Banning Chinese Newspaper Sections and Abolishing Chinese Writings." In Liao and Wang, *Taiwan*, 122–40.

Kenkō jinja shi (Record of the Kenkō Shinto Shrine). Taipei: n.p, 1928.

Ketagalan Culture Center Guide. Taipei: Taipei City Government, Indigenous Peoples Commission, n.d.

Khemir, Mounira. *L'Orientalisme: l'Orient des photographes au XIXe siècle*. Paris: Centre national de la photographie, 1994

Kinen hakubutsukan shashinchō (Album of museum commemoration). N.p. 1915.

Kitashirawaka (Biography of Prince Kitashirakawa). Taipei: Taiwan keisei shimpōsha, 1937.

Knapp, Ronald, ed. *China's Island Frontier: Studies in the Historical Geography of Taiwan*. Honolulu: University of Hawai'i Press, 1980.

Kodama Sotokufū gaisen kangei kinenchō (Photo album commemorating Governor-General Kodama's triumphant arrival). Taipei: Taiwan nichinichi shimpōsha, 1906.

Kostof, Spiro. *The City Assembled: The Elements of Urban Form through History*. London: Thames and Hudson, 1992.

Ku, Kun-hui. "Rights to Recognition: Minority/Indigenous Politics in Emerging Taiwanese Nationalism." *Social Analysis* 49, no. 2 (2005): 99–121.

Kwok, Reginald Yin-Wang, ed. *Globalizing Taipei: The Political Economy of Spatial Development*. New York: Routledge, 2005.

La Sueur, James D., ed. *The Decolonization Reader*. New York: Routledge, 2003.

Lai, Tse-Han, Ramon H. Myers, and Wei Wou. *A Tragic Beginning: The Taiwan Uprising of February 28, 1947*. Stanford, CA: Stanford University Press, 1991.

Lai, Zhengzhe 賴正哲. "Zai gongsi shangban: Xingongyuan zuowei nantongzhi yanchu dijing zhi yanjiu (Working in the Company: Research on the Performance of the New Park by the Gay Community [male "tongzhi"])." Master's thesis, National Taiwan University, 1998.

Lai, Zhizhang 賴志彰, Wei Dewen 魏德文, and Gao Chuanqi 高傳奇. Zhuqian guditu diaocha yanjiu (Research investigations of old maps of Zhuqian). Xinzhu: Xinzhushi zhengfu, 2003.

Lamley, Harry J. "The Formation of Cities in Taiwan: Initiatives and Motivation in Building Three Walled Cities in Taiwan." In Skinner, *City*, 155–209.

———. "Subethnic Rivalry in the Ch'ing Period." In *The Anthropology of Taiwanese Society*, edited by Emily Martina Ahern and Hill Gates, 282–318. Stanford, CA: Stanford University Press, 1981.

———. "Taiwan under Japanese Rule, 1895–1945: The Vicissitudes of Colonialism." In Rubinstein, *Taiwan*, 203–9.

Lau, Joseph S. M., ed. *The Unbroken Chain: An Anthology of Taiwan Fiction since 1926*. Bloomington: Indiana University Press, 1983.

Lao Taibei ren: Taibei lishi yingxian xilie (Old Taipei people: Images in Taipei history). Taipei: Taibeishi zhengfu, 1998.

Laughlin, Charles A., ed. *Contested Modernities in Chinese Literature*. New York: Palgrave MacMillan, 2005.

Lee, Ang, and James Schamus. *Two Films by Ang Lee*. Woodstock, NY: Overlook Press, 1994.

Lee, Anru. "Subways as a Space of Cultural Intimacy: The Rapid Transit System in Taipei, Taiwan." *The China Journal* 58 (2007): 31–55.

Lefebvre, Henri. *The Production of Space*. Translated by Donald Nicholson-Smith. Oxford, UK: Blackwell Publishers, 1991.

Legates, Richard T., and Frederic Stout, eds. *The City Reader*. 2d ed. London: Routledge, 2000.

Li, Lixue 李麗雪. "You dushi gongyuan fazhan de guannian tantao Taibeishi dushi gongyuan zhi yanbian" (Investigation of the changes in the Taipei City urban parks from the perspective of urban park development). Master's thesis, National Taiwan University, 1989.

Li, Qianlang 李乾朗. *Taibeifu chengqiang ji paotai jizuo yizhi yanjiu* (Investigations in the remains of the base of the battery of Taipei prefectural wall). Taibei: Taibeishi zhengfu, 1995.

———. *Taibei guchengmen* (Taipei old city gates). Taipei: Taibeishi wenxian hui, 1993.

———. *Taibeishi: Guji jianji* (Taipei City: Introduction to historical relics). Taipei: Taibeishi zhengfu, 1998.

———. *Taiwan gujianzhu tujie shidian* (Glossary and illustrations of old Taiwan architecture). Taipei: Yuanliu, 2003.

———. *Taiwan jianzhu shi 1600–1945* (History of Taiwan architecture, 1600–1945). Taipei: Beiwu, 1978.

———. *Taiwan jindai jianzhu: Qiyuan yu zaoqi zhi fazhan 1860–1945* (Taiwan modern architecture: Origins and early period, 1860–1945). Taibei: Xiongshi tushu, 1996.

Li, Qingzhi 李清志. "Taibei xin leyuan" (Taipei new pleasure garden). In Long Y, *Huidao Zhongshantang*, 164–70.

Li, Qinxian 李欽賢. "Hua Taiwan, hua Taiwan: Cong Yoshida Hatsuzo de youji ditu suyuan" (Painting Taiwan, talking Taiwan: Researching the origins of Yosida Hatsuzo's travel painting). In Zhuang Y, *Taiwan chōkanzu*, 233–37.

Li, Shuling 李淑玲. "Ererba Jianbei nabian? Shifu jianyi liangdidian" (Where to build the February 28th Monument: City government suggests two places). *Zhongguo shibao*, February 13, 1992, 14.

Li, Zi'ning 李子寧. "Linian Dashiji" (A historical record of major events). In Li Z, *Taiwan shengli bowuguan*, 306–23.

———, ed. *Taiwan shengli bowuguan: chuangli jiushinian zhuankan, 1908–1998* (Taiwan Provincial Museum, special publication on its 90th anniversary, 1908–1998). Taipei: Taiwan shengli bowuguan, 1999.

Liang Jiang wenhua yuanqu: Liang Jiang zuji jinzai Taoyuan (The culture park of the two Chiangs: The legacy of the two Chiangs in Taoyuan). Taoyuan County Government, 2008.

Liao, Chunsheng 廖春生. "Taibei zhi dushi zhuanhua—yi Qingdai sanshijie (Mengjia, Dadaocheng, Chengnei) wei li" (The urban transformation of Taipei, using the Qing dynasty three towns [Mengjia, Dadaocheng, Chengnei] as examples). Master's thesis, National Taiwan University, 1988.

Liao, Ping-hui, and David Der-wei Wang, eds. *Taiwan under Japanese Colonial Rule, 1895–1945: History, Culture, Memory*. New York: Columbia University Press, 2006.

Lin, Hengdao 林衡道. "Taibei Gongyuan shengji" (Historic relics in Taipei Park). Photography by Gao Ergong. *Taibei wenxian zhizi* 1–4 (1968): 245–68.

Lin, Li-chun Sylvia. *Representing Atrocity in Taiwan: The 2/28 Incident and White Terror in Fiction and Film*. New York: Columbia University Press, 2007.

Liu, Wenjun 劉文駿, ed. *Guditu Taibei sanbu* (Strolling Taipei in old maps). Taibei: Guoshi, 2004.

Lo, Ming-Cheng M. *Doctors within Borders: Profession, Ethnicity, and Modernity in Colonial Taiwan*. Berkeley: University of California Press, 2002.

Lo, Shih-wei. "Figures of Displacement: Modes of Urbanity in Taipei, 1740–1995." PhD dissertation, Katholieke University Leuven, Belgium, 1996.

———. "A Palimpsest of '*Fait Urbains*' in Taipei." *Journal of Architectural Education* 52, no. 2 (1998): 68–75.

Long, Yingtai 龍應台, ed. *Huidao Zhongshantang: Yangpingnanlu jiushibahao he zhouzao shenghuo gushi* (Returning to Sun Yat-sen Hall: The life story of no. 98 Yanping South Road and environs). Taipei: Tabeishi wenhuaju, 2002.

———. "Xu" (Preface). In Long Y, *Huidao Zhongshantang*, 6.

Low, Setha M. "Introduction: Theorizing the City." In Low, *Theorizing the City*, 1–33.

———. "Spatializing Culture: The Social Production and the Social Construction of Public Space in Costa Rica." In Low, *Theorizing the City*, 111–37.

———, ed. *Theorizing the City: The New Urban Anthropology Reader*. New Brunswick, NJ: Rutgers University Press, 1999.

Loyer, François. *Paris XIXe siècle: L'Immeuble et la rue*. Paris: Hazan, 1987.

Lü, Shaoli 呂紹理. *Taiwan zhanshi: Quanli, kongjian yu zhimen tongzhide xingxiang biaoshu (Exhibiting Taiwan: Power, Space and Image Representation of Japanese Colonial Rule)*. Taipei: Maitian, 2005.

Lu, Xuanfei 盧宣妃. "You shenqian dao zhuanxing: Tan guoli gugong bowuyuan jin sanshinian fazhan" (From depth to change: Development of the National Palace Museum over the last thirty years). In Cai M, *Bazheng maonian*, 183–94.

Ma, Yingjiu (Ma Yingjeou) 馬英九. "Yongxin, Chuangzao xinshijide chengshi shenghuo" (With heart, creating an urban life in the new century). In *Renzhende Taibeiren*, 5.

MacKay, George Leslie, D.D. *Far From Formosa: The Island, Its People, and Missions*. 1895. Reprint, Taipei: SMC Publishing, 1998.

Maejima, Yasuhiko 前島康彦. *Hibiya Kōen: Nihon saisho no yōfū kokumin hiroba*

(Hibiya Park: Japan's first western styled public square). Tokyo: Tokyo koen buko, 1980.

Mateo, José Eugenio Borao. *Spaniards in Taiwan*. Taipei: SMC Publishing Inc., 2001.

Meyer, Jeffrey F. "*Feng-shui* of the Chinese City." *History of Religions* 18, no. 2 (1978): 138–55.

Michalski, Sergiusz. *Public Monuments: Art in Political Bondage, 1870–1997*. London: Reaktion Books, 1998.

Mirzoeff, Nicholas. *An Introduction to Visual Culture*. London: Routledge, 1999.

Mitchell, Timothy. *Colonizing Egypt*. Cambridge, UK: Cambridge University Press, 1988.

Mitchell, W. J. T. *Iconology: Image, Text, Ideology*. Chicago: University of Chicago Press, 1986.

Morris, Andrew. "Baseball, History, the Local and the Global in Taiwan." In Jordan, Morris, and Moskowitz, *Minor Arts*, 175–203.

———. *Colonial Project, National Game: A History of Baseball in Taiwan*. Berkeley: University of California Press, 2011.

———. "The Taiwan Republic of 1895 and the Failure of the Qing Modernizing Project." In *Memories of the Future: National Identity Issues and the Search for a New Taiwan*, edited by Stéphane Corcoff, 3–24. Armonk, NY: M. E. Sharpe, 2002.

Mote, F. W. "The Transformation of Nanking, 1350–1400." In Skinner, *City*, 101–53.

Musgrove, Charles D. "Dreaming a Dream: Constructing a National Identity, 1928–1936." In Escherick, *Remaking*, 139–57.

Myers, Ramon H., and Mark R. Peattie, eds. *Japanese Colonial Empire, 1895–1945*. Princeton, NJ: Princeton University Press, 1984.

Nianqing Taibei: Taibei lishi yingxian xilie (Young Taipei: Images in Taipei history). Taipei: Taibeishi zhengfu, 1996.

Niwa, Motoji 丹羽基二. *Kamon: Sen-gohyakushu no bi to rekishi* (Family crests: The history and art of fifteen-hundred designs). Tokyo: Akita Shoten, 1969.

Osterhammel, Jürgen. *Colonialism: A Theoretical Overview*. Translated by Shelly L. Frisch. Kingston, Jamaica: Ian Randle Publishers, 1997.

Ouyang, Shengzhi 歐陽盛芝, and Li Zi'ning 李子寧. "Bowuguan de yanjiu: Yige lishide huigu" (Museum research: A historical review). In Li Z, *Taiwan shengli bowuguan*, 114–89.

Paludan, Ann. *Chinese Sculpture: A Great Tradition*. Chicago: Serindia Publications, 2006.

Peattie, Mark R. "Introduction." In Myers and Peattie, *Japanese Colonial Empire*, 3–52.

———. "Japanese Attitudes toward Colonialism, 1895–1945." In Myers and Peattie, *Japanese Colonial Empire*, 80–127.

Phillips, Steven E. *Between Assimilation and Independence: The Taiwanese Encoun-ter Nationalist China, 1945–1950*. Stanford, CA: Stanford University Press, 2003.

———. "Fighting over Peace Memorial Day: Politicians and the February 28 Com-memoration." Conference paper for Ruptures, Rivalries, and Reconciliations in Modern East Asia. Triangle East Asian Colloquium, March 25, 2006; http://web.duke.edu/apsi/events/TEAC/2005_2006/phillips_paper.pdf.

Pierce, C. S. "The Icon, Index, and Symbol." In *Collected Papers*, edited by Charles Hartshorne and Paul Weiss. Vol. 2. Cambridge, MA: Harvard University Press, 1931–38.

Pingguo de ciwei (Taste of apples). Directed by Wan Ren 萬仁. 1983.

Pong, David. *Shen Pao-chen and China's Modernization in the Nineteenth Century*. Cambridge UK: Cambridge University Press, 1994.

Ponsonby Fane, Richard. *The Vicissitudes of Shintō*. Vol. 5 of *Dr. Richard Ponsonby Fane Series* [essays from 1935 to 1936]. Kyoto: The Ponsonby Memorial Society, 1963.

Qiang (The Wall). Taipei: Guoli lishi bowuguan, 2000.

Read, Benedict. *Victorian Sculpture*. New Haven, CT: Yale University Press, 1982.

Renzhen Taibeiren: Taibei lishi yingxian xilie (Hardworking Taipei people: Images in Taipei history). Taipei: Taibeishi zhengfu, 1999.

Riep, Steven. "Renaming Taipei Streets." Manuscript.

Rigger, Shelly. *Taiwan's Democratic Progressive Party: From Opposition to Power*. Boulder, CO: Lynne Rienner, 2001.

Roden, Donald. "Baseball and the Quest for National Dignity in Meiji Japan." *The American Historical Review* 85, no. 3 (1980): 511–34.

Rojas, Carlos. "Abandoned Cities Seen Anew: Reflections on Spatial Specificity and Temporal Transience." In *Photographies East: The Camera and Its Histories in East and Southeast Asia*, edited by Rosalind Morris, 205–28. Durham, NC: Duke University Press, 2009.

———. "'Nezha Was Here': Structures of Dis/placement in Tsai Ming-liang's *Rebels of the Neon God*." *Modern Chinese Literature and Culture* 15, no. 1 (2003): 63–87.

Ross, Julia. "Taiwan Sculpture Wars." http://www.time.com/time/magazine/arti-cle/0,9171,1624901,00.html.

Roy, Denny. *Taiwan: A Political History*. Ithaca, NY: Cornell University Press, 2003.

Ruan, Changrui 阮昌銳. "Bowuguan de chuangjian" (Establishment of the museum). In Li Z, *Taiwan shengli bowuguan*, 70–77.

Rubinstein, Murray, ed. *Taiwan: A New History*. Armonk, NY: M. E. Sharpe, 1999.

Rudolph, Michael. "The Quest for Difference versus the Wish to Assimilate: Tai-wan's Aborigines and Their Struggle for Cultural Survival in Times of Multicul-turalism." In Katz and Rubinstein, *Religion*, 123–55.

Ryan, James R. *Picturing Empire: Photography and the Visualization of the British Empire*. London: Reaktion Books, 1997.

Rydell, Robert. *All the World's a Fair: Visions of Empire at American International Expositions, 1876–1916*. Chicago: University of Chicago Press, 1984.

Sato, Akira. *Landscape Planning and Recreation in Japan: With a Short History of Governmental Policies and Administration*. Tokyo: Parks and Open Space Association, 1985.

Schak, David C. "The Development of Civility in Taiwan." *Pacific Affairs* 82, no. 3 (2009): 447–65.

Schiermeier, Kris, and Matthi Forrer. *The Wonders of Imperial Japan: Meiji Art from the Khalili Collection*. Amsterdam: Van Gogh Museum, 2006.

Schinz, Alfred. *The Magic Square: Cities in Ancient China*. Stuttgart-Fellbach, Germany: Edition Axel Menges, 1996.

Segalen, Victor. *The Great Statuary of China*. Translated by Eleanor Levieux. Chicago: University of Chicago Press, 1978.

Seidensticker, Edward. *Low City, High City: Tokyo from Edo to the Earthquake*. Cambridge, MA: Harvard University Press, 1983.

———. *Tokyo Rising: The City since the Great Earthquake*. Cambridge, MA: Harvard University Press, 1990.

Selya, Roger Mark. *Taipei*. Chichester, UK: John Wiley and Sons, 1995.

Shashin kurabu: Ichimei Taiwan jimbutsu shashinchō (Photographs of the club: Photo album of famous people in Taiwan). Taipei: Taiwan shūhō, 1901.

Shengbu guanguang ditu (*Tourist Sketch Map of Taipei*). Taipei: Taiwan Tourist Bureau, 1946. Taipei City Archives, map no. 73.

Shepherd, John Robert. *Statecraft and Political Economy on the Taiwan Frontier, 1600–1800*. Stanford, CA: Stanford University Press, 1993.

Shih, Fang-long, Stuart Thompson, and Paul-François Tremlett, ed. *Re-Writing Culture in Taiwan*. London: Routledge, 2009.

Shin, Gi-Wok, and Michael Robinson, eds. *Colonial Modernity in Korea*. Cambridge, MA: Harvard Asia Center, 1999.

Shinchiku jinja gosampai (Imperial visit to Xinzhu Shinto shrine). Taipei: 1930.

Shiqi shiji Helanren huizhide Taiwan laoditu (Old Dutch maps of Taiwan from the seventeenth century). 2 vols. Taipei: Hansheng, 1997.

Shisei yonjisshūnen kinen Taiwan hakurankai shi (Proceedings of Taiwan Exposition on the forty-year anniversary of colonial rule). Taipei: Taiwan hakurankai, 1939.

Simon, Scott, "From Hidden Kingdom to Rainbow Community: The Making of Gay and Lesbian Identity in Taiwan." In Jordan, Morris, and Moskowitz, *Minor Arts*, 67–88.

Skinner, William G., ed. *The City in Late Imperial China*. Stanford, CA: Stanford University Press, 1977.

Soja, Edward W. *Postmodern Geographies: The Reassertion of Space in Critical Social Theory*. London: Verso, 1989.

Sōtokufu ho (Reports of the General Colonial Administration). Taipei: Sōtokufu.

Su, Shuobin 蘇碩斌. *Kanbujian yu kandejian de Taibei: Qingmo zhi rizhi shiqi Taibei kongjian yu quanli moshi de zhuanbian* (Invisible/visible Taipei: Changes in the forms of power and space in Taipei City from late Qing dynasty to the Japanese period). Taipei: Zuoan wenhua, 2007.

———. "Kongjian shijuehua yu xiandai zhilixing: yi Rizhi shiqi Taibei dushi xingtai bianyan wei li" (Spatial visualization and modern administration: The case of urban transformation in Taipei City during the Japanese period). *wwwsoc.nii. ac.jp/jats/archive/sushuobin2003.doc.*

Tagg, John. *The Burden of Representation: Essays on Photographies and Histories.* Minneapolis: University of Minnesota Press, 1993.

Taibei gutudi zhan. (Exhibition of old Taipei maps). August 21–October 31, 1999. Taipei: Taibeishi zhengfu, 1999.

Taibei huakan (Taipei Pictorial). Taipei: Taipei City Government, Information Office, 1967–.

Taibei Huangshi jiexiao fang: Xiuli gongcheng gongzuo baogaoshu (The widow Huang memorial arch: Report on restoration work). Taibei: Taibeishi zhengfu, 1998.

Taibei lishi sanbu: Mengjia, Dadaocheng (Walking through Taipei's history: Mengjia and Dadaocheng). Taipei: Yuanliu, 1990.

Taibei wanjiu chaowu (Twenty-something Taipei). Directed by Dai Liren 戴立忍. 2002.

Taibeishi diming yu lujie yangeshi (A history of place names and street names in Taipei City). Taipei: Taibeishi wenxianhui, 2002.

Taibeishi ditu (Map of Taipei). Taipei: Taiwan Tourist Office, April 14, 1949.

Tabeishi dushijihua cankaotu (The reference map of the Taipei City plan). Taipei: Taibeishi gongwuju (December 1971). Taipei City Archives, map no. 23.

Taibeishi dushijihua shidian (Urban Planning Glossary of Taipei City). Taipei: Taibeishi zhengfu, 1995.

Taibeishi Eererba Heping Gongyuan daolan shouce (Sightseeing handbook of Taipei's February 28th Peace Park). N.p., n.d.

Taibeishi jiedaotu (Taipei City street map). 1956. Reprint, Taipei: Chengshi huaxiang, 1999.

Taibeishi lujie shi (A history of Taipei City streets). Taipei: Taibei wenxianhui, 1985.

Taibeishi xingzheng ditu (Administrative map of Taibei City), 1952. Taipei City Archives, map no. 52.

Taibeishi zhi (A record of Taipei City). Taipei: Tabeishi wenxian hui, 1977; revised edition, 1988.

Taichū jinja shi (Taizhong Shintō Shrine record). Taizhong, 1935.

Taihoku: Daitōa kyōei no chūshinchi (Taipei: The heart of the Greater East Asia Co-Prosperity Sphere). Taipei: Taihoku City Government, 1939.

Taihoku kenhō (Taipei district reports). Taipei: Sōtokufu.

Taihoku-Matsuyama, Formosa City Plans. Washington, DC: Army Map Service, 1945.

Taihokushi seishi nijunen (Official twenty-year history of Taipei City). Taipei, 1930.

Taihoku shashinchō (Taipei photo album). N.p., 1911.

Taihoku shūhō (Taipei municipality reports). Taipei: Sōtokufu.

Taihokushi Kyōchō kaichiku kinen shashinchō (Memorial photo album of architectural changes in Kyō Ward of Taipei City). Taipei, 1931.

Tainan jinja shi (Tainan Shintō Shrine record). Tainan, 1928.

Taipei City Government, Bureau of Cultural Affairs, News Release No. 45.248. "Taibei Mazu wenhuajie dengchang: Jinmian Mazu bainian shoudu huicheng guoshou" (Taipei Mazu Cultural Festival begins: Gilt-faced Mazu returns to the city to celebrate birthday for first time in one hundred Years). May 3, 2005; http://epaper.culture.gov.tw/0045/content248.html.

———. No. 45.249. "Jinmian Mazu huiluan: Shizhang qinshou taijiao" (Gilt-faced Mazu returns to palace: Mayor carries her palanquin). May 3, 2005; http://epaper.culture.gov.tw/0045/content249.html.

Taiwan baotu (Maps of Taiwan). 1904. Reprint, Taipei: Yuanliu chuban gongsi, 1996.

Taiwan hangyō kyōshinkai kinen shashinchō (Commemorative photo album of the Taiwan Promotion of Industrialization Competition). Taipei: n.p., 1917.

Taiwan huaijiu (Taiwan nostalgia). Taipei: Chuangyili, 1990

Taiwan huixiang. (Taiwan recollections). Taipei: Chuangyili, 1993.

Taiwan jinja shi (Taiwan Shinto Shrine record). Taipei: n.p., 1930 and 1940 (two editions).

Taiwan jinja ryakushi (Taiwan Shintō Shrine brief record). Taipei: n.p., 1935.

Taiwan jinja shashinchō (Taiwan Shintō Shrine photo album). Taipei: n.p., 1931.

Taiwan meishō kyūseki shi (Taiwan scenic sites and historic ruins record in Taiwan). Taipei: Sōtokufu, 1916.

Taiwan miyage (Taiwan Souvenir). Taipei: Murata shoten, 1912.

"Taiwan Museum Director Visits China Counterpart amid Scuffles with Reporters," *Taiwan News*, February 15, 2009; http://www.etaiwannews.com/etn/news_content.php?id=866552&lang=eng_news.

Taiwan Shashinchō (Taiwan photo album). Taipei: Kyōikukai,1926.

Taiwan shishō meikan (Taiwan Businessman Directory). Taipei, 1900.

Takekoshi, Yosaburō 武越與三郎. *Japanese Rule in Formosa.* Translated by George Braithwaite. London: Longmans, Green and Co., 1907.

Tang Jiyong 湯熙勇 and Zhou Yuhui 周玉慧, eds. *Taibeishi shisi shiwuhao gongyuan: Koushu lishi zhuanji* (Taipei City parks numbers 14 and 15: A special collection of oral histories). Taipei: Wenxianhui, 1999.

Tangherlini, Timothy R., and Sallie Yea, eds. *Sitings: Critical Approaches to Korean Geography.* Honolulu: University of Hawai'i Press, 2008.

Taoyuan zhonglieci jianshao cankaoziliao (Reference materials introducing Taoyuan Shrine for Chinese martyrs). N.p., n.d.

Tardio, Felix. *Mr. Tardio Sees Taiwan: A Critical Look at the Physical Environment of Taiwan*. Taipei: private printing, 1966.

Taste of Apples. See *Pingguo de ciwei.*

Taylor, Jeremy E. "Colonial Takao: The Making of a Southern Metropolis." *Urban History* 31, no. 1 (2004): 48–71.

———. "Discovering a Nationalist Heritage in Present-day Taiwan. *China Heritage Quarterly* (Australian National University) 17 (March 2009): 1–9.

Teng, Emma Jinhua. *Taiwan's Imagined Geography: Chinese Colonial Travel Writing and Pictures*. Cambridge, MA: Harvard University Asia Center, 2004.

Thrower, Norman J. W. *Maps & Civilization: Cartography in Culture and Society*. 2d ed. Chicago: University of Chicago Press, 1999.

Ting, Jung-sheng, "The Political Architecture of the 1960s: The Architecture of the 'Chinese Cultural Renaissance.'" Translated by Chuck Eisenstein. *Discover Taipei* 2 (November 1997), 13–22.

Toushi Xingongyuan: 228 Heping gongyuan daolan shouce (A perspective on New Park—February 28th Peace Park guidebook). Taipei: Taiboguan, 2000.

Ts'ai, Hui-yu Caroline. *Taiwan in Japan's Empire Building: An Institutional Approach to Colonial Engineering*. London and New York: Routledge, 2009.

Tsurumi, Patricia. *Japanese Colonial Education in Taiwan*. Cambridge, MA: Harvard University Press, 1977.

Unno, Kazutaka. "Cartography in Japan." In Harley and Woodward, *Cartography*, 346–477.

Vickers, Edward. "Re-writing Museums in Taiwan." In Shih, Thompson, and Tremlett, *Re-Writing Culture in Taiwan*, 69–101.

Vinograd, Richard. *Boundaries of the Self: Chinese Portraits, 1600–1900*. Cambridge, UK: Cambridge University Press, 1992.

Wang, Ban. "Reenchanting the Image in Global Culture: Reification and Nostalgia in Zhu Tianwen's Fiction." In Wang and Rojas, *Writing Taiwan*, 370–88.

Wang, Chih-Hung. "Modernization Ideoscape: Imaginative Geography and Aesthetic Landscape in Taipei Rapid Transit System." In Kwok, *Globalizing Taipei*, 195–218.

Wang, Cunli 王存立, and Hu Wenqing 胡文青. *Taiwan de guditu: Ming Qing shiqi* (Old maps of Taiwan: The Ming-Qing period). Taipei: Yuanzu, 2002.

Wang, David Der-wei, and Carlos Rojas. *Writing Taiwan: A New Literary History*. Durham, NC: Duke University Press, 2007.

Wang, Yi-wen, and Tim Heath. "Constructions of National Identity: A Tale of Twin Capital Building in Early Post-war Taiwan." *Taiwan in Comparative Perspective* 2 (2008): 21–46.

Wei, Dewen 魏德文, and Gao Chuanqi 高傳棋, eds. *Chuanyue shikong kan Taibei: Taibei jiancheng 120 zhounian: guditu, jiuxinxiang, wenxian, wenwu zhan*

(Viewing Taipei through time and space: 120th anniversary of Taipei City wall: An exhibition of maps, images, documents, and historical relics). Taipei: Taibei zhengfu, 2004.

Wei, Dewen 魏德文, Gao Chuanqi 高傳棋, Lin Chunyin 林春吟, Huang Qingqi 黃清琦, eds. *Celiang Taiwan: Rizhi shiqi huizhi Taiwan xiangguan ditu, 1895–1945* (Measuring Taiwan: Taiwan-related maps from the Japanese period). Taipei: Nantian shuju, 2008.

Wei, Zhenyu 隗振瑜, ed. *Guoli Taiwan buowuguan jianjie* (Introduction to the National Taiwan Museum).Taipei: Taiwan bowuguan, 2007.

Weller, Robert P. *Discovering Nature: Globalization and Environmental Culture in China and Taiwan*. New York: Cambridge University Press, 2006.

Weng, Jiaying 翁佳音. *Da Taibei: Guditu kaoyi* (Greater Taipei: Investigations of an old map). Banqchiao: Tabeixian wenhua zhongxin, 1998.

Wright, Arthur. "The Cosmology of the Chinese City." In Skinner, *City*, 33–73.

Wu, Hung. *Remaking Beijing: Tiananmen Square and the Creation of a Political Space*. Chicago: University of Chicago Press, 2005.

Wu, Jinyong 吳金鏞. "Guozu jiangou, lishi jiyi yu jinnian kongjian—Ererba Jinnian-bei de jiangou (Nation-State Construction: Social Memory and Monumental Space—the Construction of the February 28th Monument)." Master's thesis, National Taiwan University, 1994.

Wu, Yongyi 吳永毅. "Renzhende Taibeiren." In *Renzhende Taibeiren*, 7–8.

Wyke, Terry, "Marginal Figures? Public Statues and Public Parks in the Manchester Region, 1840–1914." In *Sculpture and the Garden*, edited by Patrick Eyres and Fiona Russell, 85–97. Hampshire, UK: Ashgate, 2006.

Xia, Zhujiu. See Hsia, C. J.

Xiao, Yuanzhong 蕭淵鍾. "Xinsheng Gongyuan: Ererba Jinianbei zhi ke fan'an" (New Life Park: Possible overturn of February 28th Monument site). *Lianhebao*, April 2, 1992.

Xie, Peijuan 謝佩娟. "Taibei xingongyuan tongzhi yundong: Qingyu zhuti de shehui shijian" (Gay activities in Taipei New Park: The social practice of subjective lust). Master's thesis, National Taiwan University, 1999.

Xie Yingzong (Shieh Ying-Tzung) 謝英宗. "Kangxi Taibeihu gudili huanjing zhi tantao (The Paleography of the Ancient Taipei Lakebed in the K'anghsi Period)." *Guoli Taiwan daxue dilixi dilixuebao*, 27 (2000): 85-95.

Yamaguchi, Masao, "The Poetics of Exhibition in Japanese Culture." In Karp and Lavine, *Exhibiting Cultures*, 57–67.

Yang, Mengzhe 楊孟哲. *Taiwan lishi yingxiang* (The historical images of Taiwan). Taipei: Yishujia chubanshe, 1996.

Yao, Jen-to, "The Japanese Colonial State and Its Form of Knowledge in Taiwan." In Liao and Wang, *Taiwan*, 37–61.

Yao, Qizhong 姚其中. "Zhongshantang fenzhan jieshou" (Introduction to various components of the Sun Yat-sen Hall). In Long Y, *Huidao Zhongshantang*, 172–79.

Ye, Suke 葉肅科. *Riluo Taibeicheng: Rizhi shidai Taibei dushi fazhan yu ren richang shenghuo* (Setting sun over Taipei: Taipei City development and life during Japanese rule). Taipei: Zili wanbao chubanshe, 1993.

Yen, Chuang-ying. "Colonial Taiwan and the Construction of Landscape Painting." In Liao and Wang, *Taiwan*, 248–61.

Yin, Di 隱地. "Yuanjin Zhongshantang" (Sun Yat-sen Hall near and far). In Long Y, *Huidao Zhongshantang*, 72–76.

Yin, Zhangyi 尹章義. *Taiwan kaifashi yanjiu* (Studies of early Taiwan history). Taipei: Liangjing, 1989.

Yinshi nannü (Eat Drink Man Woman). Directed by Ang Lee. 1994.

Yip, June. *Envisioning Taiwan: Fiction, Cinema, and the Nation in the Cultural Imaginary*. Durham, NC: Duke University Press, 2004.

Yonemoto, Marcia. "The 'Spatial Vernacular' in Tokogawa Maps." *Journal of Asian Studies* 59, no. 3 (2000): 647–66.

Yu, Shuenn-Der. "Hot and Noisy: Taiwan's Night Market Culture." In Jordan, Morris, and Moskowitz, *Minor Arts*, 129–49.

Yu, Yonghe 郁永河. *Small Sea Travel Dairies: Yu Yonghe's Records of Taiwan*. Translated and with commentary by Macabe Keliher. Taipei: SMC Publishing, 2004.

Zhang, Mingxiong 張明雄. *Yuesheng de chengshi: Taibei* (The rising city: Taipei). Taipei: Qianwei, 1996.

Zhong, Jian 鍾堅. *Taiwan hangkong juezhan* (Taiwan's decisive air war). Taipei: Maitian, 1996.

Zhongwen daci dian (*The Encyclopedic Dictionary of the Chinese Language*). Taipei: Huagang, 1968.

Zhou Wanyao. See Chou, Wan Yao.

Zhu, Wanli 朱萬里. *Taibeishi dushi jianshe shigao* (Draft history of the construction of Taipei City). Taipei: Taibeishi gongwuju, 1954.

Zhuang, Yongming 莊永明. *Taibei laojie* (Old Taipei). Taipei: Shibaowenhua, 1991.

———, ed. *Taiwan chōkanzu/Taiwan niaokan tu* (Bird's-eye-view maps of Taiwan). Taipei: Yuanliu chuban gongsi, 1996 (reprint of maps dating from the 1930s)

Zhuang, Zhanpeng 莊展鵬, ed. *Taibei gucheng zhi lu* (Tour of old Taipei City). Taipei: Yuanliu, 1992.

Zijigai Zongtongfu (Build your own Presidential Palace). Taipei: Yuanliu, 1999.

Zuixin Taibeishi jie xiangtu (Latest detailed street map of Taipei), March 10, 1949. Taipei City Archives, map no. 14.

Zukin, Sharon. *The Culture of Cities*. Oxford, UK: Blackwell Publishing, 1995.

Index

considerations, 189–90; in Japan, 124–25; Moscow, 154, 226*n*54; Palace collection threats, 112–14, 219*n*5; post–World War II activity, 113–17, 119–20, 126–29, 178, 220*n*25

Museum of the Colonial Administration, 117–20

music, in *Twenty-something Taipei* film, 65–66

music pavilions, Taipei Park, 104–5, 218*n*45, 218*n*50

music performances, Sun Yat-sen Hall, 130–31

Muzha, Zhongxun temple horses, 162, 168–69

Myers, Ramon, 194

naming complications, Taipei City, 197–98

Nanjing, museum collection, 113–14

Nanputuo Temple, 99

National Assembly, 131, 222*n*59

National Defense Hall, museum exhibition, 124

National History Museum, 90, 119, 220*n*25

National Museum of History, 51

National Palace Museum, 112–17, 121–26, 219*n*5

National Taiwan Democracy Hall, 213*n*62

National Taiwan Museum, 92, 120, 178, 189–90, 231*n*50

Nationalist government, post-Chiang Kai-shek: cultural reconstruction policies, 12–16; museum/display operations, 114–15, 119–20, 120, 127–29, 220*n*25, 222*n*47; street naming policies, 85–87; subway system, 87–89; Taipei Park, 105, 109–10, 111, 218*nn*50–51

Nationalist government, under Chiang Kai-shek: arrival impact, 57; celebration anthology, 129–34; colonialism arguments, 196–97; exhibition significance, 18–20; exile of, 10–11; gate renovation, 80–81, 212*nn*44–45; Grand Hotel significance, 60; Japanese administration buildings, 34–35; Korean War impact, 11–12; museum operations, 114–15, 119–20, 126–27, 220*n*25; photographic representations, 35–36, 42–43; Shinto shrines/horses, 169–70, 171–72; street-naming policies, 82–85, 212*n*50; WWII aftermath, 9–10

neocolonial period, defined, 11, 200*n*21

Netherlands, 4–5, 20–22, 199*nn*7–8, 202*n*13

neurotic displacement, 187

New Life Movement, 223*n*1

New Life Park, 136, 137, 148–49, 150, 223*n*1

New Park. *See* Taipei Park

ni design, 34

North Gate, 25–26, 73, 76, 80–81

nostalgia, forms of, 35, 190–91

Ochi Torachi, 167

Oda family crest, 167

Old City Hall, photographic representation, 42–43. *See also* Civic Hall; Sun Yat-sen Hall

Old Maps of Taipei exhibition, 17

Old Taipei People album, 51–53

Ōmura Masujirō, 140

Ōshima Kumaji, 143

Osterhammel, Jürgen, 194, 217*n*29, 233*n*35

oxen, bronze, 178, 231*n*50

CPSIA information can be obtained at www.ICGtesting.com
Printed in the USA
BVOW01s1821201013

334101BV00001B/157/P